HISTORICAL INVESTIGATIONS IN WEST MAUI

HISTORICAL INVESTIGATIONS IN WEST MAUI

Edited by

LANCE D. COLLINS and BIANCA K. ISAKI

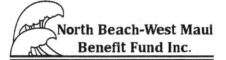

North Beach-West Maui
Benefit Fund Inc.

Lahaina, Maui, Hawai'i

29 28 27 26 25 24   6 5 4 3 2 1

ISBN 978-1-9524-6111-8 (pbk : alk. paper)

Published by the North Beach-West Maui Benefit Fund, Inc.
P O Box 11329
Lahaina, Hawaiʻi 96761

Distributed by University of Hawaiʻi Press
2840 Kolowalu Street
Honolulu, HI 96822-1888

Every effort has been made to trace copyright holders
and to obtain their permission for the use of copyright material.
The publisher apologizes for any errors or omissions and
would be grateful if notified of any corrections that
should be incorporated in future reprints or editions of this book.

This book is printed on acid-free paper and
meets the guidelines for permanence and durability
of the Council on Library Resources.

Print-ready files provided by North Beach-West Maui Benefit Fund, Inc.

CONTENTS

INTRODUCTION

Lance D. Collins

How should a history of West Maui be approached? A typical large-scale narrative of West Maui moves from Native Hawaiians to missionaries to sugar to tourism. Whales and tourists come and go. But this type of history is neither helpful nor insightful. In her Introduction to *Social Change in West Maui*, Bianca Isaki noted that "[t]here is a certain hubris in an attempt to chronicle West Maui's social history." Nevertheless, we should "discern the forms in which conflicts and crises that drive social change are realized in the material space and historical moments of West Maui." Taken together, *Social Change in West Maui* and *Tourism Impacts West Maui* sought to resist modern West Maui histories that "contort to fit new ways of explaining this place to and for tourism." Histories of recent and contemporary social struggles are often absent from those histories.

Along the same lines, in the preface to *Malu 'Ulu o Lele*, we noted that much of the focus in nineteenth- and early twentieth-century Hawai'i history has been on the high forms of political and juridical institutions, describing rules, administrative decisions and policies that applied to society as a whole. Through translations, *Malu 'Ulu o Lele* presented snapshots of the everyday lives of Hawaiians in the late nineteenth and early twentieth centuries. The transcriptions of *The Journal of James Macrae* by Brian Richardson provided a working-class outsider's observations of Hawaiians and Hawai'i at the advent of the American Calvinist missionaries' ascent in Hawaiian society in 1825—an alternative to the triumphant diaries and other writings of American missionaries that current histories typically rely upon.

Two decades into the twenty-first century, the reservoir of local historical knowledge ever recedes into the tourism abyss of the information age. History is what can be found on the plaques in Lahaina or in soundbites on a tour. While Hawaiian and Hawai'i histories are subjects in intermediate and senior high school, their placement as mandatory subjects in public education leads to how the historical fragments that are included are part of the cultural hegemony that must remove inconsistent, incompatible, and personal histories to support the state-sponsored narrative. It is a nicer story. It is a simpler story. It is a story that supports a particular kind of tourism and land development for the wealthy.

There are political reasons for supporting a single story. Partial and incomplete knowledge of historical conditions in Hawaiʻi make the current situation appear to be legitimate and natural. At the same time, the single story, with clear and important actors, limits the range of possible choices for future action. High history tends to see Hawaiʻi as a monolithic historical event affected by a uniform set of experiences that changes uniformly in response to outside influence. This further limits the range of possible choices for immediate resistance and future action. As Candace Fujikane noted in *Mapping Abundance for a Planetary Future,* "[t]he struggle for a planetary future calls for a profound epistemological shift."

Messy, local histories help to open up the range of possibilities for action by giving us additional insight into the circumstances and conditions that previous generations faced. Historical knowledge helps to frame perceptions that organize space. Local histories therefore help to render visible aspects of historical space and time that have been obscured by overarching dominant narratives and timelines. Local history can disrupt social reproduction, leading to new ways of confronting the past and imagining people, the community, and the world. Making history complicated and messy is a way to question the existing structures of understanding and existence.

The publication of *ʻOhuʻohu nā Mauna o ʻEʻeka: Place Names of Maui Komohana* told history from the perspective of place names of West Maui—both as a way to disrupt the process of erasure of native knowledge and culture and also to imagine other possible futures founded upon greater awareness for land and its meaning in non-dominant worldviews.

This collection of essays continues to extend the known histories of West Maui in multiple directions.

In the first chapter, Sydney Iaukea presents the story of Micronesian laborers in the sugar plantations in Lahaina and Kalihi, Oʻahu at the end of the nineteenth century. Micronesian labor in Hawaiʻi was paid among the least of all plantation labor, and accusations of blackbirding persist. When the Lahaina Gilbertese were finally able to go home, they came home to a British fertilizer mining colony. While nuclear testing and the U.S. military are absent in this nineteenth-century story, similar descriptions and testimonies about living as a Micronesian are echoed in Hawaiʻi today.

Adam Manalo Keawe-Camp recounts the time of Kaomi, Hawaiʻi's mōʻī kuʻi. As Keawe-Camp notes, Kaomi is "probably the least understood Hawaiian figure in 19th-century Hawaiʻi[.]" Kaomi sought an alternative vision for Hawaiʻi framed by traditional Hawaiian symbols that rejected the Calvinist values of the American missionaries. The divergent visions, and their resolution, set the stage for the fateful choices made by Kauikeaouli in the early to mid-nineteenth century that radically transformed Hawaiian society.

The third chapter focuses on a specific individual involved in one of Kauikeaouli's most impactful choices, the Māhele of 1848. The individual was Serang, also known as Lani, a "Hindu" awardee at Lahaina. Shilpi Suneja investigates the origins of Lani—likely a South Asian Muslim from the Amreli district of Gujarat, in what is today western India. Suneja's story traces the global economic networks through which a South Asian Muslim could arrive and settle in West Maui and also contrasts Lani's assimilation into the Hawaiian society of Lahaina with those of the American Calvinist missionaries.

In the next chapter, Frank Ezra Kaʻiuokalani Damas provides a modern orthography transcription and a translation of a history of Lahaina written by Judge Daniel Kahāʻulelio at the end of the nineteenth century. The story gives additional pieces of nineteenth-century Lahaina from the perspective of a nineteenth-century Hawaiian working within the legal system of the time.

In chapter 5, Ron Williams explores the foundations of the Kingdom of Hawaiʻi being one of the most literate and progressive nation-states in the nineteenth-century world, namely the development and evolution of the educational system as administered in the second tax district for the Island of Maui in the last half of that century. He follows the story of the Kingdom and its loyal subjects, the Hawaiian kumu who instructed native pupils.

Then, Bianca Isaki and Kahealani Lono investigate the story of the Lahaina famines of the 1860s. Entirely absent from English language sources, the Lahaina famines of the 1860s were described and analyzed at length by Native Hawaiian sources into the twentieth century, who understood that the shortage of food was intimately connected with the shift to industrial forms of agriculture where growing sugar displaced traditional forms of subsistence farming, which actually produced food for local consumption. These events of displacement and death were also exacerbated by unusual climatic events such as the Pacific Decadal Oscillation.

In the seventh chapter, ʻUmi Perkins pieces together the genealogy of Kale Davis, a transitional figure of nineteenth-century Hawaiʻi and West Maui. Her lands at Honokahua became the site of both massive desecration of Hawaiian burials in the construction of the Ritz-Carlton Maui Kapalua and also the ground of modern political movements to protect similar burials. Davis's grave has been cared for by her descendants up to the present. Remembering Davis's story as well as her descendants' continued maintenance of her grave gives us a glimpse at alternative futures.

In the final chapter, Lance Collins traces the legal history of land titles and the establishment of the Torrens land title registration system in Hawai'i and the Philippines—both established in 1903 by American colonial governments. He examines the first and last land court applications filed during the Territory of Hawai'i period and compares that experience with the Philippines. The analysis gives us an idea of the power dynamics at play during two key transitional periods in West Maui and how those dynamics informed control of land on a mundane, bureaucratic level.

This volume adds a few stories to local West Maui histories and creates spaces to resist the reigning cultural hegemony that erases the messiness of history so that territory and community can be rendered better fit for the needs of capital and the objectives of those in power. By offering more local histories of West Maui, we are reminded that what exists is far from expressing all possibilities and that those neglected areas of political space can be reclaimed for different stories leading to alternative, preferred futures.

CHAPTER I

ON A WING AND A PRAYER
Gilbertese Fractured Migrations to West Maui and Beyond

Sydney Iaukea

FEAR OF FLYING (IN BROKEN GILBERTESE)

I maaku
You told me ba ko tangirai
I maaku
I maaku
My arms were awkward, so ko taua baiu
I maaku
I maaku
The dancer trembles because te ruoia is a kind of sorcery
I maaku
I maaku
The frigate birds fly high above us and I'm afraid of falling
I maaku

—Teresia Teaiwa

A "fear of flying" might be crippling, even as the anticipation of soaring is liberating. But what if flying is the only option given, and the possibility of survival during flight questionable, with the return to *kainga* (home) not promised or even allowed?[1] In Teresia Teaiwa's poem *Fear of Flying*,[2] the fear is actually of falling, caused by a sense of brokenness because "Pacific culture has been damaged and disrupted [. . . resulting in a] lack of self-belief."[3] But as trembling bodies and awkward arms guide the dance of flight, self-confidence is restored by debunking the tenor of colonial narratives that drown out ancestral knowledge. The fear, both in flying and in standing still, is ultimately assuaged by learning one's *true memory* and by reweaving the genealogical connections that never actually wavered.[4]

From the mid-1800s to the mid-1900s, Gilbertese Islanders metaphorically took flight on steam ships from *te aba* (the land and people) to work abroad and on a variety of plantations—primarily of sugar, cotton, and copra.[5] Crisscrossed migratory pathways spread throughout the Pacific, Australia, New Zealand, and into parts of Peru and beyond. This resulted in approximately 9,300 Pacific laborers leaving their islands and atolls, with 2,600 headed to the sugar plantations of Hawai'i.[6] The Gilbertese made up 1,800 of these "South Sea Islanders" who migrated to Hawai'i, primarily between 1878 and 1887, and settled in plantation camps or villages across the island chain.[7] By 1903, the majority of South Sea Islanders had already returned home, but there were still two large camps of Gilbertese located at Lahaina, Maui, and Kalihi, O'ahu.

The earlier arrivals were able to return onboard the missionary ship, the first *Morning Star,* as it frequently traveled between Hawai'i and the Gilbert Islands.[8] "Return" was a condition of labor and written into their contracts by the Hawaiian Kingdom, and "South Seas islanders were guaranteed the right to free return passage upon the completion of their contract."[9] The return home clause was mandated by the Board of Immigration to the sugar-plantation owners (also known as sugar planters) once private recruiting began. The planters generally did not honor this promise, which plunged many laborers into destitution and poverty as they found it difficult to integrate into the larger local community after their contracts expired.

Some continued working at the sugar plantations as "day laborers" to earn enough money for their voyage home. But by 1903, over 200 Gilbertese migrants were still unable to leave Hawai'i. Most of them were extremely homesick and dreamed of returning to their islands, atolls, seas, family, friends—to their *te aba.* Astonishingly, as these indigenous inhabitants were immigrating wide and far, Banaba (also known as Ocean Island) and Nauru islands began undergoing geographic migrations of their own. In 1900, the Pacific Phosphate Company (PPC), which later became the British Phosphate Commission (BPC was a commission formed by representatives from Australia, New Zealand, and the United Kingdom), mined and extracted phosphate from these tiny islands until "phosphates were exhausted in 1979."[10]

In 1945, Ocean Island inhabitants were removed to Rabi Island in Fiji after World War II and the end of the Japanese occupation of the island.[11] Mining and the Japanese occupation were the two official reasons given by the government for the inhabitants' removal. In truth, islanders were essentially moved so that the BPC could mine under their homes and graves without the obstruction posed by people: "Relocating the Banabans to Rabi allowed the BPC unfettered access to all phosphate deposits, some of which were under villages, homes, and burial sites."[12]

The West Maui Gilbertese's migratory routes, their plantation/salvation experience, and their enormous effort to return home is the topic of this chapter. The Hawai'i-based Gilbertese who longed for home in the early 1900s were wishing for a *kainga* (home) that was becoming "generally inaccessible" for a multitude of reasons.[13] Idyllic images became more and more unattainable for those Lahaina-based Gilbertese who identified their land of origin as "Ocean Island" in the 1890 Hawaiian Kingdom Census. In 1903, the ship *Isleworth* passed through Hawai'i and serendipitously made a return trip to Ocean Island to transport guano to Australia.[14] Hiram Bingham II and others responded swiftly to the opportunity to help these Gilbertese and their O'ahu counterparts in Kalihi return to the Gilbert Islands via Tarawa and Ocean Island. Many years prior, Bingham's official governmental role was "Special Protector" and "Inspector of South Sea Islanders," and he befriended and spearheaded their protection on the plantations. He and his wife Minerva were longtime missionaries to the Gilbert Islands, and they lived and sermonized among the "heathens" for over five decades.[15] Along with other Hawaiian missionaries, they were not proponents of the South Sea Islander sugar-plantation labor recruitment efforts because of the heavy role that "blackbirding," or the Pacific slave trade of Kanaka workers, had played.[16] Complaints of blackbirding accompanied the Lahaina-based Gilbertese who worked at the Pioneer Mill Sugar Plantation in 1880.

Later at the group's departure, the entire population of 86, except one who decided not to go, left on the *Kinau* to O'ahu and then the *Isleworth*. After two decades, for some, they were finally going home to the vastly different Gilbert Islands, now governed by British colonial rule and controlled by the extractive phosphate mining industry. In all, their uneven diasporas were demonstrative of indigenous peoples everywhere and their desire to remain rooted and connected to their land and ocean—despite the global institutions, colonial governments, and racist narratives that fragmented identities and destroyed the places they loved. In 1903, with the return of these last Gilbertese to Oceania, those who might have been previously caught as "blackbirds" were eventually set free, one way or the other. Can there be any doubt of the fear of flying?

Frigate birds in flight. Photo by Lucy Rickards, February 10, 2014, www.flickr.com/photos/lucybraceevans/12665062684/ found in Christopher Joyce, "Nonstop Flight: How the Frigate Bird Can Soar For Weeks Without Stopping," *The Two-Way,* June 30, 2016. https://www.npr.org/sections/thetwo-way/2016/06/30/484164544/non-stop-flight-how-the-frigatebird-can-soar-for-months-without-stopping

Te Aba—The Land and The People

The word Ba-n-aba means rock land and, simultaneously, something both fixed and fluid, material and human. Banaba is the body of the land and the body of the people. To track Banaba is to track fragmented and dispersed stories, peoples, and landscapes, which throws up challenges to conventional history and literacy.[17]

Banaban Land Districts

The island of Banaba was settled in the 1600s, and the land was divided according to different hamlets, even as the people lived together as a united Banaban population.[18] Banaban cultural identity stemmed from the ancestral worship centered around the sun (te Aka), and power and societal protocols were derived

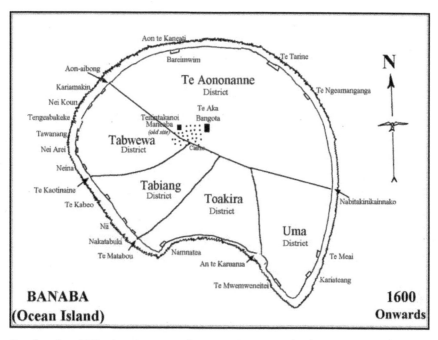

Banaban Land District 1600 onwards prior to European Settlement in 1900. ©Sigrah & King 2001; 2019. Stacey M. King and Raobeia Ken Sigrah, *Te Rii Ni Banaba, backbone of Banaba*. Banaban Vision; 2nd ed., 2019.

from their worship of the sun.[19] "Our people believe and trust that from nature, the sun is their major source of power and the very source of life itself."[20] Accordingly, rules governing society maintained the natural cycles of time and place, and were based on a relationality of people with their environment. This is often referred to as place-based understanding, whereby the place itself influences all avenues of life and informs societal norms and rules. In these understandings, "Te aba is thus an integrated epistemological and ontological complex, linking people in deep corporeal and psychic ways to each other, to their ancestors, to their history, and to their physical environment."[21]

Geographically, Ocean Island lies 400 kilometers west of the Gilbert Islands. The Gilbert Islands are made up of sixteen coral islands and atolls. The names from north to south are Makin, Butaritari, Marakei, Abaiang, Tarawa, Maiana, Abemama, Kuria, Aranuka, Nonouti, Tabiteuea, Beru, Nikunau, Onotoa, Tamana, and Arorae.[22] Both Ellice Islands and the Gilbert Islands were ruled as British Protectorates in 1892 and joined together as one British colony in 1916.[23] Ocean Island was administered by the Resident Commissioner in

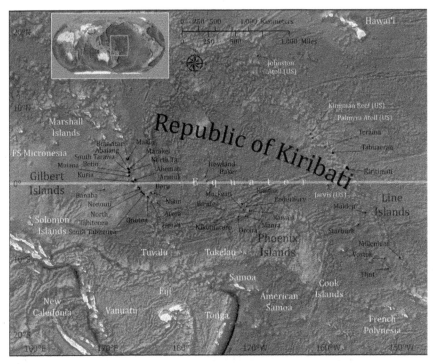

Map of the Republic of Kiribati, courtesy of Johann Lall.

1900 when phosphate mining began on the island.[24] Today, "these thirty-three islands, including Banaba, are now the Independent Republic of Kiribati,"[25] and the Gilbert and Ellice Islands are known as Kiribati and Tuvalu.[26]

In 1900, phosphate mining began on Banaba, also known as Ocean Island. Due to the fervor for phosphate extraction that immediately followed the discovery, it became a colonial center in the larger colonial periphery. Phosphate is a resource that supplies the global food chain and is the primary ingredient used in fertilizer. The phosphorous-rich rocks on Banaba and Nauru were created over centuries by petrified guano (bird droppings). New Zealander Albert Ellis accidentally discovered the phosphate in 1899, and mining and shipping began almost immediately afterward as parts of these islands were divested on one-way passages and driven by the needs of global capitalism.[27] The complete extraction of this resource caused both islands to be "consumed," as "both of these island landscapes were essentially 'eaten away' by mining."[28] This ultimately resulted in the removal of 90 percent of the surface area of Banaba, and "by the time BPC left, 22m tonnes of land had been removed."[29]

Working a Banaba Island phosphate field in the 1920s. Photo courtesy of National Library of Australia, call number PIC Album 1203 #P2/24 Physical Content-Phosphate Field, Ocean Island, found in ABC News, May 30, 1920.

The protectorate moved its headquarters there in 1908, and immigrants from both the Gilbert and Ellice Islands migrated to work in the mines.[30] "From that time until phosphate mining ended in 1979, the British Government saw the colony's problems in terms of Ocean Island phosphates and allowed the industry a major say in their attempted resolution."[31] From 1900 to 1980, the land was stripped, and 21 million tons of phosphate were taken from the island and shipped to factories for the production of fertilizer in other parts of the world.[32] Only 150 out of 1,500 acres were not mined, and in 2001, there were only 200 inhabitants left on the island, with the majority of the population

on Rabi island or located elsewhere near Fiji.[33] Today roughly 400 indigenous
inhabitants remain. Katerina Teaiwa tells us, "Ocean Island reminds us what is
at stake whenever the interests of industrial agriculture and indigenous peoples
come into conflict."[34]

In December 1945, Banaban islanders were relocated by the British to
Rabi, Fiji, located 1,600 miles away, after the Japanese occupation of the island
ended after World War II. The removal of the inhabitants further uprooted the
indigenous people, whose lifestyles were deeply embedded in their land and
ocean. Before they left, the Japanese killed 150 Banabans, and the land itself was
"so badly mauled that Britain was able to argue that the island was no longer
inhabitable."[35] Many Banabans and migrants died because of both the Japanese
occupation and the hazards and health conditions associated with working in
the phosphate mines. Mining started again after the war, once the company
reinstituted the industry after having destroyed most of its own mining equip-
ment to prevent the Japanese from taking over. In all, "the Banabans have been
tricked, betrayed, deported, and murdered. Without anyone in the rest of the
world as much as lifting a finger."[36]

Gilbertese Islander Nabetari, who lived at sea for seven months to escape the Japanese
on Ocean Island. Pacific Wrecks, Oct 1, 1945.

The tiny island of Banaba measures just over two and a half square miles, but both the island and her people have played herculean roles in international food and labor production. Today the island's *te aba* is dispersed, and "Banaba is no longer a place, an island in the middle of an ocean, but rather a flow of rocks with multiple trajectories and itineraries."[37] Likewise, the identities of the native peoples, tied to their land and ocean, are reimagined through varying environmental and sociopolitical objectives. Their uneven and fragmented diaspora continues to incite identity questions, such as: "If, ontologically, land and people are the same in the indigenous sense, then what happens when *both* the land and people are removed?"[38] "Where is your home, who are you related to, and what is your ocean and land?" That is, "Who are you?"

Being rooted is a contemporary privilege for those indigenous peoples often caught in the crossfire between global and colonial agendas. As fragmentations of Banaban land ensued, connections that informed native identity were shattered and reimagined: "If indigenous identities were or are rooted in specific landscapes and seascapes, then Banaban identities have now become coordinates between islands and continents."[39] How would they re-establish connections to *te aba* in the midst of decentering discourses and movements? How would they relate to *te aba* outside of their livelihood and labor? The cultural ability to know oneself based on genealogy and inheritance is specified in Banaban epistemology—"These three interlocking fundamentals of knowledge provide the key to Banaban identity which undisputedly connects to their land. 1. Recite your genealogy. 2. Know your family's inherited role. 3. Name your land."[40] These basic understandings were challenged and, in many ways, destroyed. In this context, the longing for home was really a longing for reconnection to one's own self and to the genealogical memory that provides knowing, by and through relationships with *te aba*.

DEPARTURE—FRACTURED MIGRATIONS

Labor migrations from Banaba and the Gilbert and Ellice Islands to other islands and continents were common during the 19th and 20th centuries. An estimated 30 percent of the Gilbertese population migrated for work between the years 1860 and 1900, as pure survival drove many to leave their own islands: "The pitiful condition of the Banaban Islanders shows the desperate plight of people ravaged by famine"[41]—so much so that "the Gilbertese, with few other means of obtaining the products of western technology and faced with the ever-pervading threat of drought, gradually developed an enthusiasm for labour migration."[42] Internal strife and wars were also defining factors, but once they left their islands, they were faced with an array of obstacles, and simple survival was still among the pervading concerns.

In Hawai'i, labor laws were enacted in 1850 by the "Act for the Government of Masters and Servants," and the roles of both "masters" and "servants" were explained therein. Ultimately, this law brought 115,000 laborers into Hawai'i from 1850 to 1897.[43] The law was printed in both Hawaiian and English in 1868, and it practically and literally indentured and bound laborers to their *lunas* (bosses).[44] "The first part of this act related to apprenticeship, [and] the contract labor provisions were found in sections 22–30."[45] The language in this law also explained penalties for desertion and those who broke their contracts: "Sec. 1410. If any apprentice or servant bound as aforesaid shall, without just cause, depart from the service of his master [...] the justice shall order the offender to be restored to his master."[46] Those escaping were also compelled "to serve double the time his absence."[47] Cruel masters could also be fined and sentenced to prison if the charges against them were found to be legitimate.[48] Regarding child labor, minors over the age of ten could be bound to work as either an apprentice or servant.[49]

Opponents of the law pointed out the advantages held by the masters and criticized their treating of labor as "chattel."[50] Gross inequity and harsh labor conditions on the plantations often resulted in labor discontent, either in the form of desertion of service or in labor strikes. Between 1876 and 1900, thousands of workers, ranging from 11 to 30 percent of the plantation workforce, were charged annually with desertion and "refusing bound service."[51] The number of masters charged with breaking the law is unknown, proving that "while in theory both servant and master were protected by the law, it was inevitable that the master should have an advantage."[52]

In the mid-1800s, discussions occurred among the sugar planters and the Hawaiian Kingdom government about what was rapidly becoming a large "labor problem" in Hawai'i. Native Hawaiians were dwindling as a labor source because they were dying due to introduced diseases and illnesses from foreigners. "The census of 1872 counted 49,044 native Hawaiians. This number fell over the years until it reached 34,346 in the 1890 census."[53] Also, "Hawaiians do not want to do hard labor" was how the sugar-plantation owners framed the issue when they pointed out that "few [Hawaiians] are tempted by the wages made in Honolulu."[54] The sugar plantations wanted docile and obedient laborers for the fields, and they paired this desire with a racial component. Race quickly became the marker by which jobs and pay were negotiated—one based on racial inferiority that assigned natives to the lowest rung and which was reinforced through Calvinist religious doctrine.

The idea of introducing "cognate races" to the workforce entered the political discourse, and recruiting similar (or "cognate") races for labor was viewed as a solution to the dwindling of the labor population. It was also thought of as a way to reinforce a Hawaiian national consciousness and allegiance.[55]

King Kalākaua (1874–1891), together with the American adventurer Walter Murray Gibson, crafted an appeal for the immigration of "cognate" races who would assimilate with Native Hawaiians and strengthen the population basis of support for his reign and for the Kingdom.[56] This meant not only Polynesians, but nearly all Pacific islanders, including Malaysians and even Japanese, were thought of as cognate to the Hawaiians.[57]

Kamehameha IV had already urged the inclusion of Polynesian migrants who could work and marry Hawaiians in order to increase the "native stock."[58] Kamehameha V enacted the policy with the advice of Walter Murray Gibson: "Gibson strenuously urged the introduction of Polynesians under the patronage of the state. In 1864 the legislature voted $36,000 for the transplanting of a considerable number of Polynesians of both sexes."[59] Gibson, a longtime political figure and journalist, was also the primary supporter of King Kalākaua's pan-Oceanianist policy in the Pacific. Though never solidified, "cognate race" recruitment might have aided the dream of creating a "Hawaiian primacy" throughout Oceania.[60] Based on Gibson's advice, the 1880 legislature approved "generous funding for political missions based on immigration treaty negotiations, as well as large subsidies for indentured migration."[61]

Pacific Islander labor recruitment was first directly implemented by the Hawaiian Kingdom government. In 1883, King Kalākaua commissioned Alfred N. Tripp as "Special Commissioner for Central and Western Polynesia."[62] Tripp was also the captain for the ship *Julia* and set forth that same year on both a "labor recruiting trip" and to "repatriate a number of Gilbertese whose labor contracts in Hawaii had expired."[63] Tripp acted as both governmental liaison and shipping captain. In his official government role, he was "to promote kindly relations between His Majesty and the various chiefs of the island."[64] He sent an invitation to two Gilbert Island chiefs for the coronation of King Kalākaua, but they did not attend.

The Hawaiian Kingdom's influence in the larger Oceania as both cousins (based on genealogical migrations of Hawaiians from Polynesia) and as the only Pacific and non-European sovereign nation (recognized in the Anglo-Franco Proclamation of 1843), accorded King Kalākaua the *kuleana* (responsibility) to act as protector and unifier of Oceania—a Pan-Oceanianism devoid of the usual acts of violence of imperialism.[65] Various Gilbertese elders and chiefs had appealed to King Kalākaua to annex their islands to the Hawaiian Kingdom, but the king deferred.[66] In 1889, John E. Bush was commissioned by King Kalākaua as Envoy Extraordinary and Minister Plenipotentiary to Samoa, Tonga, and the Cook Islands to confer to their leaders "the Royal Order of the Star of Oceania" [...] 'in advancing the good name and influence of Hawai'i in the Islands of Polynesia, and other groups of the surrounding Ocean in order to promote harmonious cooperation among kindred people and contiguous states and communities.' "[67] Gonschor writes that Bush was to then designate the Hawaiian Missionary Society (HMS) missionaries as consular agents who would "eventually work toward a Hawaiian annexation of the Gilbert Islands."[68] King Kalākaua's close ties to the people and leaders of the Gilberts is exemplified in the image below, entitled, "Showing remains of a house erected by King Kalākaua" on Ocean Island.[69]

King Kalākaua's vision of creating a "Hawaiian-led Confederation of Polynesian states" did not transpire in part because of the king's loss of political power suffered by the Missionary Party in Hawai'i when the illegal Bayonet Constitution was forced upon him.[70] But ironically, the Hawaiian missionaries in the Pacific supported the Hawaiian Kingdom's attempts and invitations to

Showing remains of a house erected by King Kālakaua.

engage as a protectorate in Oceania because it would have made their jobs easier to "regulate the evil deeds of these islands. This would speed up the advancement of the work of God in the Gilberts."[71]

On the labor recruiting front, efforts were soon handed over to private individuals who represented the sugar plantations, with the condition that they follow the laws from the Bureau of the Board of Immigration.[72] The Sugar Planters' Association took over the task of South Sea Islanders recruitment and hired their own boats and contacts to transport laborers. The Planters' Labor and Supply Company then enlisted workers in the South Pacific, with the permission of the Hawaiian Kingdom and under the Hawaiian flag.[73] Under three-year contracts, the first South Sea Islanders, totaling 86 passengers, voyaged to Hawai'i on board the ship *Stormbird* on May 29, 1878.[74] The workers were recruited from Rotuma and the Gilbert Islands.[75] Then in November 1878, the *Stormbird* delivered "128 Islanders, and was immediately dispatched for more."[76] Between 1878 and 1887, "most of the 2,403 South Seas immigrants who came to Hawaii [...] were Gilbertese. They did not intermarry with Hawaiians, nor were they valued as laborers by all plantation owners. Some plantation owners, however, favored them because of their low pay."[77]

South Sea Islanders were recruited as family units, and men, women, and children over 14 years of age were employed on the plantations. Their contracts were similar to those of Madeira laborers from Portugal in that family units were recruited, and "on-the-ground migration agents" negotiated their transportation.[78] The pay for South Sea Islanders was considerably lower than that of their Madeira counterparts, and they were paid among the lowest wages of all races. The following table explains the laborers' cost of importation, along with the average wages and living expenses garnered in 1886.

Also in 1886, and after less than a decade of recruiting South Seas Islanders to Hawai'i, the sugar planters decided to explore labor elsewhere because their efforts were proving unprofitable:

[1] The comparative cost of the several races represented on the plantations was estimated in the report of the Board of Immigration for 1886 as follows:—

	Cost of Importation	Aver. Wages (with Food)	Living Expenses
Portuguese	$112.00	$10.41 per mo.	$ 9.16 per mo.
Norwegians	130.00	9.00 "	10.00 "
Germans	100.00	12.75 "	8.00 "
Japanese[2]	65.85	9.88 "	6.32 "
Chinese	76.83	13.56 "	6.43 "
South Sea Islanders	78.50	10.16 "	5.77 "

Coman, 35.

The South Sea Islanders are obtained at lower wages than either the Japanese or Portuguese, but it is doubtful policy to obtain them as, almost without exception, they return home upon the expiration of their contracts, the expense of getting them here thereby becoming a dead loss.[79]

Unlike contract labor coming from other regions of the world, South Sea Islander contracts specified return voyages as part of the agreement:

The Government no longer tried the experiment of introducing this class of laborers, but later on, a few of the planters asked permission to secure laborers for their plantations. This was granted on the promise that they should be returned free of expense to themselves at the end of their term of service.[80]

Besides plantations flatly refusing to comply with this mandate, shipping operators did not keep track of their home islands and atolls, thus proving an enormous obstacle in returning them home. "Of all the hundreds of passenger lists of vessels entering the port of Honolulu until 1883, those of the 'South Sea Islanders' (mainly Gilbertese and New Hebrideans) are the only ones not showing the names of the immigrants and the specific place of origin."[81] Also, their contracts were later destroyed by the Territory of Hawai'i: "The government destroyed its copies of these contracts when the immigration office of the territory was moved from the custom house building to the capitol."[82] It became almost impossible to know which island was "home" after the termination of their contracts. Those fortunate enough to return to Oceania were often left to find their home island or atoll based on memory and recognition of natural markers in the environment or remembrance of the physical features of neighboring islands and atolls.

In general, the Gilbertese's contracts stipulated ten-hour work days, six days a week, for a total of 36 months, and children 14 years old and under were to be schooled in the public school system free of charge. The laws also regulated the conditions of travel, and the Board of Immigration emphasized vessel cleanliness and clear communication with workers:

1. The vessels should be fitted out with all comforts and supplied with food, water, and medicines sufficient for the number of people that the laws of the Kingdom allow them to carry, and no liquor, guns, or ammunition shall be taken for purposes of trade.

2. All acts in procuring labor shall be honest and above reproach, and no deception of any kind used. They should thoroughly interpret and explain fully to all the people what was expected of them, as well as the kind of labor, pay, and food.[83]

The Board of Immigration report in 1886 detailed other directives to the private recruiters and sugar plantations, such as the rate of pay; emphasis on the recruitment of women and children—no contracts were allowed with children, and those under 14 were to attend public schools; recruiters were to "to avoid quarrels with natives or missionaries"; and "if they so desired, they should be returned to their homes at the expiration of their contract."[84] The 1865 Ordinance 1 prohibited labor trade outside the jurisdiction of the Board of Immigration.[85] Other laws were passed in 1876, 1880, and 1884 to safeguard the laborers and ensure clean working conditions.[86]

According to immigration logs, there were twenty-nine voyages from the Gilbert Islands to Hawai'i between 1877 and 1887. The islands of origin were Rotuma, Gilberts, Tokelau, New Hebrides, Santa Cruz, Bougainville, New Ireland, Ellice, and "Manakiki." Gilberts refers to any of the islands within the island chain of Kiribati today, including Ocean Island. The primary ships carrying their passenger cargo were *Stormbird, Hawaii, Pomare, Nettie Merrill,* and *Allie Rowe,* with ship captains Jackson, Tripp, Wallace, and Tiernay, among others. The total number of islanders that arrived during these years was estimated to be between 2,383 and 2,403.[87]

The Hawaiian Kingdom's Board of Immigration laws were concise in order to guard against extracting labor as slave labor. However, some of these ships and captains were associated with the Pacific slave trade known as "blackbirding":

The term has been commonly applied to the large scale taking and carrying of people as such indigenous to the numerous islands in the Pacific Ocean during the 19th to 21st centuries. [...] They were taken from places such as the Solomon Islands, Vanuatu, Niue, Easter Island, Gilbert Islands, Tuvalu, and the Islands of the Bismarck Archipelago.... Areas such as Australia, America, the Philippines, Hawai'i, and Japan [...] took part in the slave trade in line with the notion of blackbirding.[88]

During this time, many articles in the Hawaiian newspapers covered the issue of blackbirding, and the images shared from Australia and New Zealand depicted islanders (*Kānaka*) in chains and transported like cattle to be used

Recruits, New Hebrides. "Kanaka, people, Australian South Sea Island-ers," Definition for Blackbirding Enslavement Practice, Britannica. www .britannica.com/topic/blackbirding, photo courtesy of the Australian National Library, PIC Box PIC/8179. https://nla.gov.au/nla.obj-136808374/view

as slave labor.[89] Sometimes, blackbirds were freed from distant shores, like Guatemala, and passed through Hawaiʻi en route to their homes in Oceania. A *Pacific Commercial Advertiser* article in 1904 explained:

> It should be remembered that some years ago, there was a great effort to get laborers to work on Hawaii, in South America, and elsewhere and that

Australia's Slave Trade. Nance Haxton, "Australia's Slave Trade: The growing drive to uncover secret history of Australian South Sea Islanders," ABC News. www.abc.net.au /news/2017–12–22/australian-south-sea-islanders-blackbirding/9270734 photo from the Alexander Turnbull Library.

> it was quite common to send down vessels among the islands of the Pacific to entice the simple-minded islanders, under the promise of great wages for two or three years of service. [. . .] Ah, these "labor ships" as they were called, were commanded by men of no principle, and they would often seize the islanders when they could get them on board their vessels, and carry them without any contract, never to return.[90]

According to records, one of the ships that regularly delivered laborers to Hawai'i, the *Stormbird,* was known as a blackbirding vessel: "Ships or black-birding vessels like *Stormbird* recruited 85 people [to Hawai'i] from Rotuma, Norounti, Mariana and Tabiteuea. The death rate [onboard] was 20%."[91] The boat's owner, Captain Mist, had bought the boat in Sydney, Australia and reg-istered it under the British flag. However, it was commissioned by the Hawai-ian government "to facilitate and promote immigration from the South Pacific British colonies and South Pacific islands to this country."[92] The *Stormbird's* captain from 1877 to 1879, George E. Gresley Jackson, was also known as a "blackbirder," or capturer of blackbirds, and executed his missions in often violent and forceful fashion toward islanders.

Captain Jackson was warned by the Hawaiian government to treat the

Ship *Stormbird,* National Library of New Zealand, circa 1910. Ref: PAColl-2107–04. Description: Ship *Stormbird* in Wellington Harbour, circa 1910. Photographer unknown. Photo courtesy of the Alexander Turnbull Library. https://natlib.govt.nz/records/22731380.

islanders with care. In 1878 he "received instructions to proceed to Rotumah and 'use all fair and just means to induce these people to emigrate to these Islands, and bear in mind we are anxious to have *women and children* from this Island.' "[93] That same year, Captain Jackson was reprimanded for engaging in the hostage-taking of a chief in Ponape:[94]

> Reports reached the High Commissioner for the Western Pacific telling of irregularities in the *Stormbird*'s dealings of Ponape and the Gilberts. Those regarding the Gilberts spoke of kidnapping but seem to have been merely hearsay avidly snapped up by rival Fiji recruiters from the *Patience*. What they served to do, however, was to focus British attention on the *Stormbird*, which was soon discovered to be illegally flying the British flag.[95]

This instance in Ponape was recorded in Hawai'i:

> In re. hostile attitude of the above person [Capt. Jackson] of the Brig. *Stormbird* towards the Chief & natives of Ponape. The said person had shot & wounded a native of said Island. Had the Chief put in iron & demanded

$500–as damage for the seizure of two sailors, who were taken on shore, by the Chief & held for non-payment of harbor dues & water furnished the ship.[96]

After this episode of the *Stormbird* "illegally flying the British flag," the ship was then legally registered in Hawai'i, and the Hawaiian Government again insisted on the "fair and honest treatment of the islanders."[97] Capt. Jackson also received a letter from the Board of Immigration instructing him to right his actions in Ponape, should he have the opportunity:

> *Stormbird* is placed under his command for a voyage to the South Seas for the purpose of procuring immigrants, & should he under any circumstances be near the island of Ponape, he shall visit the Chief with whom he had trouble on his first voyage & express regret on the trouble which had occurred between them, also to give presents to the Chief & the wounded man or his relative & try to settle the bad feeling existing in a pleasant way. Forbidding him not to purchase or make use of any liquor on board the vessel.[98]

The *Stormbird* continued to be besieged with blackbirding allegations, and on one of the voyages to Hawai'i, 18 men deserted upon arrival in Honolulu. S. G. Wilder requested the facts of the matter and offered to return the workers home at his own expense.[99]

In 1887, Captain Jackson's petition for pardon was referred to the Committee of Pardons by the Privy Council for a drunken fight in Honolulu.[100] Allegations of discord and mutiny followed him on his command of HMS *Kaimiloa,* the Hawaiian Kingdom's Royal Hawaiian Navy ship, on its only voyage to Samoa.[101] He was once a British Navy officer and hydrographical surveyor, and he "was hired, by contract, with the Interior Department early in 1882 [to] survey sixteen harbors of the Hawaiian Kingdom."[102] In between the two years Captain Jackson recruited laborers in the Pacific from 1877 to 1879 and the year he commanded the *Kaimiloa* from 1887 to 1888, he was sent to Maui and the districts Lahaina, Wailuku, Makawao, and Hana to "examine into and report to the Department upon the conditions of the roads and bridges in said Districts."[103]

Other labor recruiting voyages to the New Hebrides in 1880, with the ship *Pomare,* resulted in similar acts of violence between the ship's operators and the native population:

An armed raid on an Aurora village to regain a runaway was typical of Cadigan's methods [...] Cameron [second mate] did not hesitate to fire a cannon directly at attacking canoes and shore parties. Thus, what the Hawaiian government would have considered abuses occurred even when a government agent was on board.[104]

There was one recorded positive case of blackbirding aboard the *Allie Rowe* to the New Hebrides, which occurred without the Hawaiian government's consent, and on the last recruiting trip of the ship.[105] Due to sanitation and onboard rules, labor voyages to Hawai'i were generally considered better than others. Even so, the death rate of traveling to Hawai'i via steamship was exceptionally high for Pacific Islanders, and diseases were easily caught and spread in the close quarters of the ship's hold. While in Hawai'i, life on the sugar plantations was difficult, and the death rate of South Sea Islanders was the highest among all races. "The mortality rate of Gilbert Islanders in Hawaii was shocking, yet in view of the frequent drought, famine and warfare, it was probably no higher than in some years in the Gilberts."[106]

This first leg of what was supposedly a "circular migration" to Hawai'i for South Sea Islanders was strained with uncertainty and hardship. It was also highly fatal, whether in transport or on the actual plantations. Though they were leaving difficult environmental and sociopolitical conditions in their own islands and "seeing plantation work as the only escape from their 'land of heat and famine,'" obstacles to survival were also prominent in their migrations.[107] The popular use of the term "circular migrations" to describe the trans-Pacific labor movement proved to be a myth. Instead, the Gilbertese migrations resembled fractured and fragmented comings and goings. Rarely were people landed where they launched. And getting to Hawai'i was just the beginning of their journey.

Arrival—Pioneer Mill and Pu'unoa Village

In 1880, the *Pacific Commercial Advertiser* newspaper reported that approximately 90 South Sea Islander mill workers "abandoned work" and staged a strike in Lahaina, Maui.[108] These laborers then entered "a legal contest instituted [...] against their employer."[109] Four of the South Sea Islanders were charged "for desertion of service to Mr. Turton" (*sic*).[110] The Hawaiians on the plantation advised them to press the issue in court with the help of attorney J. W. Kalua.[111] Attorney Kalua contended that Turton could not file for their desertion of work because the islanders were under contract with the Board of Immigration and not contracted directly by his plantation.[112] The *Pacific Commercial Advertiser* chimed in, "These obligations we presume ought to command their services for the stipulated period" because their contracts bound them to labor.[113]

> The South Seas Islanders on Turton's plantation at Lahaina, Maui, [who] were told by a native lawyer that they could not be compelled to work on a plantation if they did not wish to, refused to work. The schooner *Nettie Merrill* was sent here for instruction from the Minister of the Interior as to what course should be pursued with the recalcitrant laborers. She returned Thursday with full instructions and was towed out of the harbor by the *Waimanalo*. Mr. Preston has taken the matter in hand (1880).[114]

Mr. Preston, the attorney for Turton, conceded that the Board of Immigration should charge them for desertion instead of Turton. The Turton case was promptly dismissed, and then Preston immediately charged the four laborers again with desertion, this time in his role as the Deputy Attorney General for the Board of Immigration. He also maintained Turton as his client because Turton was an agent for the Board as well: "Mr. Preston appeared in a new suit against the four South Sea Islanders, as Deputy Attorney General, and entered a complaint against them for desertion of service from the Board of Immigration, whose agent Mr. Turton was."[115] The case was put on hold, awaiting consultation from Hiram Bingham, who was called in to translate for the South Sea Islanders. The *Pacific Commercial Advertiser* again chimed in, "We hope to learn [...] that this disturbance of one of our most important sugar enterprises has been satisfactorily settled."[116]

For their part, the four South Sea Islanders contended they were kidnapped as slaves and brought to Maui to labor against their will:

> The defense set up that these South Sea Islanders were kidnapped, and did not understand when they left their homes, that they were to work; and, in fact, did not know where they were going or what they had to do; that Captain Wallace seduced them aboard the "Nettie Merrill," and some (not all) signed papers they did not know the purport of; that now they see they were being enticed away as slaves, and object of being such, and appeal to the courts of the Kingdom for release from contracts they did not understand. The consequences of this suit were that Mr. Turton had to stop grinding, the South Sea Islanders being the mill gang, who, on the commencement of the suit, deserted in a body.[117]

Laborers, Lahaina. Sugar-Plantation Laborers, Ark:70111/1CST, PPWD-18–3-033, Box #18, Folder #3, Image #033, Hawaiʻi State Archives.

Maui, Lahaina. Call Number PP-50–3-002. Hawaiʻi State Archives.

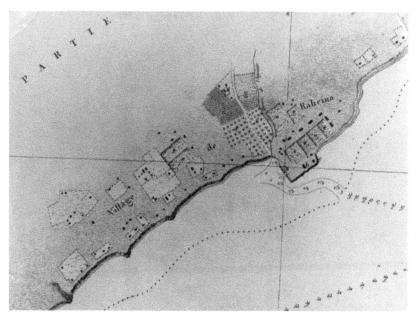

Lahaina, Maui. Call Number PP-50–3-040, Box #50, Folder #3, Image #040, Hawai'i State Archives.

Front Street, Lahaina. SP_75382, Bishop Museum Archives.

Sugar field, West Maui, Hawai'i. ca. 1945, SP_99818, Bishop Museum Archives.

This contentious encounter marked the beginning of South Sea Islander labor at the Pioneer Mill plantation in West Maui. South Sea or South Seas referred mainly to Gilbertese Islanders. The official documents of the day listed "South Sea Islander," without the "s" on Sea, while newspaper articles and other sources included the "s" and labeled them "South Seas Islanders." In any case, this group of workers made up the lowest caste of plantation labor, based on blossoming institutional racism that regarded "islanders," whether journeyed from one or plural and distinctive seas, as "savages." Assumptions of racial inferiority were primarily directed at Hawaiians. Once "civilized" through Calvinism, racism extended to their Polynesian and Pacific cousins of all island origins. Utilizing God's gospel to bring salvation to "dark-minded" and "lazy, good for nothing" islanders, newspaper articles relentlessly pondered the life and happenings of these people with equal parts wonder, fascination, distress, and contempt.[118] Attempts to "elevate" islanders to citizen-workers through 60-hour work weeks and religious doctrine were embraced wholeheartedly by plantation owners and mandated with the full force of the law.

On the one hand, images that depicted fascination and wonder about South Sea Islanders were exported to the various World Fairs, including one held in San Francisco in 1894. Lorrin Thurston went to the World Fair to sell Hawai'i "for advertising herself in the eyes of the world."[119] Besides the exhibition of a "Hawaiian village," a South Sea Island village was reproduced for curious onlookers as "it, too, will be inhabited by natives dwelling in huts of their own construction."[120] These fairs pioneered the representation of "natives" in their natural habitats and promoted illusions of "nativeness" to the world that would last until today.[121] Meanwhile, the sugar planters often used the "carrot and the stick" approach to control their laborers, and Pioneer Mill was no different in distributing equal parts incentives and punishment. Also, the power to govern the institutions themselves solidified their absolute control, as shown with the dual situation of Turton, who was both an agent for the Board of Immigration and a sugar-plantation owner.

The "Turton plantation," the Pioneer Mill Company, was in operation from 1863 to 1999. "James Campbell and Henry Turton, in partnership with Benjamin Pitman, established Pioneer Mill on land once occupied by the Lahaina Sugar Company."[122] Campbell and Turton bought land called "Mekekau at Pana'ewa and 'Ōpae'ula" in Lahaina in 1865.[123] From there, they purchased *kuleana* rights to water and land where available, while they also leased large tracts of Crown Lands, which allowed access to both land and water, from the government. Campbell and Turton added the Lahaina Sugar Company and the West Maui Sugar Company to Pioneer Mill in 1874.[124] Turton then took out loans from Hackfield & Co. to buy out Campbell, but Campbell and Isenberg paid the first promissory note owed by Turton and conveyed his interest in the company to themselves.[125]

As for labor recruitment, Hackfield & Co. brought over workers from Europe, and they played a direct role in migrations. "In Germany, Hackfield & Co. had its own agents staffed as local Hawaiian consuls and shipped indentured labourers to Hawai'i on government commission aboard its own Hawaiian-registered ships."[126] Further, "Hackfield & Co. provided assistance, though did not own the ships used."[127] Hackfield & Co. also applied for recruitment trips in the Pacific. They returned their workers onboard the *Pomare* on at least one occasion,

> subject to the regulations of the Board [of Immigration], and on the conditions accorded Mr. Turton and others. The Board undertook to return the islanders to their homes, if, at the end of their contract, any vessels under the control of the Bureau of Immigration were running to the South Seas.[128]

Also, according to the South Sea Islanders who filed charges citing slavery in 1880, at least a few of those laborers were presumed brought to Maui as black-birds onboard the *Nettie Merrill*. By 1888, the majority of South Sea Islanders worked primarily on plantations on Kaua'i, Maui, and O'ahu:

> In the whole Kingdom, there were 209 South Seas Islanders (Gilbertese) and 201 New Hebrideans employed. [...] Lihue went in strong for Gilbertese 86 out of a total 401. [...] The Horner Plantation at Lahaina, too, had a big colony of South Seas Islanders, 60 out of its 300 workers.[129]

"Horner plantation" referred to another owner and manager of the Pioneer Mill.[130] Some of the Gilbertese on Kaua'i also migrated to O'ahu and Lahaina, Maui after their three-year contracts expired because "the dry climate there suited them."[131] There were many instances where the South Sea Islanders complained about the colder weather in Hawai'i, and attempting to adapt to the weather increased their feelings of homesickness.

Pioneer Mill grew exponentially and went from cultivating 600 acres of sugarcane in 1885 to 8,000 acres in 1910.[132] They credited their success with buying up and/or leasing large tracts of land, government support and exemptions in their creation of ditches and reservoirs for water access, special access to government roads and bridges, the use of technology and the implementation of cement linings for ditches, and steam engines that streamlined operations, among other innovations. But the enormous company growth can really be credited to one thing—controlling the water flow on the entire west side of Maui.

Pioneer Mill diverted the water from the northern sections of West Maui and the West Maui Mountains' highest point, Pu'u Kukui, to the southern ends of Lahaina and Olowalu. By 1910, "the largest part of money for improvements has been spent on developing, storing, and controlling the water."[133] This massive diversion of water would have adverse and devastating impacts on the land and residents of West Maui for generations to come. "By 1866, concerns about water usage in Lahaina were being raised."[134] Court cases against Pioneer Mill for *kuleana* water rights, or court cases by Pioneer Mill to snatch those water rights away from native tenants, began early in the 1860s and continued through much of the company's history.[135]

Also aligned to the other plantations on Maui and across Hawai'i, Pioneer Mill regarded the "labor issue" as a race issue, and utilized race as a primary identifier and mechanism for control. Worker pay, hours, contracts, housing, extracurricular activities and sports—everything was categorized and managed according to race and molded by the sugar planters' fantasies about their racial inferiority. Worker pay on Maui was also strictly monitored so that no plantation offered any racial group more money than the other plantations:

> The workers were paid according to their ethnicity and the job performed. Adding to this structure was an interesting and alarming "cost comparison" done by the four Maui plantations to ensure that none of them paid their laborers more than the other plantations' wages.[136]

In this well-documented racial hierarchy, South Sea Islanders were paid near the bottom rung. The following graph relates this reality:

In the report of 1888–1890 the Board of Immigration estimated plantation wages as follows :—		
	Contract Laborers	*Free Laborers*
Hawaiian	$18.58 per month.	$20.64 per month.
Portuguese	19.53 "	22.25 "
Japanese	15.58 "	18.84 "
Chinese	17.61 "	17.47 "
South Sea Islander	15.81 "	18.56 "

Board of Immigration, plantation labor and race table. Coman, 23.

In the plantation camps and villages, Gilbertese Islanders forged strong ties to their own community, and they lived and worked closely together, often refusing to be separated. Complaints about their overcrowded plantation camp housing were reported, but they would not be socialized away from communal living. Hiram Bingham was named the South Sea Islander "Special Protector" in 1880.[137] He maintained a close relationship with the Gilbertese community in Hawai'i before and after this two-year appointment. In his records, he noted the crowded living conditions on the plantations, "but admitted this was often the Islanders' own choice."[138] As "Special Protector," Bingham's overall duties included:

> To make tours on the several islands of the group where there are South Sea islanders employed, to inspect their general treatment and condition, to report when necessary any violation of the laws, the regulations of the Board or the conditions under which they are engaged, to inspect the quarters, food, and arrangements for medical care and enquire into any complaints that they may have to make, explaining to them their rights and their duties and helping them by advice to obtain redress in case of wrong; to see that

their children are given the facilities for education in district schools, and report to the Board such modification of contracts or other arrangements as might to him appear to conduce to the well-being of the people, as also all statistics that he may gather.[139]

Besides housing, Bingham encountered other issues in this role: Children under 15 were being made to labor, and "suitable" food was not being served. He additionally advocated for "sufficient medical attendance," and he insisted on "clean and proper" lodging conditions.[140] The islanders expressed gratitude to Bingham for his role: "His appointment was a source of satisfaction to the Islanders [who] were yet glad to be visited by one who spoke their language and whom they regarded as a disinterested friend."[141]

No other race had an official "protector" on the plantations, but the tracking and categorization of all races were undertaken by both the government and the plantations themselves. The Hawaiian Kingdom Census of 1890 coincided with the Comparative Table and Sugar Plantation Statistics in 1888 and 1890. The following tables list the sugar plantations' "nationality" tracking.

The Hawaiian Kingdom Census in 1890 further classified races according to regions. For example, a partial count from the island of Maui, region of Lahaina, is listed here with those who responded with "Ocean Island" to the question: *Aina Kahi i Hanau Ia Ai, Na Haole Vale no* (Where were you born? Haole only). "Ocean Is" was included after the name of their home island or

COMPARATIVE TABLE
SHOWING NUMBER AND NATIONALITY OF LABORERS EMPLOYED ON PLANTATIONS, JANUARY, 1890 AND 1888.
(From Report of President of Board of Immigration, 1890.)

NATIONALITY.	Men day Labor.	Men under Contract.	Women.	Minors.	Totals, 1890.	Employed 1888.
Hawaiian	954	900	19	....	1873	2062
Portuguese	1867	463	272	416	3017	3132
Japanese	952	6558	1114	....	8624	3299
Chinese	4214	303	....	....	4517	5727
South Sea Islanders	123	252	58	....	433	470
Americans	98	3	....	....	101	888
British	79	1	....	....	80	
Other Nationalities	253	61	....	....	314	
	8540	8541	1462	416	18959	15578

Board of Immigration, 1890. "Comparative Table, Board of Immigration, 1890." Hawai'i State Archives.

SUGAR PLANTATION STATISTICS.

(Compiled from Report of President Board of Immigration to the Legislature, 1890.)

TABLE SHOWING NUMBER AND NATIONALITY OF PLANTATION LABORERS.

NATIONALITY.	Men day labrs.	Men under contrct	Wo- men.	Mi- nors.	Total Jan. 1890.	Total 1888.	Decrse	Incrse
Hawaiians	954	900	19	......	1,873	2,062	189	......
Portuguese.......	1,867	463	272	416	3,017	3,511	494	......
Japanese.........	952	6,558	1,114	......	8,624	3,299	......	4,261
Chinese..........	4,214	303	......	......	4,517	5,727	1,210	......
South Sea Islanders	123	252	58	......	433	470	37	......
Americans	98	3	......	......	101	} 888	393	......
British...........	79	1	......	......	80			
Other Nationalities	253	61	......	......	314			
Totals........	8,540	8,541	1,462	416	18,959	15,957	2,323	4,261

Sugar Plantation Statistics. "Sugar Plantation Statistics, 1890."
Hawai'i State Archives.

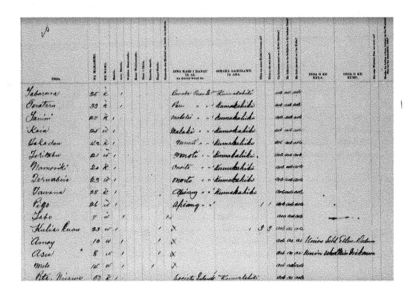

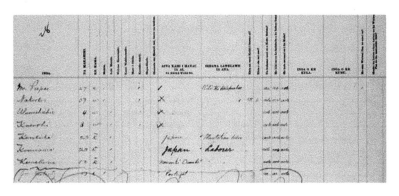

atoll. Ocean Island was recorded as a general identifier and perhaps viewed as the center in the periphery for these islanders.

In 1890, the Lahaina, Maui South Sea Islanders were:

Tabarena, 35, Banaba, Ocean Island
Terataru, 33, Peru, Ocean Island
Yanimi, 27, Makatei, Ocean Island
Kaia, 25, Makaki, Ocean Island
Takadau, 42, Monoiti, Ocean Island
Teritabu, 21, Monoti, Ocean Island
Namoriki, 30, Onoito, Ocean Island
Teruabeia, 23, Onoito, Ocean Island
Tawana, 28, Apaiang, Ocean Island
Pigo, 26, Apaiang, Ocean Island
Pita Niuewe, 50, Society Islands
Kamekune, 52, Monoiti, Ocean Island[142]

This is obviously not a complete list of the 86 South Seas Islanders who lived at the Pu'unoa Village in Lahaina by 1903, but it represents those who took part in the 1890 census. By 1910, in the "Statistics for Hawaii" United States Government Census, "South Sea Islands" was no longer part of the descriptive discourse or the U.S. census count. This ethnic redistribution occurred alongside the illegal overthrow of the Hawaiian Kingdom and the taking of Hawai'i by the United States—aspects that transformed the social and political life since the last census count of 1890. In this mix, the South Sea Islander classification was erased from bureaucratic memory and reclassified as "Other."[143]

Pu'unoa Village was the name of the camp community in Lahaina where the South Sea Islanders lived: "By 1900 there were two permanent settlements of Gilbertese, one in Honolulu and one at Lahaina, Maui. The Hawaiian, Lutera, was given charge of the Gilbertese at Puunoa, Lahaina."[144] The Pu'unoa Village was located just north of Lahaina town, on the beach, and south of Mala wharf.[145] By 1927, many years after the South Sea Islanders had departed, Pu'unoa was listed in Pioneer Mill's records as a camp that housed mainly Filipino and Portuguese workers.

While the South Sea Islanders inhabited Pu'unoa Village, *The Maui News* recorded tales of their eventful lives and vibrant community. There were articles of a capsized boat and a South Sea Islander swimming ten miles to get help to save the remaining crew members.[146] There were descriptions of singing events

Watergate. Maui S.
Waik. Call Number
PP-50–7-025, Box #50,
Folder #7, Image #025,
Hawai'i State Archives.

Late 19th Century South Sea Islander Sugar Plantation Laborers

Olowalu Mill, Maui. Call Number PPBER-2–6-010, Box #2, Folder
#6, Image #010, Photo Credit: Bellinghausen, Brother Gabriel Bertram
(1849–1933), Hawai'i State Archives.

Olowalu Mill, Maui. Call Number PPBER-2–6-010, Box #2, Folder #6, Image #009, Photo Credit: Bellinghausen, Brother Gabriel Bertram (1849–1933), Hawai'i State Archives.

South Sea Islander Sugar Plantation Laborers. Hank Soboleski, "New Hebridean Immigrants Ben and Lizzie Ramson of Kauai," *The Garden Island, Island History,* November 12, 2019. www.thegardenisland.com/2017/11/12/lifestyles/new-hebridean -immigrants-ben-and-lizzie-ramson-of-kauai/.

Lahaina Mill. c. 1890s, SP_104112. Bishop Museum Archives.

Pioneer Sugar Mill, Lahaina, Maui. CP_56449. Bishop Museum Archives, Honolulu, Hawaiʻi.

PIONEER MILL COMPANY, LTD.
(Name of Plantation)

PLANTATION CENSUS - **February 28, 1927.**
(Date)

Camp or Village (Full Name)	JAPANESE			FILIPINO			PORTUGUESE		
	Men	Wn.	Chdn.	Men	Wn.	Chdn.	Men	Wn.	Chdn.
Crater Village	38	24	80	41	16	17	3	4	11
Otani Camp	7	4	8						
Mahinahina Camp	22	14	47	4			1	1	2
Honokowai Village	39	25	59	7	4	9			
Kahana Camp	13	11	27	14	5	4			
Landing Camp	4	3	8	10	7	16			
Puukolii Camp	142	115	277	183	65	118	14	11	39
Kiawe Camp	1	1	4	136	17	32			
Kapunakea Village	47	27	86	4	3	5			
Mala Village	1	-	2	30	13	30	10	12	19
Kahua Village	42	29	92	59	11	24			
Mill Camp (Old)	22	18	34	17	8	15	4	3	9
Kilawea Village	37	39	102	1	1	1			
Tezaoka Camp.	6	6	19				2	3	13
Chan Hau Camp				5	1	1			1
Catholic Mission Camp	3	2	2						
Puunoa Village				3	2	5	5	8	12
Lunaville	2	2	5				5	4	12
Wainee Village	51	50	163	121	12	18	1	1	3
Makila Camp	20	12	45	12					
Naruehi Camp	4	2	6	9	1				
Inoye Camp				6					
Kauaula Camp	14	9	26	20	3	8			
Kirei Camp	3	2	5	31	13	19			
Joe Lua Camp				5	4	2			
Jno. Lua "				1					
Old Clubhouse	7			1			1	1	1
Totals	525	395	1093	940	180	324	46	49	121

SKILLED EMPLOYEES LIVING IN LAHAINA CITY.

	Men.	Women.	Children.
	24	16	17
Americans.	8	11	12
Japanese	9	10	10
Filipinos	2	1	2
Portuguese	21	11	62
Hawaiians	10	15	9
Chinese	1		2
Others	1	1	
	66	56	102

Pioneer Mill Company, Ltd., Plantation Census, February 28, 1927. Hawaiʻi Sugar Planters Association Archives, Hamilton Library, University of Hawaiʻi, Mānoa.

Boat house built by Gilbert Island immigrants at Lahaina, Maui, ca. 1903. F_20074, Bishop Museum Archives.

Homes constructed by Gilbert Island immigrants at Lahaina, Maui, Hawaiʻi, ca. 1903. F_20075, Bishop Museum Archives.

and community festivities: "At the South Sea Island village, the young people attend a singing school every evening."[147] However, the main narratives that accompanied the South Sea Islanders in Lahaina, besides work at Pioneer Mill, referred to their religious indoctrination through the efforts of Bingham, Reverend Martin Lutera, and Ellice Island missionary Mr. Isaia.

Reverend Lutera was a primary figurehead for this group. He was born on the island of Lāna'i, attended the Royal School in Honolulu, was a cabin boy on a British vessel, and eventually became a missionary in the Gilbert Islands. When he returned to Hawai'i, he served the Gilbertese in Lahaina, "and a considerable portion of their church was built with his own hands."[148] Reverend Lutera was aided by Mr. Isaia, a missionary from Ellice Islands who married a Gilbertese and came to Hawai'i on board the ship *John Boyd* when it was commanded by Capt. Jackson. Both were employed by the Board of the Hawaiian Evangelical Association.[149] The two precipitated a "revitalization" of religious fervor among the Gilbertese:[150] "There has been a religious revival in the colony of South Sea Islanders at Lahaina, and the aliens have ceased flying kites on Sunday."[151] The dedication of the clergy sustained the Gilbertese while they labored in the hot sun of Lahaina and their efforts were reportedly "met with much success" by other missionaries.[152]

Mr. Isaia was able to return with the rest of the Gilbertese in 1903. In 1904, the church Reverend Lutera built for them was torn down, and a Japanese Hongwanji temple was built in its place: "The church building which Martin Lutera constructed for the South Sea Islands has been torn down. Near the site of the demolished structure, a handsome Japanese Buddhist temple has been built by the flourishing Hongwanji sect."[153] Reverend Lutera died in 1908 as "one of Maui's Most Prominent Ministers."[154] As for Pioneer Mill, their early history was rife with worker discontent and "militancy." Two years after the Gilbertese laborers left in 1903, Pioneer Mill contended with a riot that resulted in

> the death of a worker. Alarmed by the militancy of the workers, the governor called out the militia, and the United States Army sent a squad of Signal Corps troops, even though the manager had made several important concessions, including the dismissal of the foreman.[155]

Early worker strikes on the various plantations eventually led to the unionization of workers in the form of the International Longshoremen's and Warehousemen's Union (ILWU) in 1946. Power rearranged itself away from plantation paternalism and along union and political-party lines.[156]

RETURN—HOME

One young man whose gaze was centered upon the ridges back of Honolulu was asked whether he really wanted to go to the Gilbert Islands. There was a silence for a few seconds, when he replied in a voice earnest and deep: "Well, there's much up here to enjoy—but I'm glad to go back, because it's, it's—home." And that expressed the feelings of all.[157]

We sweat and cry salt water, so we know the ocean is in our blood.[158]

On the morning of October 18, 1903, the ship *Isleworth* left Honolulu "with her human freight on board and bound for Tarawa, the seat of British Government for the Gilbert and Ellice Islands protectorates."[159] *Isleworth* would transport most of the South Sea Islander immigrants from Hawai'i to Tarawa, where a British officer met them and assisted in getting them to their home islands.[160] Those staying on board continued to Ocean Island and then disembarked. The *Isleworth* would also exchange the cargo of lumber she was carrying, alongside the Gilbertese, for guano and continue en route to Spencer Gulf, South Australia.[161] Nothing would disrupt this final voyage of Gilbertese Islanders to their homes and the transportation of guano to their fields.

The *Hawaiian Annual* reported on the "Exodus of Gilbertese:"

> Practically the whole colony of Gilbert Islanders of Honolulu and Lahaina, some 220 in number, took advantage of the opportunity which presented itself to them to return to their coral island home in October last, by the S.S. *Isleworth,* as that vessel was getting ready for her return to the South Seas. Notwithstanding the short notice and lack of funds among a majority of these people, through the personal efforts of Rev. H. Bingham, Mr. J. T. Arundel, British Consul W. R. Hoare, C. L. Wright and others, funds were provided, and all arrangements were satisfactorily carried through so that they departed, as above stated, October 17th.[162]

In 1903, cargo movement of both humans and raw materials was orchestrated along the well-worn routes of colonization and globalization. This voyage answered the call of the Gilbertese, who had long since outstayed their three-year contracts, some by more than twenty years. Only one out of the remaining 86 islanders in Lahaina decided to stay, saying, "I get plenty to drink up here—no get down there."[163] The others from the Lahaina group joined the Honolulu-based Gilbertese, who resided at the Kalihi Detention Camp, leaving a total of 220 migrants making the long-awaited voyage home.

Going home was a constant theme and perhaps the glue that kept the two Gilbertese communities so tightly woven in their places. Some were able to leave in 1886 onboard a vessel that made a stop in Hawai'i from Mexico and was headed to the Gilbert Islands, but about 80 workers who arrived after this episode were completely stuck with no way to return, and only 25 of the last group of 80 survived.[164] Hiram Bingham noted that out of approximately 1,500 workers, around 300 had died while in Hawai'i, and about 900 returned home.[165] Many did not return immediately after their three-year contracts expired, most did not have any savings with which to return home, and few sought remedy in the courts for their return voyage. "They were scattered over these islands: thinking they had been deceived."[166]

By 1901, Hiram Bingham II was trying to help the roughly 200 Gilbertese former plantation laborers go home.[167] Also, in 1901, the Board of Health threatened to remove the "South Sea Island squatters occupying land on the naval station. It had become insanitary."[168] The Kalihi South Sea Islander community sprang up from 23 makeshift shacks put together after the big fire in Chinatown on Maunakea Street had destroyed most of their belongings.[169] They lived in a colony at Kaka'ako behind the quarantine wharf. Later, they were moved to the Kalihi camp, which was known as the Kalihi Detention Camp and once housed bubonic plague victims in 1900.[170] They survived by fishing and braiding hats and mats. The ones still there were more than likely brought between 1880 and 1882, and the Gilbertese who arrived during that same time and were laborers at the Koloa plantation on Kaua'i had already returned "according to [the] agreement."[171]

In 1903 with news that the ship *Isleworth* would be passing through Honolulu en route to Ocean Island, Bingham and others rushed to organize both camps. On Maui, Reverend Lutera and Mr. Isaia helped with the effort, as Mr. Isaia was also returning home to the Gilbert Islands with them. The Lahaina South Sea Islanders went to Honolulu a day early on the *Kinau* to await passage on the ship *Isleworth*: "There was a happy lot of Gilbertians on the *Kinau* when they arrived [...] The anticipation of once more living at 'home' as they termed the distant islands of their birth, caused them to smile on the least provocation."[172] Hastening their belongings together and finding the funds to pay for the O'ahu voyage was the exciting yet daunting precursor for the larger voyage they would take collectively with the Kalihi-based Gilbertese. They were met by Bingham once they docked in Honolulu, and they then camped overnight onboard the *Isleworth* with the Kalihi group under tents and tarps that were set up in anticipation for their voyage home. At their meeting, "the slit-eared, poorly clad, but happy people from Lahaina and Honolulu mingled and renewed acquaintances."[173]

The Lahaina group consisted of Gilbertese and "a couple of Tongans," and who were wealthy compared to their Oʻahu compatriots, as 19 of them had $856.70 in the bank.[174] The $300 needed for the Lahaina group to travel on the *Isleworth* came from this total. The Lahaina group also paid $250 for travel on the *Kinau* to Oʻahu.[175] Of the Oʻahu group, only 21 of them had any money in the bank.[176] Bingham held $1,700 in trust for the entire group, and they raised $1,500 for the trip with the help of Bingham, Arundel, and others.[177] The voyage itself cost $1,000, and it was paid by 38 of the Gilbertese, with more than half of the money contributed by two men.[178] Besides the transportation fee, there were food and provisions to purchase for the approximately 20-day voyage home.[179] They also returned with almost $1,000 in savings among them, and therefore might have seemed like "plutocrats" on arrival.[180]

Bingham had negotiated the voyage with British Consul Hoare and the charterer of the *Isleworth*. Planning the Lahaina group's arrival to coincide with the departure of the *Isleworth* while organizing the Kalihi group took finessing. Bingham had originally contacted Consul Hoare to send a British vessel from Fiji to transport them. But when this opportunity arose, they jumped to action. According to one writer, "They have been clamorous and pathetic in their requests to Rev. Bingham to be deported in some way to their former homes."[181] Their request was eventually formalized with correspondence from Sir Henry M. Jackson, the Britannic Majesty's High Commissioner. Sir Jackson's reply read:

> Sir: I have the honor to acknowledge the receipt of your dispatch [...] on the subject of the repatriation of a number of Gilbert Islanders who have long been resident in Hawaii: and I have hereby to express the thanks of his Majesty's Government to yourself and to all concerned with you in the matter, for your philanthropic efforts on behalf of these people.[182]

Besides curiosity of their fate and if home would be met as anticipated, some in Honolulu wondered at the continuation of hat-making as the Gilbertese in Kalihi took this Hawaiian cultural art and excelled with the sale and production of hats—"the Gilbert Islanders, as well as the natives, but not the present generation, are born hat weavers."[183] "Lewalewa" was the term used for South Sea Islander hat-makers, and "the Honoluluans will miss the Gilbert Islanders from the streets on which they appeared barefooted and generally with about half a dozen of the cheap hats in their hands."[184] The women primarily made hats while the men fished. These were their main sources of survival and how they earned money that paid for their weekly community feasts. Those residing at the Kalihi Detention Camp could stay there rent-free as long as they abided by the "laws of the land."[185]

On the day of the departure, the *Isleworth* stayed the night just outside the harbor because the company chartering the boat was awaiting cablegrams.[186] With their happiness on display, some in the community suggested their departure would be a good "opportunity for securing some very choice pictures" of the "picturesque Gilbertese."[187] The curious onlookers noticed no musical instruments on board, but "every old woman seemed to own a pipe and a woven bag in which tobacco was carried."[188] It was reported that "the night before the *Isleworth* arrived at Tarawa, the Islanders held a big prayer meeting, singing as a closing hymn, 'God Be With You Till We Meet Again.' "[189] After their departure, numerous newspaper articles wondered at their voyage and what had transpired. News came from the ship *Sierra* two months later that the Gilbertese had arrived at Tarawa at the end of October and that both a baby boy and girl were born on board. The British Commissioner met them at Tarawa and helped transport them to their home islands.

Prayer meetings and religious hymns accompanied their passage to Tarawa, and the captain of the ship reported back, "We had a fine run down, lots of singing and praying."[190] Hiram Bingham II and his wife, Minerva, had introduced religious doctrine to Apaiang, Gilbert Islands, many years prior in 1857 on board the first *Morning Star*. They set off on their Micronesian mission with the American Board of Foreign Missions and were intent on "the evangelization of heathen tribes inhabiting islands of the Pacific."[191] His parents, Rev. Bingham and Sybil Bingham, were part of the first company of Calvinist Missionaries that arrived in Hawai'i in 1820. They returned to the U.S. when Hiram II was ten years old, and he returned many years later with his wife, a missionary who directly descended from the *Mayflower* missionaries. Upon arrival in Honolulu as an adult, Kawaiahao Church asked Bingham to be their pastor, but he declined, saying, "I would prefer to go with such Hawaiian Christians as might be ready, to Micronesia, to co-operate with them and the Hawaiian churches in giving similar blessings to the benighted heathen of those distant and neglected lands."[192] For 51 years, until his death in 1908, Bingham and his wife worked closely with the Gilbertese, either in the Gilbert Islands or in Hawai'i, and he knew 20 of the 21 Hawaiian missionaries who were sent to the Gilbert Islands.[193]

Bingham translated the Bible into Gilbertese in 1890. In 1892 and 1893,

Lauhala Hats, Mats, and Fiber. I-102,688.26, Bishop Museum Archives.

Hat making. C, 1900–1910, SP_3182, Bishop Museum Archives.

Bingham went to New York to oversee the printing of the Gilbertese Bible. He prided himself in "bringing a language" to the Gilbertese and indoctrinating them into the teachings of God:

> I was enabled to preach for years to thousands who had never heard of Jesus, to give the Gilbertese churches the entire Bible in their own tongue, to prepare them a Commentary on the Four Gospels, a Hymn and Tune Book, and a Bible Dictionary, and my dear wife was enabled, among other things, to give their school books.[194]

Gilbertese Islander Moses Kaure helped him in his translations with the Bible and the Gilbertese Dictionary while in Honolulu, living with him for over a year. Bingham was praised by fellow missionaries for his works after his death in 1908:

> Few men have had the opportunity and the ability mentally and physically, together with scholarship sufficient for the task, to reduce a language to writing and translate into that language the whole Bible, to prepare commentaries on many of its books, and at last to produce a dictionary which shall give it a clear place among the written languages of the world.[195]

After his death, much was also written about the "treacherous" conditions the Binghams had faced in the Gilbert Islands. On Apaiang, he had apparently dealt with "the gross ignorance and nakedness of those they sought to teach."[196] At the death of his wife Minerva in 1903, the "harshness" of their journey in Apaiang was deciphered in newspaper articles:

> What a cheerful spirit she had: what loving patience: but how her house-wifely soul must have been tried when her savage neighbors, animated by curiosity, presented themselves, in season and out of season, and seating their well oiled bodies on her clean, fresh matting, left huge grease spots as witness of their prompt recognition of these strangers in their midst.[197]

Besides residing in Apaiang, Minerva and her husband traveled while they could and before both were afflicted by various illnesses. Bingham was the captain of the second *Morning Star* ship built in 1866. They sailed to and from Honolulu to Marquesas and Micronesia to visit the various mission stations of the Hawaiian Board of Missionaries. Minerva was referred to as his "private

Reverend Hiram Bingham, "*Morning Star* Sketch, Story of the *Morning Star;* The Children's Missionary Vessel," American Board Missionary House, 33 Pemberton Square, 1866. www.trussel.com/kir/mornstar.htm

mate." He stopped sailing in 1868 when he started to have health problems, and they both returned to Apaiang. They soon came back to Honolulu due to health issues that they both faced.[198]

Bingham died while away from Hawai'i in Baltimore when he went East to proofread and make corrections to his Gilbertese Dictionary before printing; "he therefore died on duty."[199] After his death in 1908, the missionary schooner *Hiram Bingham* was named after him and delivered these Gilbertese Bibles from San Francisco, with a replenishing stop and religious ceremony in Honolulu, en route to the Gilbert Islands. "The printing of this Bible was the culmination of all his years of missionary labors on behalf of the Gilbert Islanders, and the fruits are now on the way to be distributed among the natives."[200] Bingham was regarded by his fellow missionaries as "the maker of a language" and savior of a people.[201]

Soon after, a Missionary School for Boys was built on Ocean Island by Missionary Channon and his wife from the island of Kusaie. The mission's boys' and girls' schools were destroyed on Kusaie by a typhoon a couple of years prior, and the girls' school had already been rebuilt on that island. They decided to build the boys' school on Ocean Island and name it after Hiram Bingham:

> We go therefore to Ocean Island to re-establish the school for boys of the Gilbert Islands there. It is to be known hereafter as the Bingham school in honor of Dr. Bingham, the first missionary to the Gilbertese, who with his devoted wife reduced their language to writing.[202]

They chose Ocean Island for the rebuilding of the school because of the phosphate industry and the ease to travel as missionaries between islands by jumping on board the various ships that were coming and going for the industry. There were an estimated 1,300 Gilbertese employed for the mines and about 100 "whites" living there, and it gave them ample opportunity "to minister to a larger number in one place than would be possible anywhere else in the group."[203] They also enthused that the phosphate company welcomed them to Ocean Island with open arms and "extend[ed] us every help it can."[204]

The now-familiar joint indoctrination of religion and industry followed the Hawai'i-based immigrants into their return home. The Gilbertese "circular migrations" were finally completing their trajectory. *Isleworth* was already voyaging to the northernmost point of the Gilbert Islands and would easily transport the Gilbertese as commissioned.[205] They were perhaps "crossing the beach" for the final time.[206] They carried within them the "deep histories" of their ancestors and had also lived the deep outbreaks of violence that occurred during and because of their migrations.[207] By all accounts, the early Gilbertese experience in Hawai'i was not an easy diaspora of non-broken linear flows of departure, arrival, and return. Instead, they presented in fractured starts and stops. With the objective finally completed, many in Hawai'i were left wondering what became of them and if they really found their way home. The Gilbertese had garnered a niche in local culture, and their exodus attracted the attention of the larger community. For the Gilbertese, despite uncertainty as to their final destinations, they knew they wanted to leave and had wanted to leave for many years because "all of them [were] homesick."[208]

In 1904, the ship *Inger* came from Ocean Island and transported 2,600 tons of guano to Hackfield & Co. in Hawai'i and "Capt. Johannson reports that several of the Gilbertese who once lived at Lahaina are now working in the fertilizer beds at Ocean Island."[209] The returned Banabans would meet religious doctrine on Ocean Island in the familiar personage of the Bingham legacy with the naming of the mission's boys' school after him. The home they returned to was even more reminiscent of where they had left, and they were once again caught between religion and industry in their homeland. How would they connect or reconnect to *te aba?*

Since land and people are one in Gilbertese, as in the term *te aba,* the control by the phosphate industry, missionaries, and global food agendas silenced not only the inhabitants but destroyed the agency of the land and the islands themselves. International markets, the chains of supply and demand, and a crisscrossing of routes and the ties that bind are reminiscent of the global marketplace that demands importation and deportation of laborers and land, disposable and available for all regions and for the global marketplace. Assumptions based on race and ideas of racial inferiority were and continue to be at the forefront of such destruction. "The global recitation of ethnic deficiencies was a part of the worldwide psychological rationalization of labor exploitation."[210]

Racial inequalities and deficiencies were also the mantras that fueled Christianization and the "salvation" of entire populations of Pacific Islanders in Oceania during this era. Consequently, the treatment of people regarded as less than human carried with it strong social and political stigma and formidable methods of discipline mixed with desire to subjugate and control. This Banaban flow and movement of both land and people across ocean spaces was actuated to serve and placate global desires and needs, and during the turn of the last century, the diaspora was guided by colonial voices and agendas that systematically silenced and sought to destroy the Gilbertese voice of both the land and people.

'Iwa

The frigate bird represents strength and fortitude in Banaban culture. In Hawai'i, the frigate bird is the 'iwa bird and symbolic of "survival and prophecies."[211] The 'iwa bird spends 90 percent of its life flying, and it can soar with the sophisticated knowledge of using the cumulus clouds to help it climb and soar over enormous distances and for months-long time spans.[212] No one knows how the 'iwa survives in the turbulence of the clouds, and only recently have their feats of survival in freezing temperatures and through extraordinarily long flights been understood by scientists. They liken the movements to hang gliders, aerialists, who are also able to navigate an entire metauniverse of weather and strength obstacles. The 'iwa are also unable to walk on land, and they cannot land on the ocean—they could drown, as their wings are not waterproof.[213] Incredible feats of migrations. One scientist commented:

I have seen them in the air and they fly just so beautifully it takes your breath away. Then I have seen them on land and they just stand in place, totally out of sorts. They don't walk, they just stand there. But soon enough they are jumping back into the air, where they belong.[214]

There is no fear, only freedom in the flight and mystery in the observation—like the incredible migrations and survival of those from the "land of frigates," where Banaba is the center of their world as the *buto*.[215] Though systematically decentered by outside agencies and agendas, the center still exists and continues to guide her people to search for cultural longevity and genealogical continuity, whether in Rabi or on their home island.

KA ʻIWA

> This is a song for you
> The ʻiwa bird so relaxing
> Gliding easily
> Gliding easily
> By the front of the cliffs
> His back is as straight as a cliff
> His face as bright as the moon
> It's a beautiful sight
> It's a beautiful sight
> You are my sweetheart
> Your eyes are tantalizing
> They're drawing the heart
> It's just like the beauty
> It's just like the beauty
> Sitting in the shade of the ʻōhia tree
> The birds gather about
> To enjoy your appealing scent
> You are likened to the Mākalei
> You are likened to the Mākalei
> Always being attractive forever more
> To all my story is told
> Of the ʻiwa bird, quietly poised
> Gliding easily
> Gliding easily
> Before the face of the cliffs.

—Mary Kawena Pukui[216]

NOTES

1. Katerina Martina Teaiwa, *Consuming Ocean Island: Stories of People and Phosphate From Banaba,* Indiana: Indiana University Press, 2015, 7.
2. Teresia Teaiwa, "Fear of Flying (in Broken Gilbertese)," Poetry Foundation.
3. Gregory Walker, "Poetry," Apr. 1, 2019.
4. Pierre Nora writes that *true memory* "installs remembrance within the sacred." ("Between Memory and History: Les Lieux do Memoire." *Representations 26* [Spring 1989]: 7–25). Sydney Iaukea further explains, "Ingrained in natural cycles, and celebrating the larger patterns of existence, *true memory* involves many more actors, more agency, and more complications in its construction. Nonlinear and generational, this form of knowing the past demands that we track ourselves through the narrative itself as opposed to the representation of the narrative." Sydney Iaukea, *The Queen and I: A Story of Dispossessions and Reconnections in Hawai'i,* Berkeley: University of California Press, 2012, 32.
5. Katerina Teaiwa, 7.
6. Nicholas B. Miller, "Trading Sovereignty and Labour: The Consular Network of Nineteenth-Century Hawai'i," *The International History Review,* (Routledge 42:2): 260–277, 262.
7. Barrie Macdonald, *Cinderellas of the Empire: Towards a history of Kiribati and Tuvalu,* Canberra: Australian National University Press, 1982, 57. The terms South Sea Islanders and Gilbertese are used interchangeably in this chapter.
8. "Exiles From Their Birthplace: The Remnant of Many Importations of Gilbertese Waiting to be Taken Home," *The Hawaiian Star,* Oct 28, 1902, p. 6, col. 3. The first *Morning Star* missionary ship sailed from Boston, under Captain Hiram Bingham II, to Honolulu in 1866. The purpose was to "make yearly trips from the Gilbert Islands to Ponape, one thousand misses northwest, visiting other mission islands on the way, bringing supplies and occasionally transporting missionaries." "The Missionary Packet Morning Star, Boston, November 12, 1866," Arader Galleries; Prints, Watercolors, and Rare Maps," https://aradergalleries.com/products/the-missionary-packet-morning-star-boston-november-12–1866. There were a total of five *Morning Star* ships, each used for the same purpose of Hawaiian missionary work in the Pacific. Albert S. Baker, *Morning Stars and Missionary Packet,* printed in "The Friend," Honolulu, Hawai'i: Board of Hawaiian Evangelical Association, 1942–1943.
9. Miller, 271.
10. British Phosphate Commissioners, "Records of the British Phosphate Commissioners," 1919–1982, *The National Archives.*
11. Katerina Teaiwa, 19.
12. Ibid.
13. Katerina Teaiwa, 24.
14. The names Banaba and Ocean Island are used interchangeably in this chapter.

15. J. A. Bennett, "Immigration, 'Blackbirding,' Labour Recruiting? The Hawaiian Experience 1877–1887," *The Journal of Pacific History, 1976,* vol. 11, no. 1, Labour Trade [Part 1]: 2–37, 19 (in "Wodehouse to Grenville," *Slave Trade,* no. 8 [Aug 23, 1889], British Consulate Records, HSA).

16. Blackbirding was the practice of kidnapping and/or tricking islanders to labor abroad. This practice was primarily associated with the Kanaka slave trade to Australia, and in other places throughout Oceania, that recruited cheap labor for large plantations.

17. Katerina Teaiwa, xvi.

18. Stacey M. King and Raobeia Ken Sigrah, *Te Rii Ni Banaba, backbone of Banaba.* Banaban Vision; 2nd ed., 2019.

19. Stacey M. King, "Te Rii Ni Banaba—The Foundation of Traditional Law," *Banaba Culture, Customs, and Tradition.*

20. Raobia Ken Sigrah and Stacey M. King, *Te Rii Ni Banaba,* Institute of Pacific Studies: University of the South Pacfic, 2001.

21. Katerina Teaiwa, 8.

22. "Japan captures Gilbert Islands," *Enemy in the Mirror.* www.enemyinmirror.com/japanese-forces-take-gilbert-islands-dec-8–1941/

23. Macdonald, vi.

24. Ibid.

25. Janice Cantieri, "Our Heart Is on Banaba: Stories From The Forgotten People of the Pacific," *National Geographic Society Newsroom.*

26. Macdonald, v–vi.

27. Kaushik Pattowary, "Banaba: A tropical Paradise Destroyed by Mining," *Amusing Planet.* Ellis discovered the rock in the Australian office, when it was being used as a doorstop, of the Pacific Island Company (later called the Pacific Phosphate Company). He discovered the properties of the rock when he decided to test it. The following year he went to Banaba to negotiate a one-sided agreement with the Banabans to mine the island. In 1906, he signed a similar agreement with Nauru. Teaiwa, 43–49.

28. Katerina Teaiwa, 5.

29. Kaushik Pattowary and Joshua McDonald, "The Island With No Water: How Foreign Mining Destroyed Banaba," *The Guardian.*

30. Macdonald, 75.

31. Ibid.

32. McAdam.

33. K. Sigrah and S. M. King, "Banabans Living on Banaba Today," *Come Meet the Banabans: Our Homeland Our Past Our Identity Our Future,* 2001.

34. Katerina Teaiwa, "Consuming Ocean Island" video, Jan 5, 2015.

35. Bob Hawkins, "Nearly Gone: Pacific Islands Refugees From 'Development,'" *New Internationalist* (July 1981, is. 101).

36. Kalle Dixelius, "The Island of Yearning Has Sunken Below the Horizon," *Abara Banaba*, 2001.

37. Katerina Teaiwa, 11.

38. Ibid., 22.

39. Ibid., 11.

40. King.

41. Bennett, 16.

42. Macdonald, 54.

43. Katherine Coman, "The History of Contract Labor in the Hawaiian Islands." *Publications of the American Economic Association* (Aug. 1903), 3rd Series, vol. 4, no. 3: 1–61, 11.

44. Coman, 10.

45. Ralph S. Kuykendall, *The Hawaiian Kingdom, Vol. 2, 1854–1874, Twenty Critical Years*, Honolulu: University of Hawai'i Press, 1953, 185.

46. Hawaiian Kingdom Civil Code, Chapter XXX Of Masters and Servants, Sec. 1410. www.hawaiiankingdom.org/civilcode/CHAPTER_XXX.shtml

47. Hawaiian Kingdom Civil Code, Chapter XXX Of Masters and Servants, Sec. 1410.

48. Kuykendall, The Hawaiian Kingdom, Vol. 2, 185.

49. Hawaiian Kingdom Civil Code, Chapter XXX Of Masters and Servants, Sec 1397.

50. Kuykendall, The Hawaiian Kingdom, Vol. 2, 186.

51. Edward D. Beechert, "Patterns of Resistance and the Social Relations of Production in Hawaii," in Brij V. Lal, Doug Munro, and Edward D. Beechert, eds., *Plantation Workers: Resistance and Accommodation*, Honolulu: University of Hawai'i Press, 53 in "Cases of Deserting and Refusing Bound Service," Reports of the Chief Justice, Hawaiian Kingdom, 1876–1900, Summary of Civil Cases in District Court.

52. Kuykendall, The Hawaiian Kingdom, Volume 2, 185.

53. Bennett, 3.

54. Beechert, 48.

55. Beechert, 48 & 50.

56. Miller, 267.

57. Kuykendall, The Hawaiian Kingdom, Volume 2, 181–182.

58. Coman, 13.

59. Ibid.

60. Ralph S. Kuykendall, *The Hawaiian Kingdom, Volume 3: The Kalakaua Dynasty, 1874–1893*. Honolulu, University of Hawai'i Press, 1979, 314.

61. Miller, 267.

62. Ralph S. Kuykendall, The Hawaiian Kingdom, Volume 3: The Kalakaua Dynasty, 1874–1893, 314.

63. Ibid.

64. Ibid.

65. Lorenz Gonschor, *A Power in the World: The Hawaiian Kingdom in Oceania*, Honolulu: University of Hawai'i Press, 2019, 94 from *Statutes of the Royal Order of the Star of Oceania*, Honolulu, Elele Office, 1886, 111.

66. Gonschor, 141.

67. Ibid., 145.

68. Gonschor, 96 from Jason Horn, "Primacy of the Pacific under the Hawaiian Kingdom, M.A. Thesis, University of Hawaii, 1951, 107.

69. "Showing remains of a house erected by King Kālakaua," Title: Islands, Ocean, Call Number PP-45–11–002, Hawai'i State Archives.

70. Gonschor, 106.

71. Kealani Cook, *Return to Kahiki: Native Hawaiians in Oceania,* United Kingdom: Cambridge University Press, 2018, 58 from George Haina to Bingham, Nov 27, 1878, Micronesia Collection Archive, HMCS; George Haina, "Parish Report of Tarawa, 1878–79," HMCS-Micronesia; Henry Nalimu to Bingham, Feb 4, 1879, Micronesian Mission Archives, HMCS.

72. "Report of the President of the Board of Immigration to the Legislative Assembly of 1886," Honolulu: Daily Bulletin Steam Printing Office, 1886, 147.

73. Bennett, 9.

74. "Report of the President of the Board of Immigration to the Legislative Assembly of 1886," 103.

75. Ibid.

76. Ibid., 146.

77. Sandra Rennie, "Contract Labor Under a Protector: The Gilbertese Laborers and Hiram Bingham Jr. in Hawaii, 1878–1903." *Pacific Studies*, vol. 11, no. 1 (November 1987): 81–106, 82.

78. Miller, 271.

79. "Planters' L. and S. Co.: Annual Meeting of the Shareholders," *Pacific Commercial Advertiser*, Oct 19, 1886, col. 2.

80. Hiram Bingham, "Gilbert Islanders: Rev. H. Bingam Pertinent Query, Where Shall These People Go? History of the Little Settlement on the Sea Front—The Home Sick Strangers," *Pacific Commercial Advertiser*, June 7, 1901, p. 11 col. 3.

81. Bennett, 9.

82. "Exiles From Their Birthplace: The Remnant of Many Importations of Gilbertese Waiting to be Taken Home."

83. "Report of the President of the Board of Immigration to the Legislative Assembly of 1886," 147.

84. Ibid., 147–148.

85. Ibid., 21.

86. Coman, 20.

87. Bennett, 26–27.

88. Suh Hillary Sama and Kenfack Tonnang Florence, "Slavery and slave Trade Activities: The case of Blackbirding in the Pacific Ocean and Interiors from the 19th to the 21st Centuries Period." *International Journal of Advanced Engineering Research and Science*, Vol. 8, Issue 2 (February 2021): 36–51, 40.

89. *Kanaka* is described as Pacific Islander labor in "near-slave status" taken to work in Queensland, Australia, from 1847 onward to work on sugar plantations. www .britannica.com/topic/Kanaka

90. "The Story of Mataio, A Gilbert Islander," *Sunday Advertiser*, Sep 25, 1904, p. 6, col. 1.

91. Suh Hillary Sama, et al., 45.

92. Bennett, 4, found in "Mott Smith to Mist, Honolulu, n.d. (c. July 1877)," Interior Miscellaneous 53 (hereinafter IM53), Immigration—South Seas Islanders, 1877–98, Hawai'i State Archives.

93. "Report of the President of the Board of Immigration to the Legislative Assembly of 1886," 147.

94. Bennett, 5.

95. Bennett, 5, found in WPHC Correspondence, "Mist to Jackson" and "Seed to High Commissioner," March 1878.

96. "Capt. Jackson to Int. Dept," Bk. 15, p. 163, Apr. 17, 1878, Hawai'i State Archives.

97. Bennett, 6.

98. "Capt. Jackson to Pres. of the Board of Immigration," Dept. Bk. 15, p. 165, July 5, 1878. Hawai'i State Archives.

99. "Report of the President of the Board of Immigration to the Legislative Assembly of 1886," 149. Samuel Gardner Wilder was a royalist to the Hawaiian Kingdom, friend and politician under King Kalākaua, shipping magnate, and businessman.

100. Punawaiola, Curated Digital Collections; Privy Council Records, "Minutes Privy Council, 1881–1882," vol. 14, pp. 229–231. http://punawaiola.org/es6/index.html ?path=/Collections/PCMT/PCMT1881001.pdf and "Police Court," *The Daily Herald*, Mar 15, 1887, col. 2.

101. George Edward Gresley, d. 1907, M-349, Hawai'i State Archives and "Samoan Affairs, Interview with Mr. J. D. Strong Jr., Doings of the Hawaiian Embassy and Movements of the Kaimiloa, Mr. Poor's Influence Averts a Fight Between Supporters of Malietoa and Those of Tamassasi, Details of the Kaimiloa Mutiny," *Pacific Commercial Advertiser*, Aug 3, 1887, col. 1.

102. "George Edward Gresley Jackson, d. 1907."

103. "Capt. Jackson from Min. of Interior," Int. Dept. Bk. 18, p. 77, Sept. 30, 1880, Hawai'i State Archives.

104. Bennett, 8.

105. Ibid., 11.

106. Ibid., 22.

107. Doug Munro and Stewart Firth, "Samoan Plantations: The Gilbertese Laborers' Experience, 1867–1896" in Beechert, et al., 106.

108. "Correction," *Pacific Commercial Advertiser*, Dec 18, 1880, col. 4.

109. Ibid.

110. "Lahaina Correspondence: Court News—An Important Question," *Pacific Commercial Advertiser*, Dec 18, 1889, col. 7.

111. Ibid.

112. "Correction."

113. Ibid.

114. "Topics of the Day," *Pacific Commercial Advertiser*, Dec 18, 1880, col. 6.

115. "Lahaina Correspondence: Court News—An Important Question."

116. "Correction."

117. "Lahaina Correspondence; Court News—An Important Question."

118. "A Call to Labor: People Urged to Aid Foreign Mission Enterprise, Rev. Dr. Bingham's Appeal." *Pacific Commercial Advertiser*, June 12, 1899, p. 3 and "Chasing the Rainbow," *The Hawaiian Star*, Oct 19, 1903, p. 4, col. 1.

119. "Hawaii at the Fair," *Daily Pacific Commercial Advertiser*, Sept 19, 1893, col. 2.

120. Ibid.

121. Ibid.

122. Sydney Iaukea, *Keka'a: The Making and Saving of North Beach West Maui*, Lahaina, Hawai'i: North Beach West Maui Benefit Fund, 2014, 46.

123. " 'Ko Lahaina Ahahui Hana Ko': Association of Lahaina Sugar Makers, An Overview of Sugar Plantations in Lahaina (ca. 1849–1999)," 1.

124. Iaukea, Keka'a: The Making and Saving of North Beach West Maui, 46.

125. Ibid., 47.

126. Miller, 273.

127. Miller, 271 from Knut M. Rio, "From Adventure to Industry and Nation Making: The History of a Norwegian Sugar Plantation in Hawai'i," *Navigating Colonial Orders: Norwegian Entrepreneurship in Africa and Oceania*. New York: Berghahn Books, 2015, 254–57.

128. "Report of the President of the Board of Immigration to the Legislative Assembly of 1886," 148.

129. "Gilbertese at Lihue," *Honolulu Record*, vol. 9, no. 19 (December 6, 1956), 3.

130. Iaukea, Keka'a: The Making and Saving of North Beach West Maui, 48.

131. Edward Joesting, *Kaua'i: The Separate Kingdom,* Honolulu: University of Hawai'i Press, 1984, 224.

132. Iaukea, Keka'a: The Making and Saving of North Beach West Maui, 54.

133. Ibid., 57, from "Report of the Pioneer Mill Co. Ltd. For Fifteen Months Ending December 31, 1910," Hawai'i Sugar Planters Association Archives, Hamilton Library, University of Hawai'i at Mānoa.

134. "Ko Lahaina Ahahui Hana Ko," 2.

135. "Ko Lahaina Ahahui Hana Ko," 1. The Kuleana Act of 1850 assured "native tenants" fee simple titles and rights of access on Government and other lands (sec. 1–7). Hoakalei Cultural Foundation, *The Kuleana Act of 1850.* www.hoakaleifoundation .org/documents/kuleana-act-1850

136. Iaukea, Kekaʻa: The Making and Saving of North Beach West Maui, 70–71.

137. On 2 Nov. 1880, a letter was read from the Rev. Mr. Bingham accepting the appointment of inspector and protector of South Sea immigrants, "Report of the President of the Board of Immigration to the Legislative Assembly of 1886," 150.

138. Bennett, 19 in Bingham to Armstrong, 28 Mar. 1882. IM 53, HAS; Bingham to Bush, 31 Oct. 1882, IM 53, HAS.

139. Coman, 16.

140. "Report of the President of the Board of Immigration to the Legislative Assembly of 1886," 155.

141. Ibid.

142. "1890 Census of the Hawaiian Islands, Lahaina and Lanai," Census Track #5, Hawaiian and Pacific Collection, University of Hawaiʻi at Mānoa. The census is handwritten. Any error in spelling is attributed to the chapter's author. guides .library.manoa.hawaii.edu/hawaiicensus1890.

143. "Thirteenth Census of the United States Taken in the Year 1910," Statistics for Hawaii: Containing Statistics of Population, Agriculture, and Manufactures for the Territory, Counties, and Cities, Washington Government Printing Office, 1913. www2.census.gov/library/publications/decennial/1910/abstract/supplement -hi.pdf.

144. Rennie, 100.

145. Refer to the "Puʻunoa Village and Vicinity Map" and the "Lahaina Area Map" at the Lahaina Restoration Foundation's website at https://lahainarestoration.org /pioneer-mill-camp-maps/ to view the Puʻunoa camp map alongside the locations of the other plantation camps in West Maui.

146. "A Long Swim," *Evening Bulletin*, Mar 29, 1897, col. 2.

147. "Lahaina Lines," *The Maui News*, Aug 1, 1903, col. 3.

148. "Lahaina Lines," *The Maui News*, Oct 24, 1903.

149. "What the Gilbertese Will Find," *The Hawaiian Star*, Nov 11, 1903, p. 6, col. 3.

150. "Isleworth Take All But Three of the Gilbertians: Two Hundred and Twenty Leave For Their South Sea Homes Today." *Sunday Advertiser*, Oct 18, 1903.

151. "Local Brevities," *Pacific Commercial Advertiser*, Nov 16, 1897.

152. "What the Gilbertese Will Find."

153. "Lahaina Lines," *The Maui News*, Dec 31, 1904, col. 2.

154. "Death of Rev. Lutera: Was One of Maui's Most Prominent Ministers," *The Maui News*, Dec 5, 1908, p. 6, col. 2.

155. Edward D. Beechert, "Patterns of Resistance and the Social Relations of Production in Hawaii," in Beechert, et al., 58 from Ernest Wakuwaku, *A History*

of the Japanese in Hawaii (Honolulu, 1938), 133–134; Governor, Report, 1905: 64–65.

156. "1946: The Great Hawai'i Sugar Strike: Rice & Roses," Center for Labor Education and Research, University of Hawai'i, West O'ahu. www.hawaii.edu/uhwo /clear/home/1946.html.

157. "Isleworth Take All But Three of the Gilbertians: Two Hundred and Twenty Leave For Their South Sea Homes Today."

158. "Teresia Teaiwa, Biography and Background," Apr 4, 2019. https://teaiwa484508714 .wordpress.com/

159. "Young Gilbertese are Disgusted with Their First View of Homeland," *Pacific Commercial Advertiser*, Jan 6, 1904, p. 1, col. 1.

160. "Gilbert Islanders May Go On Isleworth," *The Hawaiian Star*, Oct 15, 1903, p. 1, col. 3.

161. "Isleworth Take All But Three of the Gilbertians: Two Hundred and Twenty Leave For Their South Sea Homes Today."

162. Thos G. Thrum, "Exodus of Gilbertese," *Hawaiian Almanac and Annual for 1902*, Honolulu, 1901, 206.

163. "Isleworth Take All But Three of the Gilbertians: Two Hundred and Twenty Leave For Their South Sea Homes Today."

164. "Gilbert Islanders: Rev. H. Pertinent Query, Where Shall These People Go?" *Pacific Commercial Advertiser*, June 7, 1901, p. 11 col. 3.

165. "Gilbert Islanders: Rev. H. Pertinent Query, Where Shall These People Go?"

166. Ibid.

167. "Isleworth Takes All But Three of the Gilbertians: Two Hundred and Twenty Leave For Their South Sea Homes Today."

168. "South Sea Island Village To Go." *The Hawaiian Star*, Aug 29, 1901.

169. "Lewalewas May Go: Gilbert Islanders May Leave on Isleworth."

170. "At the Gilbertese Village: All is Excitement in the South Sea Island Section of the Kalihi Camp—Notable Examples of Generosity Among Those With Money to Help Those Without," *The Hawaiian Star*, Oct 16, 1903.

171. "Lewalewas May Go: Gilbert Islanders May Leave on Isleworth." *Hawaiian Gazette*, Oct 16, 1903, p. 5, col. 1.

172. "Isleworth Take All But Three of the Gilbertians: Two Hundred and Twenty Leave For Their South Sea Homes Today."

173. Ibid.

174. Ibid.

175. "Going to Where They Will Be Plutocrats," *The Hawaiian Star*, Oct 19, 1903, p. 1, col. 2.

176. "At the Gilbertese Village: All is Excitement in the South Sea Island Section of the Kalihi Camp—Notable Examples of Generosity Among Those With Money to Help Those Without," *The Hawaiian Star*, Oct 16, 1903.

177. "Lewalewas May Go: Gilbert Islanders May Leave on Isleworth."

178. "What the Gilbertese Will Find."

179. "Exiles From Their Birthplace: The Remnant of Many Importations of Gilbertese Waiting To Be Taken Home," *The Hawaiian Star*, Oct 28, 1902, p. 6, col. 3.

180. "Going to Where They Will Be Plutocrats."

181. "Gilbert Islanders May Go On Isleworth."

182. "Repatriation of the Gilbertese," *Hawaiian Gazette*, Dec 18, 1903, p. 7, col. 3.

183. "Lauhala Hats Scarce When Gilbertese Leave Honolulu: Art of Hat Making is Falling Into Decadence Among the Hawaiians and Was Chief Industry Among the South Sea Islanders," *Pacific Commercial Advertiser*, Oct 17, 1903, p. 3, col. 2.

184. "Lauhala Hats Scarce When Gilbertese Leave Honolulu: Art of Hat Making is Falling Into Decadence Among the Hawaiians and Was Chief Industry Among the South Sea Islanders."

185. Hiram Bingham, "Were Not the Gilbert Islanders," *Pacific Commercial Advertiser*, Oct 25, 1902, p. 14, col. 2.

186. "Famous Man in Company: Gilbert Islanders Spend Day on Isleworth Holding Prayer Meetings," *Pacific Commercial Advertiser*, Oct 19, 1903, p. 2, col. 2.

187. "The Picturesque Gilbertese: Their Embarkation Today Will Be Analogous in Some Respects to the Acadians," *The Hawaiian Star*, Oct 17, 1903.

188. "Isleworth Takes All But Three of the Gilbertians: Two Hundred and Twenty Leave For Their South Sea Homes Today."

189. Gilbert Islanders Reached South Sea Homes Safely," *Pacific Commercial Advertiser*, Dec 16, 1903. p. 1, col. 5.

190. "Gilbertese Taxed Too Much," *The Hawaiian Star*, Jan 29, 1904, p. 5, col. 3.

191. "A Call To Labour; People Urged to Aid Foreign Mission Enterprise, Rev. Dr. Bingham's Appeal."

192. Hiram Bingham, "Kawaiahao Is Given a Site for Personage," *Pacific Commercial Advertiser*, Aug 31, 1903, p. 1, col. 1.

193. "Kawaiahao is Given a Site for Parsonage."

194. Ibid.

195. "Rev. Hiram Bingham's Gilbertese Lexicon," *Pacific Commercial Advertiser*, Apr 10, 1908, p. 10, col. 2.

196. "A Tribute of Sorrow: The Hawaiian Board on the Late Rev. Dr. Hiram Bingham," *Pacific Commercial Advertiser*, Dec 17, 1908, p. 12, col. 2.

197. "Women Laud Life of Micronesian Missionary: Tributes to the Memory of the Late Mrs. Hiram Bingham by the Woman's Board of Missions," *Pacific Commercial Advertiser*, Dec 2, 1903, p. 5, col. 2.

198. "A Tribute of Sorrow: The Hawaiian Board on the Late Rev. Dr. Hiram Bingham."

199. "Rev. Hiram Bingham Dies in Baltimore Hospital: Honolulu Divine, Famous as a Missionary Among the Gilbertese Islanders, Succumbs to an Operation," *Pacific Commercial Advertiser*, Nov 3, 1908, p. 1, col. 2.

200. "Missionary Schooner Arrives," *Sunday Advertiser*, Dec 6, 1908, p. 1, col. 2.
201. "Hiram Bingham—The Maker of a Language," *Pacific Commercial Advertiser*, Nov 20, 1908, p. 5 col. 3.
202. "A Missionary From Micronesia: Rev. And Mrs. Channon of Kusaie Are Going to Ocean Island," *Pacific Commercial Advertiser*, Dec 10, 1907, p. 2, col. 2.
203. Ibid.
204. Ibid.
205. "Lewalewas May Go: Gilbert Islanders May Leave on Isleworth."
206. Greg Dening in *Islands and Beaches* ponders the encounter between Marquesas and outsiders, with the beach providing the border and place of encounter. Greg Dening, *Islands and Beaches, Discourse on a Silent Land: Marquesas 1774–1880.* Dorsey Press, 1988.
207. "Deep history" is an anthropological term used to describe pre-contact and pre-modern histories.
208. "Lewalewas May Go: Gilbert Islanders May Leave on Isleworth."
209. "Inger Arrives From South Seas," *Pacific Commercial Advertiser*, Nov 4, 1904. p. 10, col. 2.
210. Beechert, 57.
211. Brittany Lyle, 'Iwa: The Great Frigate Bird is a Master-Thief, a Harbinger of Storms and the World Champion of Aerial Endurance, *Hana Hou! The Magazine of Hawaiian Airlines*, is. 20/5: Oct/Nov 2017.
212. Ibid.
213. Ibid.
214. Ibid.
215. Katerina Teaiwa, 8.
216. Mary Kawena Pukui, "Ka 'Iwa Poetry Analysis," Oct 21, 2020. www.youtube.com /watch?v=nEc2dmMvDlQ

BIBLIOGRAPHY

"1946: The Great Hawai'i Sugar Strike: Rice & Roses." Center for Labor Education and Research. University of Hawai'i, West O'ahu. www.hawaii.edu/uhwo/clear /home/1946.html

Baker, Albert S. *Morning Stars and Missionary Packet,* printed in "The Friend." Honolulu: Board of Hawaiian Evangelical Association, 1942–1943.

Beechert, Edward D. "Patterns of Resistance and the Social Relations of Production in Hawaii." Edited by Brij V. Lal, Doug Munro, and Edward D. Beechert, *Plantation Workers: Resistance and Accommodation.* Honolulu: University of Hawai'i Press, 1993.

Bennett, J. A. "Immigration, 'Blackbirding,' Labour Recruiting? The Hawaiian Experience 1877–1887." *The Journal of Pacific History, 1976,* vol. 11, no. 1, Labour Trade [Part 1]: 2–37.

Bingham to Armstrong, 28 Mar. 1882. IM 53, HAS; Bingham to Bush, 31 Oct. 1882, IM 53. HAS.

www.britannica.com/topic/blackbirding

www.britannica.com/topic/Kanaka

British Phosphate Commissioners. "Records of the British Phosphate Commissioners." 1919–1982, *The National Archives.* https://discovery.nationalarchives.gov.uk /details/r/C497

Cannon, Sara. "Counting Down Fieldwork in the Gilbert Islands." March 3, 2018. https://saracannon.ca/2018/03/03/countdown-to-fieldwork-in-the-gilbert -islands/

Cantieri, Janice. "Our Heart is on Banaba: Stories From The Forgotten People of the Pacific." National Geographic Society Newsroom. https://blog.nationalgeographic .org/2015/10/14/our-heart-is-on-banaba-stories-from-the-forgotten-people-of-the -pacific/

"Capt. Jackson from Min. of Interior." Int. Dept. Bk. 18, p. 77, Sept. 30, 1880, Hawai'i State Archives.

"Capt. Jackson to Int. Dept." Bk. 15, p. 163, Apr. 17, 1878. Hawai'i State Archives.

"Capt. Jackson to Pres. of the Board of Immigration." Dept. Bk. 15, p. 165, July 5, 1878. Hawai'i State Archives.

"Cases of Deserting and Refusing Bound Service." Reports of the Chief Justice, Hawaiian Kingdom, 1876–1900. Summary of Civil Cases in District Court.

Coman, Katherine. "The History of Contract Labor in the Hawaiian Islands." *Publications of the American Economic Association* (Aug. 1903), 3rd Series, vol. 4, no. 3: 1–61.

Cook, Kealani. Return to Kahiki: Native Hawaiians in Oceania. Cambridge University Press, 2018.

Dening, Greg. Islands and Beaches, Discourse on a Silent Land: Marquesas 1774–1880. Dorsey Press, 1988.

Dixelius, Kalle. "The Island of Yearning Has Sunken Below the Horizon." *Abara Banaba,* 2001.

DX News.com, "T33HA Banaba Island." https://dxnews.com/t33ha_banaba-island _kiribati/

www.geographicguide.com/oceania-maps

"George Edward Gresley Jackson, d. 1907." M-349, Capt. Jackson from Min. of Interior, Int. Dept. Bk. 18, p. 77, Sept. 30, 1880. Hawai'i State Archives.

"Gilbertese at Lihue." *Honolulu Record.* vol. 9, no. 19, Dec 6, 1956.

Gonschor, Lorenz. A Power in the World: The Hawaiian Kingdom in Oceania, Honolulu: University of Hawai'i Press, 2019.

Haina, George to Bingham. Nov 27, 1878. Micronesia Collection Archive, HMCS.

Haina, George. "Parish Report of Tarawa, 1878–79." Micronesia Collection Archive, HMCS.

Hawaiian Kingdom Civil Code, Chapter XXX Of Masters and Servants. www .hawaiiankingdom.org/civilcode/CHAPTER_XXX.shtml

Hawkins, Bob. "Nearly Gone: Pacific Islands Refugees From 'Development,'" *New Internationalist* (July 1981, is. 101). https://newint.org/features/1981/07/01/guano

Haxton, Nance. "Australia's Slave Trade: The growing drive to uncover the secret history of Australian South Sea Islanders." abc news. www.abc.net.au/news/2017–12–22/australian-south-sea-islanders-blackbirding/9270734

Hoakalalei Cultural Foundation. *The Kuleana Act of 1850.* www.hoakaleifoundation.org/documents/kuleana-act-1850

Horn, Jason. "Primacy of the Pacific under the Hawaiian Kingdom." M.A. Thesis, University of Hawai'i, 1951.

Iaukea, Sydney. Keka'a: The Making and Saving of North Beach West Maui. Lahaina, Hawai'i: North Beach West Maui Benefit Fund, 2014.

Iaukea, Sydney. The Queen and I: A Story of Dispossessions and Reconnections in Hawai'i. Berkeley: University of California Press, 2012.

"Japan captures the Gilbert Islands." *Enemy in the Mirror.* www.enemyinmirror.com/japanese-forces-take-gilbert-islands-dec-8–1941/

Joesting, Edward. *Kaua'i: The Separate Kingdom.* Honolulu: University of Hawai'i Press, 1984.

Joyce, Christopher. "Nonstop Flight: How the Frigate Bird Can Soar For Weeks Without Stopping." *The Two-Way,* June 30, 2016. www.npr.org/sections/thetwo-way/2016/06/30/484164544/non-stop-flight-how-the-frigatebird-can-soar-for-months-without-stopping

King, Stacey M. "Te Rii Ni Banaba—The Foundation of Traditional Law." *Banaba Culture, Customs, and Tradition.* www.banaban.com/post/banaban-culture-customs-and-tradition

"'Ko Lahaina Ahahui Hana Ko': Association of Lahaina Sugar Makers, An Overview of Sugar Plantations in Lahaina (ca. 1849–1999)."

Kuykendall, Ralph S. The Hawaiian Kingdom, Vol. 2, 1854–1874, Twenty Critical Years. Honolulu: University of Hawai'i Press, 1953.

Kuykendall, Ralph S. The Hawaiian Kingdom, Volume 3: The Kalakaua Dynasty, 1874–1893. Honolulu, Hawai'i, University of Hawai'i Press, 1979.

Laborers Lahaina." Sugar-Plantation Laborers, Ark:70111/1CST, PPWD-18–3-033, Box #18, Folder #3, Image #033. Hawai'i State Archives.

Lyle, Brittany. "'Iwa: The Great Frigate Bird is a Master-Thief, a Harbinger of Storms and the World Champion of Aerial Endurance." Hana Hou! The Magazine of Hawaiian Airlines, is. 20/5: Oct/Nov 2017.

Macdonald, Barrie. Cinderellas of the Empire: Towards a history of Kiribati and Tuvalu. Canberra: Australian National University Press, 1982.

McAdam, Jane. "Caught between Homelands." *Inside Story.* https://insidestory.org.au/caught-between-homelands/

McDonald, Joshua. "The Island With No Water: How Foreign Mining Destroyed Banaba," *The Guardian.* www.theguardian.com/world/2021/jun/09/the-island-with-no-water-how-foreign-mining-destroyed-banaba

Miller, Nicholas B. "Trading Sovereignty and Labour: The Consular Network of Nineteenth- Century Hawai'i." *The International History Review* (Routledge 42:2): 260–277.

"Mott Smith to Mist, Honolulu, n.d. (c. July 1877)." Interior Miscellaneous 53 (here-inafter IM53), Immigration—South Seas Islanders, 1877–98, Hawai'i State Archives.

Munro, Doug & Firth, Stewart. "Samoan Plantations: The Gilbertese Laborers' Experience, 1867–1896." Edited by Brij V. Lal, Doug Munro, and Edward D. Beechert, *Plantation Workers: Resistance and Accommodation,* Honolulu: University of Hawai'i Press, 1993.

Nalimu, Henry to Bingham. Feb 4, 1879, Micronesian Mission Archives, HMCS.

National Library of Australia. "Working a Banaba island phosphate field in the 1920s." ABC News, May 30, 1920. www.abc.net.au/news/2019-05-31/working-a-banaba -island-phosphate-field-in-the-1920s-1/11091280?nw=0

Nora, Pierre. "Between Memory and History: Les Lieux do Memoire." *Representations 26* (Spring 1989): 7–25.

Pacific Wrecks. "Gilbertese Islander Nabetari who lived at sea for seven months to escape the Japanese on Ocean Island." Oct 1, 1945. https://pacificwrecks.com/provinces /kiribati/ocean/1945/3902596.html

Pattowary, Kaushik. "Banaba: A tropical Paradise Destroyed by Mining." *Amusing Planet.* www.amusingplanet.com/2018/10/banaba-tropical-paradise-destroyed -by.html

Pukui, Mary Kawena. "Ka 'Iwa Poetry Analysis," Oct 21, 2020. www.youtube.com /watch?v=nEc2dmMvDlQ

Rennie, Sandra. "Contract Labor Under a Protector: The Gilbertese Laborers and Hiram Bingham Jr. in Hawaii, 1878–1903." *Pacific Studies,* vol. 11, no. 1 (November 1987): 81–106.

"Report of the Pioneer Mill Co. Ltd. For Fifteen Months Ending December 31, 1910." Hawai'i Sugar Planters Association Archives, Hamilton Library, University of Hawai'i at Mānoa.

"Report of the President of the Board of Immigration to the Legislative Assembly of 1886." Honolulu: Daily Bulletin Steam Printing Office, 1886.

Rio, Knut M. "From Adventure to Industry and Nation Making: The History of a Norwegian Sugar Plantation in Hawai'i." Navigating Colonial Orders: Norwegian Entrepreneurship in Africa and Oceania. New York: Berghahn Books, 2015, 254–57.

Sama, Suh Hillary & Florence, Kenfack Tonnang. "Slavery and Slave Trade Activities: The Case of Blackbirding in the Pacific Ocean and Interiors From the 19th to the 21st Centuries Period." International Journal of Advanced Engineering Research and Science, vol. 8, is. 2 (February 2021): 36–51.

Sigrah, K. & King, S. M. "Banabans Living on Banaba Today." *Come Meet the Banabans: Our homeland Our past Our identity Our future,* 2001. www.banaban.com/banaba -today, 2001.

Sigrah, Raobia Ken & King, Stacey M. *Te Rii Ni Banaba; backbone of Banaba.* (USP 2001: Banaban Vision: 2019).

Statutes of the Royal Order of the Star of Oceania, Honolulu, Elele Office, 1886.

Teaiwa, Katerina Martina. Consuming Ocean Island: Stories of People and Phosphate From Banaba. Indiana: Indiana University Press, 2015.

Teaiwa, Katerina. "Consuming Ocean Island," video, January 5, 2015. www.youtube .com/watch?v=asGdMroQqo8

Teaiwa, Teresia. Biography and Background." Apr 4, 2019. https://teaiwa484508714 .wordpress.com/

Teaiwa, Teresia. "Fear of Flying (in Broken Gilbertese)," *Poetry Foundation.* www .poetryfoundation.org/poetrymagazine/poems/89735/fear-of-flying-in-broken -gilbertese

"The Missionary Packet Morning Star, Boston, November 12, 1866." Arader Galleries; Prints, Watercolors, and Rare Maps." https://aradergalleries.com/products/the -missionary-packet-morning-star-boston-november-12–1866.

"Thirteenth Census of the United States Taken in the Year 1910," *Statistics for Hawaii: Containing Statistics of Population, Agriculture, and Manufactures for the Territory, Counties, and Cities,* Washington Government Printing Office. 1913. www2 .census.gov/library/publications/decennial/1910/abstract/supplement-hi.pdf

Thrum, Thos. G. "Exodus of Gilbertese." *Hawaiian Almanac and Annual for 1902.* Honolulu, 1901.

Walker, Gregory. "Poetry." Apr. 1, 2019. https://teaiwa484508714.wordpress.com/

"Wodehouse to Grenville." *Slave Trade,* no. 8 (Aug 23, 1889). British Consulate Records, HSA.

Wakuwaku, Ernest. *A History of the Japanese in Hawaii* (Honolulu, 1938), 133–134; Governor, Report, 1905.

WPHC Correspondence. "Mist to Jackson" and "Seed to High Commissioner." March 1878.

Newspapers

Daily Herald
  "Police Court." Mar 15, 1887, col. 2.
Evening Bulletin
  "A Long Swim." Mar 29, 1897, col. 2.
Hawaiian Gazette
  "Lewalewas May Go: Gilbert Islanders May Leave on Isleworth." Oct 16, 1903, p. 5, col. 1.
  "Repatriation of the Gilbertese." Dec 18, 1903, p. 7, col. 3.
Hawaiian Star
  "At the Gilbertese Village: All is Excitement in the South Sea Island Section of the Kalihi Camp—Notable Examples of Generosity Among Those With Money to Help Those Without." Oct 16, 1903.
  "Chasing the Rainbow." Oct 19, 1903, p. 4, col. 1.
  "Exiles From Their Birthplace: The Remnant of Many Importations of Gilbertese Waiting to be Taken Home." Oct 28, 1902, p. 6, col. 3.
  "Gilbert Islanders May Go On Isleworth." Oct 15, 1903, p. 1, col. 3.
  "Gilbertese Taxed Too Much." Jan 29, 1904, p. 5, col. 3.
  "Going to Where They Will Be Plutocrats." Oct 19, 1903, p. 1, col. 2.
  "South Sea Island Village To Go." Aug 29, 1901.

"The Picturesque Gilbertese: Their Embarkation Today Will Be Analogous in Some Respects to the Acadians." October 17, 1903.

"What the Gilbertese Will Find." Nov 11, 1903, p. 6, col. 3.

Maui News

"Death of Rev. Lutera: Was One of Maui's Most Prominent Ministers." Dec 5, 1908, p. 6, col. 2.

"Lahaina Lines." Aug 1, 1903, col. 3.

"Lahaina Lines." Oct 24, 1903.

"Lahaina Lines." Dec 31, 1904, col. 2.

Pacific Commercial Advertiser

"A Call To Labour; People Urged to Aid Foreign Mission Enterprise, Rev. Dr. Bingham's Appeal." June 12, 1899, p. 3.

"A Missionary From Micronesia: Rev. And Mrs. Channon of Kusaie Are Going to Ocean Island." Dec 10, 1907, p. 2, col. 2.

"A Tribute of Sorrow: The Hawaiian Board on the Late Rev. Dr. Hiram Bingham." Dec 17, 1908, p. 12, col. 2.

Bingham, Hiram. "Gilbert Islanders: Rev. H. Bingham Pertinent Query, Where Shall These People Go? History of the Little Settlement on the Sea Front—The Home Sick Strangers." June 7, 1901, p. 11 col. 3.

Bingham, Hiram. "Kawaiahao is Given a Site for Personage." Aug 31, 1903, p. 1, col. 1.

Bingham, Hiram. "Were Not the Gilbert Islanders." Oct 25, 1902, p. 14, col. 2.

"Correction." December 18, 1880, col. 4.

"Famous Man in Company: Gilbert Islanders Spend Day on Isleworth Holding Prayer Meetings." Oct 19, 1903, p. 2, col. 2.

"Gilbert Islanders Reached South Sea Homes Safely." Dec 16, 1903, p. 1, col. 5.

"Gilbert Islanders: Rev. H. Pertinent Query, Where Shall These People Go?" June 7, 1901, p. 11 col. 3.

"Hawaii at the Fair." Sept 19, 1893, col. 2.

"Hiram Bingham—The Maker of a Language." Nov 20, 1908, p. 5 col. 3.

"Inger Arrives From South Seas." Nov 4, 1904, p. 10, col. 2.

"Isleworth Take All But Three of the Gilbertians: Two Hundred and Twenty Leave For Their South Sea Homes Today." Oct 18, 1903.

"Lahaina Correspondence: Court News—An Important Question." December 18, 1889, col. 7.

"Lauhala Hats Scarce When Gilbertese Leave Honolulu: Art of Hat Making is Falling Into Decadence Among the Hawaiians and Was Chief Industry Among the South Sea Islanders." Oct 17, 1903, p. 3, col. 2.

"Local Brevities." Nov 16, 1897.

"Missionary Schooner Arrives." Dec 6, 1908, p. 1, col. 2.

"Planters' L. and S. Co.: Annual Meeting of the Shareholders." October 19, 1886, col. 2.

"Rev. Hiram Bingham Dies in Baltimore Hospital: Honolulu Divine, Famous as a Missionary Among the Gilbertese Islanders, Succumbs to an Operation." Nov 3, 1908, p. 1, col. 2.

"Rev. Hiram Bingham's Gilbertese Lexicon." Apr 10, 1908, p. 10, col. 2.

"Samoan Affairs, Interview with Mr. J. D. Strong Jr., Doings of the Hawaiian Embassy and Movements of the Kaimiloa, Mr. Poor's Influence Averts a Fight Between Supporters of Malietoa and Those of Tamassasi, Details of the Kaimiloa Mutiny," Aug 3, 1887, col. 1.

"The Story of Mataio, A Gilbert Islander." September 25, 1904, p. 6, col. 1.

"Topics of the Day." Dec 18, 1880, col. 6.

"Women Laud Life of Micronesian Missionary: Tributes to the Memory of the Late Mrs. Hiram Bingham by the Woman's Board of Missions." Dec. 2, 1903, p. 5, col. 2.

"Young Gilbertese are Disgusted with Their First View of Homeland." Jan 6, 1904, p. 1, col. 1.

CHAPTER 2

KA WĀ IĀ KAOMI
The Time of Kaomi

Adam Keawe Manalo-Camp

The Hawai'i of the 1820s and 1830s was a difficult time for Kānaka Maoli in identity and nation-building. Into this political and cultural malaise came forms of resistance to the new order that was being established. Hawai'i was thrown into a global economy, and with the end of the Hawaiian religious system in 1819, questions of identity arose. Out of this emerged the "time of Kaomi." Kaomi had an intimate relationship with King Kamehameha III. The time that Kaomi was *Mō'ī ku'i* marked a shift from complying with missionary-inspired social order to resisting it. Kaomi is probably the least understood Hawaiian figure in nineteenth-century Hawai'i due to a lack of written sources drafted by him or his followers. Missionary descriptions of him emphasize his Tahitian ancestry allowing an "othering" of him and his influence. His life was also primarily reduced to acting as a morality play instructing Hawaiian Christians not to "backslide." But what is known about Kaomi is that he had a temporary yet profound impact on the discourses of his day.

KANAKA MAOLI AND MĀ'OHI CONNECTIONS

Throughout Hawaiian history, Kānaka Maoli[1] and Mā'ohi[2] have been interconnected by navigation (Henry, 1995), migrations, spirituality, place names, and cultural exchange. The term "Kahiki" in Hawaiian itself had come to mean not just the place name Tahiti, but a realm of the ancestors. Pa'ao, who is generally attributed to be Mā'ohi from Ra'iātea, helped to shape the Hawaiian religious system for 300 years and is alleged to have brought blood rituals to Kānaka

Maoli along with a stricter observance of religious laws (Kalākaua, 1972). Lono rituals are believed to have originated with Oro rituals from Tahiti. Heiau and place names such as Kapukapuakea (Taputapuatea in Tahitian) are named after Tahitian place names, thereby showing a spiritual genealogy of mana. Hawai'i itself shares the ancient place name of the sacred island of Ra'iātea, Havai'i. Pele, the *akua wahine* (female god) who resides at Kīlauea, originates from Bora Bora. A famous chant attributed to the navigator Kamahualele expresses the sentiment that:

> Eia Hawai'i, he moku, he kanaka
> He kanaka Hawai'i, e—
> He kanaka Hawai'i
> He kama na Kahiki
> He pua ali'i mai Kapa'ahu
> Mai Moa'ulanuiākea Kanaloa
> He mo'opuna nā Kahiko, laua o Kapulanakehau....
> *Behold Hawai'i, an island, a man*
> *A man is Hawai'i*
> *A man is Hawai'i*
> *A child of Kahiki*
> *A royal bud from Kapa'ahu*
> *From Moa'ulanuiākea Kanaloa*
> *A descendant of Kahiko and Kapulanakehau*... (Fornander, 1916)

Long-distance navigating on the Ke-ala-ke-Kahiki route[3] would stop for 200 years. Tahiti or Kahiki was never forgotten in the Hawaiian historical memory. Tupaia and Mai (Omai), two Mā'ohi navigators, would play a pivotal role in Captain James Cook's expeditions, leading to Polynesian populations being decimated by introduced foreign diseases. In the re-opening of long-distance navigation traditions and the emerging global economy that the islands were forced to be a part of, Kānaka Maoli and Mā'ohi joined sailing crews that took them to the Pacific Northwest of Turtle Island (North America), China, and Europe. It also brought Mā'ohi and Kānaka Maoli to each other's islands for the first time in centuries.

Due to existing political dynamics and the need to establish nation-states similar to what existed in Western Europe, the Kingdom of Tahiti was unified under Pōmare I, while at the same time, the Kingdom of Hawai'i was unified under Kamehameha I. Hawaiian and Tahitian kings had been eyeing marriages amongst themselves as a way to legitimize themselves and build alliances (Jarves, 1843). In the meantime, Christianity was gaining a foothold in Tahiti due to the missionary efforts of the London Missionary Society. In 1818, some two years before the arrival of the American Calvinist missionaries to Hawai'i, a Tahitian named Toketa was attached to the household of John Adams Kuakini. Kuakini was the younger brother of the most influential consort of Kamehameha, Ka'ahumanu, and governor of Hawai'i Island. Toketa would witness the passing of Kamehameha I and the abolition of the Hawaiian religious system known to Westerners as the "Kapu System." He would also see the rise of Ka'ahumanu as she became Kuhina Nui[4] in 1919 and the arrival of American Calvinist missionaries in 1820. When the Calvinists arrived, Kuakini had three Tahitians in his household, including Toketa (Barrere & Sahlins, 1979). Toketa himself seems to have been exposed to Christianity and may have been a convert.

Toketa, sometime between 1820 to 1822, would then move to Maui and join the household of Hoapili. On Maui, a woman claimed that Pele had taken possession of her and warned of destruction if other Kānaka Maoli would adopt the new religion. Toketa represented the missionaries possibly because of his Mā'ohi roots. Ma'ōhi converts at this point became intermediaries between the religious practices allegedly brought by Pa'ao and the new religion of Christianity (Ralstom, 1985). They also were able to communicate in ways that the white missionaries could not because of their ancient shared history and a similar worldview with Kānaka Maoli. Due to the degree of prestige, Mā'ohi also served as political emissaries between different Hawaiian *ali'i* (aristocratic) factions, particularly in the power vacuum left by Kamehameha I. Toketa's role was no different in this regard, but would earn the displeasure of missionaries who wanted that role for themselves.

Toketa would support the newly arrived Calvinist missionaries for the next few years. He assisted the Hawaiian converts in worship and the creation of the Hawaiian language in the Latin alphabet. When Elisha Loomis struck the first printed material in the Hawaiian language on January 7, 1822, Kuakini was there. Toketa learned the new alphabet after an hour and, on February 8th, wrote a letter on behalf of Kuakini to the Rev. Hiram Bingham requesting copies of spelling books. This marked the first correspondence written entirely in the new alphabet of the Hawaiian language. However, despite Toketa's role in helping the missionaries and teaching the new alphabet to Hawaiian chiefs, Toketa was denied baptism and membership into the congregational church (Barrere & Sahlins, 1979).

In May of 1822, another Mā'ohi missionary by the name of Auna would arrive in Hawai'i as part of a visiting delegation that included the Rev. William Ellis and several Mā'ohi Christian converts. Auna soon found himself invited to stay and became attached to the court of Kuhina Nui Ka'ahumanu and her other consort, King Kaumuali'i of Kaua'i. Auna was introduced to the Kuhina Nui through his brother-in-law, Jack Moe.[5] Jack Moe was a native of Bora Bora and married Kahuamoa, a Hawaiian woman (Kamakau, 1992). Moe had been in Hawai'i for some years, and perhaps due to his wife, he had become a friend of Ka'ahumanu. Moe was a seaman before arriving in Hawai'i, and was at one time aboard HMS *Bounty*. Due to the invitation of Ka'ahumanu and Moe, Auna and his wife, Auna Wahine, decided to stay on O'ahu, where Auna would open a school with some 60 chiefly students (Barrere & Sahlins, 1979). One of the pupils was Auna's nephew, Kaomi.

The role that Mā'ohi played in the early history of Christianity in Hawai'i is often overlooked, but by 1825, nearly every important ali'i had Mā'ohi teachers within their household. Tau'ā and his wife, Tau'ā Wahine, as well as a female teacher, Ka'aumoku, were also part of the Ellis delegation. The three of them became part of the household of Keōpūolani and, after her passing, Hoapili. Stephen Pupuhi or Popohe arrived with the second batch of Calvinist missionaries and was trained in New England. He became part of Boki's household for a time before joining Kalanimōkū. Kahikona, who was friends with Toketa and Auna, became the teacher and chaplain of Aaron Keali'iahonui (Barrere & Sahlins, 1979). Aaron Keali'iahonui was the son of King Kaumuali'i of Kaua'i and was another consort of Kuhina Nui Ka'ahumanu. Therefore the presence of Toketa, Auna, Jack Moe, and the many other Mā'ohi within ali'i circles was not unusual. It fits a historical pattern going back centuries before Western contact.

Kaomi and his parents were part of the household of Ka'ahumanu. By 1826, Kaomi became a pupil of the Rev. Hiram Bingham and was listed as a native teacher employed by the missionaries and led prayer groups (Ralstom, 1985). He taught Ka'ahumanu's households on O'ahu and Maui in bible studies and literacy. However, Kaomi became close to Boki and learned in the *la'au lapa'au* (indigenous herbal medicine) (Kamakau, 1992). It was due to his healing skills that he attracted the attention of King Kamehameha III, as explained by the historian Samuel Kamakau:

> He was a friend of Ka-'ahu-manu's brother, Ka-hekili Ke'e-au-moku, and became a favorite of the king not because he was well-educated and intelligent, but because he knew something of the art of healing, could tell the symptoms of diseases, had learned from Boki and Ka-'o'o how to diagnose

a disease by feeling the body of a patient and [could prescribe] the proper medicine to cure it. Since his advice was successful the king conceived a great liking for him. He had moreover the power to tell a funny story entertainingly, and for these reasons he was admitted to intimacy with the king... (Kamakau, 1992).

King Kamehameha III and Kaomi were both in their late teens or early twenties and became attracted. This attraction became well known to chiefs and foreigners alike. Before her passing, Ka'ahumanu tried to extinguish the relationship by punishing the young king. Rather than abandoning Kaomi, the King replied to Ka'ahumanu, "Let me work at hard labor as the law that I have made for my kingdom says" (Kamakau, 1992, pp. 334–335). Kamehameha III was compelled to build a cattle fence for Hiram Bingham. Interestingly, in English translations, the king was punished for "adultery." But in the Hawaiian translation, he was punished for "moe kolohe." *Moe kolohe* covers a wide range of sexual behavior that the missionaries frowned upon, including adultery, polygamy, homosexuality, homosexual acts ("sodomy"), prostitution, and incest. As the king was unmarried at the time and his punishment was directly a result of his relationship with Kaomi, he was not being punished for adultery *per se,* but for his romantic and sexual relationship with Kaomi. This is further alluded to in a statement from Hiram Bingham:

> Several young men, belonging to a class attached to the king, and distinguished from the rest of their countrymen by the term Hulumanu (Feather or Bird-Feather), were among the advocates of a system of loose morals and vile sports. Among these, Paki, Namauu, and Kaomi were, for a time, conspicuous. The latter was a native born son of a naturalized Tahitian, by a Hawaiian mother, and possessed considerable shrewdness. He early manifested a desire to be instructed, and for a time made good progress—became a teacher and exhorter of his countrymen, and after four or five years desired baptism. But this was granted. Then, getting entangled in love affairs, he denied the authority of God's Word, attached himself to the irreligious, and declared he tried religion, and found nothing in it... (Bingham, 1848, p. 539).

Māhū and Moe Aikāne

Before the arrival of the missionaries, *māhū* and *aikāne* had been a normal part of Hawaiian society. *Māhū* was described as "homosexual" in early twentieth-century Hawaiian dictionaries but is now is used to describe "third gender," "transgender," "queer," or someone "in the middle" of the Euro-American gender binary. Kānaka Maoli did have gendered responsibilities, but women could and did exercise political and spiritual authority in their own name, unlike many of their contemporaries in the U.S. and Europe. Women were involved in combat, and prestigious titles were inherited matrilineally. Relationships based on genealogy seemed to have mattered more than gender. Māhū, in this context, could be more described as occupying a fluid *wā* (space) that both men and women could occupy and, in some ways, embodied both gender roles. It was up to the person what that embodiment meant. Māhū was widely accepted in Hawaiian society. Māhū also had traditional roles in spiritual matters. The term "māhū" in Tahitian has essentially the same meaning.

Moe Aikāne, on the other hand, was a same-gender relationship or "deep friendship." The attraction was not based on gender but the other person's character. While māhū occupied a wā, moe aikāne was explicitly a type of sanctioned relationship between two individuals who became aikāne to each other. These individuals could each be men, women, or māhū. Moʻolelo, including those involving Hiʻiaka, have aikāne relationships, which were celebrated. As noted by foreigners, including Captain Cook, having an aikāne relationship was typical among the aliʻi. Kamehameha I had several aikāne.

These types of relationships were deeply discouraged by the Calvinist missionaries due to their understanding of the Christian gospel and their ideas of gender roles and belief in capitalism, which they referred to as "civilized behavior." Many prominent missionaries believed in early forms of the prosperity gospel, meaning that wealth was tied to personal industry and was a sign of one's predestination towards salvation within the Kingdom of God. Therefore, poverty was a personal moral failing and punishment by God due to laziness and irreligiosity. To paraphrase the political economist and historian Max Weber:

> It is salvation anxiety that drives the desire to pursue with rigor a secular calling in the world. The pastoral literature of English Puritans revealed to him the depth of this uncertainty. The unknowable nature of God pushed Calvinists to seek signs of election in the world, yet, as the Dutch of the seventeenth century experienced, believers did not allow themselves to enjoy the fruits of acquisition. To ease the tension between their piety and their prosperity, wealth was instead to be reinvested in society, promoting an ascetic discipline in which commerce could be converted to the service of God. This "ethical" form of capitalism was seen to be consonant with Reformed teaching....[6]

Missionaries, therefore, believed that their own nuclear family structures enforced these ideas of "work ethics" and hierarchy, which they tried to impose on Kānaka Maoli. Kānaka Maoli were to be remade into an idealized version of themselves.

These notions of what constituted a "family" differed from the concepts that Kānaka Maoli and other Pacific Islanders had. Traditionally for Kānaka Maoli, one's ʻohana or family unit was composed of generations of family, relatives, adopted children, and polyamorous relationships, including aikāne. This way of viewing a family within the context of a larger communal relationship can be seen in Hawaiian genealogical terms, where the concern is placed on generational rather than individual relationships. The Kanaka Maoli term for parent is *makua.* The term for father is *makuakāne,* with the suffix *kāne* (male) being added, as Hawaiian, like other Austronesian languages, is a gender-neutral language. *Makuahine* (makua + suffix (wa)hine) is mother. The traditional Kanaka Maoli term for uncle is makua. *Makuahine* could also mean aunt. This is because a child's parent and a child's aunt or uncle are of the same generation and therefore have a similar relationship within the context of the entire family lineage.

These nuclear family structures also reinforced Euro-American gender roles, particularly patriarchy, with the men leading both the State and the Church. Māhū and aikāne relationships were considered emasculating and sinful because they violated God's law, but also what they saw as the "man's role." Women were the property of their husbands, and sexual relations were only for the purposes of procreation. As part of the missionary effort, Kanaka Maoli women were trained to be "civilized." Missionary and wife of Gerrit Judd, Laura Fish Judd, records:

> ... To help these degraded beings up and out of the depths of heathenism; to teach them how to become better wives, better mothers, and better neighbors, is indeed a work that angels covet, especially when these efforts seem to be accepted of God and are crowned with success... (Judd, 2017).

The obvious *aikāne* relationship between the king and Kaomi directly challenged the missionaries in political power and their authority over religious and social structures. Whether or not Kaomi himself was *māhū* or simply in a *moe aikāne* is a matter of speculation, although it has been suggested that a reason for Kaomi's request for baptism by the Church was because he was *māhū.* After this rejection, Kaomi rejects Christianity and embraces a return to traditional

Hawaiian values. The king, who seemed to care deeply for Kaomi, previously had his own misgivings about the new religion. Still, the missionaries placed the entirety of the blame on Kaomi, who is repeatedly referred to as "the infidel" in missionary writings (Bingham, 1848). It is also assumed that they could not directly attack the king as that would sway more aliʻi to the king's side.

Furthermore, Kaomi is linked to the *Hulumanu* ("Bird feathers"). The Hulumanu was established around 1826 and consisted of favorites of the king. The Hulumanu at first acted as a retinue of the king and even had uniforms and daily parades (Ralstom, 1985). Although described by missionary sources as a cult, they were revivalists. They participated in traditional Hawaiian arts, sports, and spiritual practices—all frowned upon by the missionaries and the Kanaka Maoli Christian converts. They did not at first directly attack Christianity itself but the form of Christianity that the Calvinists were trying to impose. They were also against the Kaʻahumanu-backed elites that displaced other aliʻi families from their traditional lands. The Hulumanu members formed the closest opposition movement that Hawaiʻi had to the missionaries and Kaʻahumanu. After the passing of Kaʻahumanu, their opposition turned to her successor, Elizabeth Kīnaʻu.

KĪNAʻU

In 1832, Kaʻahumanu became gravely ill and decreed that her successor as Kuhina Nui was Elizabeth Kīnaʻu. Elizabeth Kinaʻu was the half-sister of Kamehameha III and was adopted by Kaʻahumanu. Kīnaʻu was also probably one of the most pro-Calvinist missionary Hawaiian aliʻi of her time. She was known to have more hardline views than Kaʻahumanu and believed in the Calvinist vision of Hawaiʻi. Having been appointed by Kaʻahumanu without first consulting the king caused instant resentment by Kamehameha III and Governor Liliha of Oʻahu. On June 5, 1832, Kaʻahumanu passed away, and Elizabeth Kīnaʻu is recognized by most of the powerful chiefs as Kuhina Nui Elizabeth Kīnaʻu Kaʻahumanu II.

Kamehameha III gives the title of mōʻī kuʻi to Kaomi. The title of mōʻī originates from Maui. Kamehameha III is the first to officially use it to correspond to the English word "King." King Kamehameha I was called mōʻī after his conquest of Maui, but he never officially adopted the title because although he was a conqueror, his genealogical rank did not necessarily allow him to hold that title. In adopting the title, Kamehameha III was claiming not just his inheritance from his father, but also his high-ranking mother, Keōpūolani of Maui. The second definition of the Hawaiian dictionary defines *Kuʻi* as: "To join, stitch, sew, splice, unite; joined; seam" (Pukui & Elibert, 1986). It is this definition that renders Mōʻī Kuʻi to mean joint or united ruler. Samuel Kamakau confirms this:

> When the king took up sinful ways he gave Kaomi the title of "joint king, joint ruler" (moi kuʻi, au-puni kuʻi), appointed chiefs, warriors, and guards to his service, and made his name honorable. Any chief, prominent citizen, member of the king's household, or any man at all who wanted land, clothing, money, or anything else that man might desire, applied to Kaomi. He had the power to give or lend for the government. Landless chiefs were enriched by Kaomi and landless men also received land through him... (Kamakau, 1992).

Mōʻī Kuʻi is a higher title than the title of "Kuhina Nui." It can be interpreted to mean a consort with equal sovereign powers, similar to William III and Mary II of England. In doing this, Kamehameha III was not just undermining the new Kuhina Nui but also showing his opposition to the worldview of the missionary establishment. It is also interesting to note that missionaries refused to acknowledge this title. Bingham uses the title "kelii kui" and translates it as "engrafted king" (Bingham, 1848). Laura Judd also uses the title of "kelii kui" and translates it as "grafted king" (Judd, 2017). By not acknowledging the term *mōʻī* as Kamakau does, it lowers Kaomi's rank. Mōʻī is one of the highest titles an aliʻi may hold, and although the king is sharing this title with Kaomi, this too was being denied to him by the missionaries.

Around this time, Hoapili and others tried to persuade the king to return to Maui and separate himself from Kaomi. Ever since the passing of Kaʻahumanu, the king had been staying in Waialua, Oʻahu with Kaomi and the Hulumanu. Waialua is significant because it is home to several sacred sites, including Kapukapuakea heiau and Mahuka heiau, which overlooks Laniakea (*Raʻiātea* in Tahitian). A famous place for martial arts, Keawawaihe ("Valley of the Spears") is also located in Waialua. These sacred and historical sites became associated with the Hulumanu (Bingham, 1848). Kamehameha III could not be persuaded to leave Waialua, which left the government, located on Maui, in an awkward situation.

In March of 1833, Kamehameha III announced his age of majority and called a special council of chiefs that "he wished to take into his position the lands for which his father toiled, the power of life and death, and the undivided sovereignty" (Bingham, 1848, p. 540). The king at the time was 17 or 18 years old. It is unknown if this council took place on Oʻahu, but it more likely took place on Maui, as Lahaina was the kingdom's capital, and most of the important chiefs were present at these meetings (including Hoapili). At this meeting, a rumor spread that Kīnaʻu was about to be ousted, and Hoapili and others made preparations to resist the king's will if he did so. Kinaʻu walked to the king and said, "We cannot war with the Word of God between us!" (Bingham, 1848, p. 540). King Kamehameha backed down and confirmed her appointment.

The following day, another meeting was held in which the king wanted to regulate alcohol. Alcohol had previously been banned, but a black market arose. Kīnaʻu, Governor John Adams Kuakini of Hawaiʻi Island, Governor Kakioʻewa of Kauaʻi, and Governor Hoapili of Maui were against lifting the ban and refused to issue licenses within their jurisdictions. Kaomi, however, offered a different solution and urged for the regulation of alcohol, as banning it deprived the government of revenue, and Kanaka Maoli-owned businesses complained that foreigners constantly asked to buy alcohol from them; thus, the ban also deprived them of income. There was also smuggling, and Kaomi urged Kamehameha to regulate this "necessary evil" as was done in other countries (Bingham, 1848). Ultimately, the decision was left to the governors, and only Governor Liliha of Oʻahu exercised the prerogative to grant liquor licenses on her island.

Missionaries and Hawaiian converts deplored this and exaggerated Kaomi's influence. For example, Kamakau claims that:

> The king's love of pleasure grew, and evil ways that had been stamped out were revived. The natural impulses of the old days—prostitution, liquor drinking, the hula—came back. The liquor distilleries were again opened. Only in the district of Waialua was the distillation of liquor not allowed. All kinds of indulgence cropped up. People poured in from Hawaii, Maui, and Kauai, for on Oahu, the marriage laws were not observed, but on the other islands, the rulers were strict in their enforcement of Kau-i-ke-aouli's law. Such infringements of the law as knocking out the teeth, tattooing, tobacco smoking, and other small sins were punished by working on the road. [...] No one of the chiefs dared attempt to turn the king back to right living. Not even his foster mothers, Kinaʻu and Ke-ka-ulu-ohi, could utter a word. The king's mind was set... (Kamakau, 1992).

Alcohol had a devastating effect on indigenous populations everywhere. Understandably, a ban would be enforced. However, Kamakau does not mention that King Kamehameha had brought that issue up in council, as Bingham mentions in his memoir. Kamakau suggests that Kaomi himself made alcohol legal and that the king had no say in the matter. But all of the problems attributed to Kaomi had already existed. By the 1820s, foreigners owned pubs and brothels throughout Nuʻuanu Avenue, which they called "Fid Street" (Carr, 2014). While a ban on alcohol had been placed, the Hawaiian government was reluctant to enforce it on foreign nationals due to fears of rioting and gunboats, thus leaving these foreigners with a monopoly. The partiality of how the alcohol ban was enforced on Kānaka Maoli and their businesses could have been the real reason why Kaomi pushed for regulation.

It should also be noted that Waialua did not allow distilleries. Although the missionary sources also accused Kaomi of rum production, Kaomi had an association with ʻō *kolehao,* a liquor made of ti leaf, and may have been the first Kanaka Maoli to produce it (Middleton, 1971). ʻŌ kolehao is traced back to Captain Portlock, a member of Captain Cook's crew who used it to try to treat scurvy. Kaomi somehow became involved in this, perhaps due to its possible value as a form of anesthesia.

In November of 1833, another incident occurred. A rumor had spread that Kīnaʻū was again going to be ousted.

> The party consisted of Elizabeth Kinaʻu, Ke-ku-anaoʻa, and two armed men, Kani-ku and Ka-ʻai-puaʻa; Ke-ka-ulu-ohi and Ka-naʻina with two armed men, Halali and Kilinahe; and Ulu-maheihei Hoa-pili with Ke-kauaʻi and Ka-ʻumiʻumi. The yard was lined with soldiers armed with guns and swords, foreigners behind them, and officers mounted on horses and carrying swords. Ulu-maheihei went first, then the young women, and after them the escort. In defence of the dignity of their rank as chiefs they risked their lives, and did not wait to be announced as daughters of Kamehameha. As they drew close to the white soldiers they were recognized and someone told the king. He called out, "Come in!" and wept aloud as he kissed his foster mothers whom he saw again for the first time, and the foreign soldiers hearing the wailing withdrew. The king asked Hoa-pili, "Why did you come here?" Hoa-pili replied, "We came because we had heard rumors that you were going to appoint Liliha premier of the kingdom. You must first kill me before making my daughter premier lest I be blamed as her parent. Here is the daughter of the house of Kamehameha. Let her serve you. My daughter is but a tenant here." The king answered, "I love these two and I also love Liliha, but these two I love because they keep my laws." Hoa-pili

said, "Do me this favor to place the duties of the kingdom upon her who is
here ready to serve you." "I consent, but Liliha must hear of this," said the
king. Liliha was called and was found drunk... (Kamakau, 1992, p. 337).

At this point, it became clear that Kīna'u and her followers were willing
to use force in order to maintain power. The young king seems to have been
shaken by this incident and consented to confirm Kīna'u as Kuhina Nui again.
Through this intimidation, Kīna'u also replaced Liliha as governor of O'ahu
and was appointed command over the fort in Honolulu. This meant that in
effect, Kīna'u commanded her own military force. Again, one wonders how
much influence Kaomi had in political matters. In Kīna'u's case, missionary
writers paint a different picture of her.

> Kinau stood nobly in defense of virtue, decency, and good order, but the
> king refused to listen to her advice, and even threatened her with personal
> violence, if she dared to venture into his presence.
>
> In her despondency she made us [Judd family] a visit one day, and
> said, "I am in straits and heavy-hearted, and I have come to tell you my
> thought. I am quite discouraged, and can not bear this burden any longer.
> I wish to throw away my rank, and title, and responsibility together, bring
> my family here, and live with you, or we will take our families and go to
> America. I have money" (Judd, 2017, pp. 51–52).

It was in this period that the Hulumanu became more active. Laura
Judd adds:

> Vile heathen songs, games, and shameless dances, which had gone out of
> use, were revived. Rum and wretchedness became rampant; and the quiet
> of our lovely dells and valleys were disturbed with bacchanalian shouts and
> the wild orgies of drunken revelry. Family ties were sundered, husbands
> forsook their wives, and wives left husbands and helpless little children, to
> follow drunken paramours... (Judd, 2017, p. 51).

She probably was referring to the performances of *hula,* and a rejection of
missionary-imposed values. The Kanaka Maoli population was rapidly collaps-
ing primarily due to introduced diseases. In the midst of this, a new political
and social order arose, radically different and alien to Kanaka Maoli culture.
Missionaries and many of the ali'i refused to acknowledge that the masses of

Kānaka Maoli were dealing with all of this trauma and trying to figure out who they were as a people. Kamehameha III had maintained regular contact with Hewahewa, his father's *kahuna nui* (high priest). Hewahewa lived in Waialua at this time. When asked about the indigenous Hawaiian religion subjects by the king or by Boki, he assisted. In conversations with missionaries, Hewahewa admitted he had been invited to join the Hulumanu by the king, but declined as he was a Christian (Ralstom, 1985). This implies that the Hulumanu had a genuine interest in reestablishing the former indigenous religion. Kamehameha III and the Hulumanu threw a Christian funeral for his pet baboon, which allegedly mocked the missionaries (Daws, 1968). Kamehameha III told a foreign consul that he was eyeing land in the Pacific Northwest of Turtle Island (Ralstom, 1985). This hinted that Kamehameha III was aware of the threats to his rule and was considering alternatives. However, the Hulumanu represented the first honest attempt at reconstructing the Hawaiian religious and political system since the Battle of Kuamoʻo in 1819.

In early 1834, factions within the aliʻi came to a head with the kidnapping of Kaomi and the attempt on his life.

> Some of the chiefs murmured against the king because his mind was so fixed on evil ways, and they made a secret plan to kill Kaomi, and a certain chief named Ka-iki-o-ʻewa was to carry it out. He went with a servant named Ka-ihu-hanuna, carrying a war club in his hand, to the yard of Kaomi (near the present publishing house of the Kuʻokoʻa) and ordered the servant to tie Kaomi's hands behind his back with a rope. Kaomi did not order the guards to kill Ka-iki-o-ʻewa in accordance with the law that "the chief who enters Kaomi's house shall die." He allowed himself to be bound and put to death if death it was to be. Ka-iki-o-ʻewa led him into the presence of Kinaʻu inside the fort. When she saw Kaomi with his hands tied behind his back she cried out in alarm to her uncle, "Alas! what are you doing to the king's favorite? The king will think that I have a share in this. Let him go, or this crime will rest upon us all!" Ka-iki-o-ʻewa said, "Who is ruler over the kingdom? You are the ruler. Give your consent to the death of this trouble-maker." At this moment the king hurried in, dressed in the scant clothing he was wearing when a guard had run to inform him that, "Kaomi is being killed by Ka-iki-o-ʻewa." The king himself untied Kaomi's bonds. Ka-iki-o-ʻewa sprang forward and grappled with the king, over and under they fought until the king held Ka-iki-o-ʻewa fast. Then words poured from Ka-iki-o-ʻewa's mouth declaring, "You are not the ruler over the kingdom

if you keep on indulging yourself in evil ways!" but the king did not answer him. (Ka-iki-o-'ewa must have been insane.) Kaomi was released and went back with the king to Ka-hale-uluhe [former palace of Boki located near St. Andrew's Cathedral], and the king's place was made tabu; no one was allowed to enter it... (Kamakau, 1992, pp. 398–339).

This marked the first time that anti-queer-related violence was documented in Hawaiian history. Missionary sources do not mention this attempt on Kaomi's life. Immediately after this, coup rumors were spread that Kīna'u would replace Kamehameha III as ruler (Kamakau, 1992).

Kamehameha III and Kaomi went on a circuit of the islands. This circuit could be explained as a way for Kamehameha III to re-assert his authority. After the circuit, Kaomi removed himself and disappeared from court. Being that there was a continued threat on his life, Kaomi may have ended the relationship to preserve the power of the king. By 1836, Kaomi reportedly died alone in Lahaina while the king was on O'ahu (Dibble, 1843). No ceremonies were given, and it is believed that he was buried in an unmarked grave. Nāhi'ena'ena, the king's beloved sister, also passed away around the same time. In 1837, Kamehameha III agreed to an arranged marriage with Kalama Hakaleleponi Kapakuhaili, the adopted daughter and niece of the high-ranking ali'i Charles Kana'ina.

Kaomi's life after that was used as a warning against resisting the new status quo. Hawaiian language newspapers such as the *Ka Hae Hawaii* printed out the story of Kaomi as a warning. As Noenoe Silva explains:

Related to the admonitions to conform to Euro-American gender behavior were condemnations of well-known aikāne, in articles such as "Ka wa ia Kaomi".... Many missionary-inspired laws were openly transgressed while Kaomi was an intimate of the king: Kamakau states that "fight, murdering, adultery, prostitution, plural marriage, disregard of the marriage laws, drunkeness, and the distilling of liquor went on all over O'ahu".... In the story, Kaomi was in the end abandoned by the young king, deserted to wander, ill and destitute, until he died. The story is meant to be a lesson in Calvinist morality, and to reinforce the discourse of salvation and civilization through labor (Noenoe, 2004).

Why did Kaomi get such bad press? Until 1861, all newspapers in Hawai'i were printed on presses owned by the missionaries. The government newspaper, *The Polynesian,* was also published on missionary-owned presses. So writers such as Samuel Kamakau, David Malo, and other notable Hawaiians had their works censored. This ensured that anything positive about Kaomi would not be printed, and the missionary-approved accounts of him would be the official accounts. This also meant that anything positive about the ancient indigenous Hawaiian religious system would not be printed. Eventually, 22 Kānaka Maoli, including David Kalākaua, formed the 'Ahahui Ho'opuka Nūpepa Kūikawa o Honolulu and bought their own printing press (Noenoe, 2004). In 1861, this group printed out *Ka Hoku o Pakipika,* the first independent newspaper in the Hawaiian language, and marked the beginning of a free press for Kānaka Maoli. It was not until the publication of works by Kanaka Maoli scholars in the twentieth century such as Drs. Noenoe Silva and J. Kēhaulani Kauanui that Kaomi began to be re-evaluated.

But as pointed out, when Kaomi was mentioned, it was as if it were a morality play. Bingham and other missionaries did use Kaomi as a tool to convert more Kānaka Maoli and extend the reach of the church. Bingham, for example, writes:

> The six hundred members of the church, in different parts of the islands, for the most part stood their ground firmly. Samuel J Mills, and the young princess[7], and a few others, were drawn into the snare of the devil, and occassioned disappoinment and grief. But during the year after Kaomi's commotion, there was one hundred and twenty-four additions to the churches—a number greater than the average annual additions, during the seven years of Ka'ahumau's membership....Scarcely more than half a thousand were admitted to the church at the Sandwich Islands during the Christian life of the queen regent, though tens of thousands availed themselves of schools and other means of improvement availed themselves of schools....Never, perhaps, has the king had a better demonstration that the new religion had struck deep root in Hawaiian soil, than at the time when the influence of the infidel Kaomi, and his coadjutors, was applied to check or destroy it; and his young majesty was constrained to say openly, "The Kingdom of God is strong" (Bingham, 1848, pp. 542–543).

All of the major missionary writers from Bingham to the Judds as well as Hawaiian language newspapers allowed to be published at the time all specifically mention Kaomi in the same triumphalist tone.

In addition, missionary sources and Kamakau consistently refer to Kaomi as either part-Tahitian or part-Bora Bora to further "othering" of Kaomi. This also allowed missionaries to degenerate the contributions of Kaomi as he was a foreigner, but also the contributions of Māʻohi throughout Hawaiian history, and especially in the early proselytization of Christianity. Kaomi was a Kanaka Maoli. He was probably born on Maui, as Kaʻahumanu had her principal household there, but was raised on Oʻahu. He probably knew of Māʻohi traditions from his father and uncle, but he was still raised in Hawaiʻi. He was as much a Kanaka Maoli as anyone at the royal court he served, and certainly more than the New England missionaries.

Kaomi, in the context of his time, can be seen as the first break with the Calvinist impositions on Kānaka Maoli. His role in history could not be denied as even the official chronologies found in Hawaiian dictionaries used in the Hawaiian Kingdom's public schools included his era (Andrews, 1865). He was an aikāne and a joint ruler with Kamehameha III. His time saw the short-lived revival of the hula and Hawaiian sports and martial arts. He questioned Christianity and restored land to chiefs who had been displaced. His lineage as being part of a long tradition of Māʻohi among Kanaka Maoli aliʻi further gave him legitimacy, not removing it, as missionary writers tried to do. Even though Kaomi never directly insulted the missionaries, he questioned the type of nation Hawaiʻi should be: would it be a Kanaka Maoli nation or a Calvinist one? All of these things earned him the ire of the establishment. He represented the first leader since Kekuaokalani in 1819 to have attempted to revive the indigenous religion. After Kaomi, Hawaiʻi was pushed into essentially colonizing itself and leaving a wound in Kānaka Maoli. Although King Kalākaua in the 1880s would attempt to heal this wound, he too was pushed out of power. The Hawaiian Renaissance of the 1970s in some ways mirrors what both Kaomi and King Kalākaua were attempting to do in restoring a Hawaiian sense of place and identity. Kaomi still resonates with those who could view Kaomi not just as a "queer icon," but as an early Polynesian leader of resistance to assimilation.

Notes

1. Native Hawaiian.
2. Indigenous people from Tahiti and/or the adjacent Tōtaiete mā (Society Islands).
3. Traditional oceanic route starting from Kahoʻolawe and ending at Tahiti.
4. Often translated as "regent," "viceroy," "premier," or "prime minister." Kuhina Nui was the most powerful executive officer after the king, and during the lifetime of Kaʻahumanu, acted as co-ruler.
5. Young, Peter (2017). Auna. Images of Old Hawaiʻi. https://imagesofoldhawaii .com/auna/

6. Gordon, Bruce. Calvinism and Capitalism: Together Again? *Reflections:* Yale Divinity School. https://reflections.yale.edu/article/money-and-morals-after -crash/calvinism-and-capitalism-together-again

7. Princess Nāhiʻenaʻena, the king's sister.

BIBLIOGRAPHY

Andrews, L. (1865). *Dictionary of the Hawaiian Language: To Which is Appended an English-Hawaiian Vocabulary and Chronological Table of Remarkable Events.* Honolulu: Whitney.

Barrere, D., & Sahlins, M. (1979). Tahitians in the early history of Hawaiian Christianity. *Hawaiian Journal of History, Vol 13,* 19–35.

Bingham, H. (1848). *A Residence of Twenty-One Years in the Sandwich Islands.* New York: Huntington.

Carr, J. (2014). *Hawaiian Music in Motion.* Chicago: University of Illinois Press.

Daws, G. (1968). *Shoal of Time: A History of the Hawaiian Islands.* Honolulu: University of Hawaiʻi Press.

Dibble, S. (1843). *A History of the Sandwich Islands.* Lahaina: Press of the Missionary Seminary.

Fornander, A. (1916). *Hawaiian Antiquities and Folk-Lore.* Honolulu: Bishop Museum.

Henry, T. (1995). *Voyaging Chiefs of Havaiʻi.* Honolulu: Kalamaku Press.

Jarves, J. J. (1843). *History of the Hawaiian Islands.* Boston: Tappan and Dennet.

Judd, L. (2017). *Sketches of Life in the Hawaiian Islands (Revised 1880).* Oregon: Helps Communication.

Kalakaua, K. (1972). *The Legends and Myths of Hawaii.* Vermont: Tuttle.

Kamakau, S. (1992). *Ruling Chiefs of Hawaii (Revised Edition).* Honolulu: Kamehameha Schools.

Middleton, W. S. (1971). Early Medical Experiences in Hawaii. *Bulletin of the History of Medicine, Vol. 45,* 444–460.

Noenoe, S. (2004). *Aloha Betrayed: Native Hawaiian Resistance to American Colonialism.* Durham: Duke University Press.

Pukui, M. K., & Elbert, S. H. (1986). *Hawaiian Dictionary: Hawaiian-English, English-Hawaiian.* Honolulu: University of Hawaiʻi Press.

Ralstom, C. (1985). Early Nineteenth Cenury Polynesian Millennial Cults and the Case of Hawaiʻi. *Journal of the Polynesian Society, Volume 94,* 307–331.

CHAPTER 3

THE STORY OF SERANG, AKA LANI, HINDU MĀHELE AWARDEE AT LAHAINA

Shilpi Suneja

Because the Māhele is considered one of the most significant chapters in the modern history of Hawai'i, land parcels distributed through it have become indelibly attached to the names of the Māhele grantees. One such name making its mark on Lahaina history is "Serang aka Lani," a sailor from India who found his way to Maui in the early 1820s. The six pieces of land awarded to him during the Great Māhele continue to bear his name in the official records. And yet, many details of his life remain shrouded in mystery. In this essay, I attempt to construct a narrative for the man whose name continues to be attached to Lahaina history and to the genealogy of Lahaina lands. In doing so I hope to shed light on the very first South Asian refugee-transplants on the Hawaiian Islands in modern history.

I. Beginning with the End

Inevitably, we must begin with the end: with Serang's obituaries, which supply the most detail as well as a narrative about his life. The first obituary, published in the *Pacific Commercial Advertiser* on February 21, 1861, states the following:

ANOTHER LANDMARK GONE—Died at his residence in Lahaina, Feb. 11, Sheik Mahomet, more generally known among foreigners as "Serang," and by the natives as "Lani." Serang was one of the *old residents,* having arrived at these islands in the *Pickering,* somewhere about 1822. From the

A 1916 map of Lahaina indicating the Land Commission Awards. Lani's lands are highlighted in rectangles. Source: Hawaiʻi State Archives.

account he gave of himself, he left Bombay (his native city) in the *Paragon,* for Boston, as the boatswain or "Serang" (whence his name), of a gang of his fellow countrymen, who engaged as seamen on board the vessel. He was promised a return passage from Boston, but no opportunity offering, he shipped on board the *Pickering,* on a voyage to the Northwest and Bombay. Arriving here, he was induced to run away, and became domesticated. He was at one time engaged in trade, and conducted quite a thriving and lucrative business. Among his papers are found large bills for merchandise, bought of Pierce & Brewer, E. & H. Grimes, Stephen Reynolds, O. P. Ricker, and other merchants of the olden time. Before his death, he became reduced in circumstances, but died quietly in his own home, attended by his wife and friends.

The second obituary for Serang, published in *Saturday Press* on October 27, 1883, reads as follows:

Died at Lahaina, February 11th, an old East Indian, named Sheik Mahomet, generally known however among the foreign residents as "Serang" or Boatswain. He was a very old resident, having arrived on the islands in 1822. By his own statement, he left Bombay in the ship "Paragon," for Boston, as *serang* or boatswain over his fellow countrymen, seamen on the same vessel. Arrived at Boston, and failing to get an opportunity to return to Bombay, he shipped on the brig *Pickering,* for a voyage to the north-west Coast of America. The vessel touching at these islands, Serang ran away from her and from thenceforth resided either at Honolulu or Lahaina. He at one time kept a retail dry goods store and carried on a pretty large business, as was evidenced by papers found after his death, showing large purchases of merchandise from such old-time houses as—Pirce & Brewer, E. & H. Grimes, Stephen Reynolds, O. P. Ricker, and others. Later he had become poor and so died, aged about 80 years.

Serang was so called because of his profession—he was a head lascar, in charge of other lascars. But who were the lascars?

II. Serang as a Head Lascar

Lascars were South Asian sailors who both manned the British and American ships and participated in capturing enemy vessels in the fifteenth century (likely beginning even earlier), filling in the gaps left by British and American deserters. As was the case with their liminal, in-between-lands employment, the origin of the word "lascar" is also liminal, sharing roots in both the Persian and the Portuguese languages: from the Persian word "lashkar," which means army, and the Portuguese word "lascari," which means soldier.

The Sessional Papers of the British Mercantile Marine Committee of 1903 define the lascars thus:

> Lascars are in most cases hereditary sailors, and have special qualifications for work as firemen in hot climates. They are temperate, and those who came before us made a most favourable impression upon us. The evidence shows that they make most amenable and contented crews. In consequence their employment as firemen has grown almost universal in the tropics, and they are also largely employed in vessels trading between ports within the tropics and the United Kingdom (vi).

It is important to note that lascars and serangs not only stoked the fires onboard the ships, but also participated in the fights that ensued between their and the enemies' ships. The British Royal Navy conscripted hundreds of lascars during wartime (Fisher 144–5). An article in the August 12 1904 edition of *Hawaiian Gazette* describes how 21 lascars and a serang were sent onboard an enemy ship to sink her.

Lascars were ubiquitous on all the major ports of the world, even in Honolulu. Lascars were so popular, the merchant Stephen Reynolds mentions in his journal a ship named *Lascar* arriving on the Hawaiian ports. The missionaries active in Hawai'i in the early 1800s describe numerous encounters with lascars. Cochran Forbes describes a lascar manning his ship during his journey from New Bedford to the Hawaiian Islands taken between November 26, 1831, and September 21, 1832:

> I could not but admire our little steward (who is a Lascar, pretty dark, stout and thick set, with a turban on his head and an apron tucked close around his waist) as he would come dodging along from the caboose or cook-house to the cabin, with a tin mug in each hand, full of Indian meal gruel or something of the kind. He would keep his feet and run from the caboose to the cabin stairs and dodge down to his pantry with the greatest grace while the passengers would be holding on for life by a rope or something else, waiting for the ship to come to a level again that they might

take a step or two to some other secure position, before she pitched on the other side (4).

On October 2, 1900, The *Hawaiian Star* carried the following story about lascars and a serang onboard the American vessel *Samoa:*

One of the queerest crews that ever went down to the sea in a ship is now on the Pacific on board the steamer Samoa which is carrying nearly a thousand horses to China for the German troops.

Every one of the sixty-six men of the Samoa's crew is a native of India. In the galley and the saloon are seven other East Indians who in appearance are exactly like the men in the fo'castle, with the exception that the men before the mast invariably wear little round caps, a dingy red in color, while the seven others are mostly barren of head covering. All are the same hue, as far as complexion is concerned, the prevailing shade being a deep coffee color.

The sixty-six men before the mast are Mohammedans: the seven in the gally and saloon are Roman Catholics.

Every morning as the sun appears on horizon the sixty-six face the orb of day and then throw themselves prone on the deck while one of their number cries "Allah il Allah!" (God is God), and recites passages from the Koran. Five times during the day this ceremony is gone through with. In addition there are other and more extended prayers twice a day, the "Serang" or head man of the crew, leading the devotions.

The seven and sixty-six hold no intercourse that is not absolutely necessary. They have nothing in common save the dangers of the ocean. Their food is not the same, and they do not eat together. The sixty-six Mohammedans will eat no meat but mutton, and this they must kill and prepare themselves. The Samoa carries a large number of live sheep out of deference to religious scruples of the sixty-six. A Mohammedan would much prefer to be hanged than forced to eat the flesh of an animal that had been killed by "an unbeliever."

The Mohammedans are docile and make good sailors.

They are very seldom insubordinate, and when one of them is guilty of an infraction of discipline his punishment is swift and severe. The Serang ties the culprit's hands and then lashes the malefactor with a rope's end until tired of the amusement.

Among the sixty-six of the Samoan's Mohammedan is a boy of 16.

Although hampered with the appellation of Mahomet Said Ziderbarr, this boy has attained a degree of worldly wisdom that is startling. He can quote you off hand the gaming rules and customs in vogue in half the ports of the world. He has decided views as to the duty that wives owe their husbands, although he says of the husband's responsibility to the wife. On marital matters this boy should be something of an authority, considering the fact that he was married to his first wife about nine years ago. The wife lives in a little village east of Bombay, where Mahomet hopes to join her some day, when he has saved enough money to permit of his doing so. Ad Mohemet receives ten rupees, about $3 a month for his services. He figures that it will be several years before he can afford the luxuries of housekeeping.

Every one of the sixty-six black men in the fo'castle is married. Nearly all of them send the money they earn to their wives in India, retaining only a rupee or two to squander on themselves.

The greatest advantage in having a crew of Mohammedans, say the officers of the Samoa, is the fact that the men never become intoxicated. Their religion forbids them to drink strong liquors, and this obligation is rarely violated.

By 1903, the word "lascar" came to mean East Indian sailor, because by then thousands and thousands of Indian sailors were employed on English and American merchant ships. Despite prejudices against them and the sometimes reluctance of the East India Company to hire them, their numbers grew exponentially: in 1808, 1,336 lascars arrived in London (Visram 34). By 1944, *Life* magazine reported 59,000 lascars sailing around the world. Based on these numbers alone, it is easy to gauge the importance of lascars to British and American trade. "Britain owes a debt to these sailors (lascars and Chinese seamen)," writes Rozina Visram in *Ayahs, Lascars, and Princes*, "for carrying here the wealth of the East which helped to build up British maritime wealth and prosperity" (34).

Apart from their abundant numbers, another reason why the lascars were so useful to the British merchant ships is because they came comparatively cheap. The shipowners could get away with paying the lascars "one-sixth and one-seventh of the European rate of pay" (Visram 34). Lascars were also given less space, fewer provisions, and less prize money for capturing enemy ships (Linden & Behal 38). The work of sailors was difficult, and desertion from British and American sailors was common; lascars rose to fill these gaps, and for far less pay.

Despite their large numbers, and perhaps because of it, lascars faced discrimination. Visram speaks thus about their mistreatments:

> Mirza Abu Talib Khan described how the ship on which he was travelling
> to Europe was delayed on the way because "sixteen of our best lascars being
> much disgusted by the treatment received on board this ship, deserted and
> hid themselves in the woods; and it was discovered that the remainder of the
> crew only waited the approach of the night to follow the example of their
> comrades." Incidents of this kind were not uncommon; Joseph Salter, the
> Missionary to the Orientals and Africans, recorded some harrowing tales of
> mistreatment. In one case the entire lascar crew of Muslims deserted after
> the ship docked in the Thames. Their complaint, confirmed by the Euro-
> pean members of the crew, was that they "had been hung up with weights
> tied to their feet, flogged with a rope"; they were forced to eat pork, and
> "the insult carried further by violently ramming the tail of a pig into their
> mouths and twisting the entrails of the pig round their necks." One lascar
> tried to escape this vicious treatment by jumping overboard: he drowned.
> In another instance Salter (an English missionary) met lascars who had
> been flogged: one had his teeth missing after being hit with a chain; another
> could not walk straight. The most gruesome story concerned nine lascars
> who had died because of wounds inflicted by the captain; their bodies were
> then thrown overboard. Others arrived in England in a state near to death.
> In court the sad tale of Abdullah was narrated: he had been flogged, tied to
> the windlass and doused with salt water. Abdullah died (35–36).

If they somehow managed to survive the mistreatments on the voyage, things only got worse for the lascars once they landed on Western shores. Unaccustomed to the cold climes, often penniless and starving, the lascars had very shabby and unhygienic accommodations at the lodging houses. There were no beds or furniture; the lascars slept on the floor. The sick weren't quarantined (Visram 44). Because of overcrowding, fights broke out among lascars, such that many lascars died. "The death rate was high, especially in winter. It was estimated by some that before 1810, 130 lascars died in Britain each year. According to the lascars themselves the figure was double that" (Visram 40). An East India Company official visited the barracks and found

> two or three hundred of them (lascars) . . . [they] were ill-fed and badly
> treated by a person (a superior lascar) who had command of them, both as

to food, clothes and settling disputes among them. He frequently whipped them.... The buildings were like warehouses, very dirty.... There were two or three large cupboards of the height of sentry boxes (*Life of William Allen,* Vol. I, pp. 188–9. Quoted in Visram 41).

When a cupboard was opened "out came a living lascar" who'd been confined for "quarreling and bad behavior" (41).

From the citizens of the Western shores, the lascars earned some sympathy. A 1784 English pamphlet complained thus:

Those poor sons of misery, who strangers to the climate, to the manners, and to the people of this country, have traversed the town naked, penniless and almost starving in search of subsistence. Their situation is as singular as it is deplorable; they have been brought into this country as the friendly assistants of natives.... While the dispute lasted as to who should maintain them they have been left a prey to melancholy and distress. The dispute, you know, has been between the husband of the ships and the Directors of the East India Company. (*A Letter to Archibald Macdonald Esq., on the Intended Plan for Reform in what is called the Police of Westminster,* 1784, p. 17. Quoted in Visram 36).

The share of responsibility for the upkeep of the lascars fell somewhere between the East India Company and the shipowners. Neither wished particularly to feed, clothe, and house the East Indian sailors; thus, the lascars were left to suffer on foreign shores until they found passage home. In most cases, the lascars had to wait for several months. During this time of waiting, they "fell prey to the more wily inhabitants of the slums of Wapping and Shadwell in the east end of London. Robbed of their money and clothes, some arrived in the lodging houses of St Giles as beggars" (Visram 38–39).

In the October 1, 1850, edition of *The Friend,* a Honolulu newspaper, a writer laments the miserable condition of a crippled lascar who'd lost both legs and was abandoned to a life of begging on Honolulu streets:

Being no longer useful on board, and unable to go "aloft" he must go ashore: but where? To "Little Greenwich," no he is not an Englishman, but a foreigner. He may work for the Englishman, but if sick and crippled, he must hobble and beg, like his Portuguese brother. This too, is wrong! It is unjust! It is inhuman! English vessels should not be allowed to ship foreign seamen under the British flag, unless the law protect and provide for those seamen when sick and crippled. Reader, if you chance to meet in the streets of Honolulu the poor Portuguese, hobbling on *three* legs, or the poor Lascar hobbling on *four*, give him a shilling, or a sovereign, which is more than the American or British Consular Representatives are *allowed to do in their official capacity*. We hope to witness still greater improvements in the navigation laws of the two countries.

The March 13, 1852 edition of *Polynesian* reports the suicide of a lascar thus:

> SUICIDE.—A Lascar committed suicide on the evening of the 21st ultimo, at Puleha, Maui. He had long been insane, and knives and razors had been kept out of his way. On the evening above specified, he obtained a razor, and destroyed himself at once. he had the reputation of being a quiet and inoffensive man of about 35 years of age.

Quite likely, our Lani witnessed and survived gruesome mistreatments of the kind quoted above. Lani originated from Bombay, a major port on the western coast of India. Quite likely, he originated from the bhádela caste of Muslim sailors who lived in the Amreli district of Gujarat, a state adjacent to Bombay (*A Glossary of Castes, Tribes & Races in the Baroda State* 8). At times he claimed the name Sheik Mahomet, more a title than a name, but one that signifies his religious affiliations. That Serang, aka Lani, came from the Muslims of India matches with the ethnic breakdown of lascars conducted by Joseph Salter, an English missionary who wrote about Indian migrants in England, in 1873 and 1874. Out of the 3,271 sailors he counted on 40 ships, he found that most of the lascars came from India and were mostly Muslim: 1,653 East Indians. Hindu Indians were far less likely to work as lascars because crossing the black international waters constituted a religious taboo, punishable with excommunication and the loss of one's caste status.

Our Serang was a head lascar, or a *ghat serang*: someone who recruited other lascars for the British ships. As such, he wielded power over his subordinates. He liaised between the British officers on the ships and the lascars, negotiated salaries and enforced discipline. He intervened between the British sailors and the lascars, which indicates that he was adept in conversational English or a version of Pidgin that the sailors used, a mixture of Hindi-Urdu, English, and Persian. Given his esteemed position among other lascars, it is very likely that he had sailed on the British ships many times before boarding the *Paragon* for Boston.

While he most likely suffered mistreatment at the hands of his superior white officers, as a serang, Lani would not have suffered the beating of another lascar, being in charge of them:

> No boatswain of an ordinary British merchant vessel has such complete control over the crew he has to work and manage to the same extent as a serang—the boatswain's equivalent—has over his Lascars. No leading fireman or engine-room petty officer of an ordinary British steamer can compete with the engine-room serang in keeping control of the black squad (Hood 50).

The January 24, 1944, edition of *Life* magazine showcased stories of twelve lascars living in New York at the British Merchant Navy Club for Indian Seamen. The magazine reported that 59,000 lascars were sailing the world at that time, defending the allied powers' various ships in World War II. The twelve lascars portrayed (complete with color pencil drawings of their faces) depict the wide range of ethnic and educational backgrounds. One lascar, nineteen, was "the best educated" of the men profiled by the magazine. He spoke good English. Another lascar, around 50, had been at sea for 30 years. A third lascar gave up farming for the slightly more profitable job of a fireman on a freighter. "Result: he has waited between ships in U.S. for the past five months." Another lascar named Mohidin, from the village of Udyawar in the South Kanara district near Bombay, was torpedoed in the South Atlantic by a U-boat, that "machine-gunned the survivors." Mohidin boarded the only remaining life raft and survived on it for 35 days. "Once a heavy man, he is now very thin," reports *Life.* The life of a seaman was rough and unpredictable, and their work left them stranded on unfamiliar ports for months on end. The traumatic experience of storms, sharks, and fighting—in the nineteenth century the sea trade was never safe from competition with the French—caused the lascars to suffer emotional and physical scars.

Given the harsh conditions of his job, it is easy to understand why Lani was reported in his obituary to have "run away" as soon as his ship reached the Hawaiian shores. Like all lascars, he undoubtedly contemplated desertion many times, long before his voyage to Boston onboard the *Paragon.*

III. Onboard the *Paragon*

The *Paragon* that brought Lani from Bombay to Boston could have been an English trader ship, a Boston trader ship, or a ship that belonged to the East India Company. *Lloyd's Register* of 1799 mentions three ships named *Paragon:* the first belonging to G. Cushing with its home port as New England, the second belonging to J. Dean and home port of Boston, and the third belonging to Hemsley and home port of Stockton. The 1800 *Lloyd's Register* mentions two ships named *Paragon:* the first belonging to E. Thacker with the home port of Stockton, and the second belonging to Whitmore with the home port of New England. Rowan Hackman's *Ships of the East India Company* also lists two ships by the name of *Paragon:* the first launched on January 1, 1800 by Fishburn & Brodrick, Whitby for J. Woodcock & Co., and the second a United States ship chartered for one voyage direct to Bengal, operational in 1796–1797, built at Boston for Deane & Co. Captain James Deane (Hackman 304). Our Lani could have served aboard any one of these ships—the muster rolls from 1800 contain only crew numbers and no names. In any case, Sheik Mahomet is likely a title Lani gave himself in the later years of his life; this search wouldn't yield any useful information on Lani.

Still, what is apparent from the plethora of ships traversing the Atlantic between English, American, and Asian ports is the fluency of international trade. The East India Company traded with India and China and other ports in the southeast, and until 1815, America imported cloth from India. American textile trade with India thrived until 1816 when Congress imposed a tariff on such imports to encourage the nascent US textile manufacturing industry (Bean 43). The textiles imported into America were also exported to Africa, Europe, and European colonies in the Caribbean and South America. In fact, the robust trade between Bombay and Calcutta and Salem inspired the founding of the East India Marine Society in Salem in 1799, "composed of persons who have actually navigated the seas beyond the Cape of Good Hope...as masters or supercargoes of vessels belonging to Salem" (Whitehill).

American newspapers were always abuzz with news of American ships bound to and from Indian ports such as Bombay, Calcutta, and Madras. For example, in the January 1, 1800 issue of *The Salem Gazette,* there is a mention of a Boston ship destined to Bombay headed by Captain Stutson, but no name for the ship is provided. Alongside the shipping news can be found advertisements for Indian textiles: muslins, Patna handkerchiefs, white cotton and also dyed cottons, silks, and woolen Kashmir shawls.

IV. Transferring to USS *Pickering*

According to the 1903 Sessional Papers of the British Mercantile Marine Committee, a lascar could transfer from ship to ship, but was dischargeable in India alone. He could be transferred "from one ship to another of the same owner,

U. S. REVENUE CUTTER PICKERING.

Drawing of USS *Pickering*. (NH 85146). Source: Naval History and Heritage Command. https://history.navy.mil

and return to India without practically breaking his agreement" (48). After the transfers, and to be discharged, he would be put on a ship returning to his original port. As per his obituary, this was the reason our Lani transferred to the *Pickering*—because no other return passage to Bombay was available.

Unlike *Paragon, Pickering* isn't a very popular ship name. *Lloyd's Register* of 1800 does not mention a *Pickering*. The only mention of a ship named *Pickering* begins in the archives from 1798, and it is undoubtedly an American ship.

USS *Pickering* was quite the pride and joy of the American naval force, and all references to it in the archives celebrate its victory over competing French ships that it captured in the quasi-French-American war. Built in Newburyport, Massachusetts, she departed Boston on her first cruise in August 1798. In her short but illustrious career, she defeated more heavily armed French ships, most notably the French privateer *L'Egypte Conquise* after a nine-hour battle on 18 October 1799. She also captured 13 American ships and four more French ships. Her last voyage, the voyage that our Lani was on, took place on 20 August 1800. She was being sent to join Commodore Thomas Truxtun's squadron on the Guadalupe Station in the West Indies. But on that voyage, she encountered a hurricane and was lost at sea. She is said to have left no trace. The officers who served on her were reported in the newspapers of 1800 as "in her yet," and "still in Pickering," and later, reluctantly, "lost with her." It is impossible to confirm without any doubts if our Lani was upon this very *Pickering* as the muster rolls of its last voyage were lost with her. (*Naval Documents Relating to the Quasi-War Between the United States and France* 334).

But if indeed Lani was lost at sea with the *Pickering* in August 1800, how did he resurface on the Hawaiian Islands in the 1820s, how did he survive the shipwreck, and what did he do for those lost twenty years?

Another possibility, although we have no way to confirm it, is that Lani misremembered the ship's name, boarded a different vessel, returned to Bombay, and worked as a serang for the next two decades until a different ship brought him to the Hawaiian ports in the 1820s. Two reasons why I entertain this hypothesis are that first, his obituary is silent on the matter of the *Pickering's* shipwreck, a significant detail that a survivor would remember and share. And second, twenty years of working as a boatswain and surviving the mistreatments of European sailors and the rough seas might explain why Lani did not wish to return to sea.

And yet, it is not out of the realm of possibility that Lani survived the *Pickering's* wreck, surfaced on a different island or continent, worked as a serang on other ships, and eventually made his way to the Hawaiian Islands.

V. In Hawaiʻi and Destitute

The earliest mention of our Lani on the Hawaiian Islands appears in the 1821 *Missionary Herald* journal kept by missionaries Hiram Bingham, Asa Thurston and Elisha Loomis. Loomis reports of an excursion that Brothers Bingham and Thurston took one day when they happened upon the house of two lascars. He writes:

> Returning from the excursion, Brs. B. & T. fell upon the cottage of two Lascars, who had a year ago applied to us for medical aid. One of them is exceedingly emaciated, reduced to a skeleton, sitting on the ground at the door of his hut, an emblem of poverty & wretchedness. Br. B. asked him if he thought seriously of Jehovah, the great God. He replied, "me no see him—Where is your God?" pointing upward he pronounced the name Jesus Christ—"Is Jesus C. your God?" "Yes, Jesus Christ & Mahomet, is all the same, & Mahomet is my God"—Here Serang, his companion, added, "In my bible he is called Mahomet, but in your bible he is called Jesus Christ—

all the same." "No, they are not the same—M. is one. & J.C. is another—M. is an imposter—Jesus a savior—M. cannot make your heart better,—Jesus can—M. cannot take you to heaven—Jesus can, if you believe in him."

This encounter happened in Honolulu on December 15, 1821. Whether our Lani surfaced in Honolulu after a shipwreck, or whether he surfaced after a long and tiring bout of working as a serang, we can believe that he would be found on the streets of Honolulu, destitute and attempting to desert his work contract, very much like the tormented lascars we have discussed in Section II. The above archival evidence of Lani's presence in Honolulu is key in confirming the great travails of his job as a head lascar, his faith in Islam as a marker of his identity, and his desire to stop sea travel and pick up different trade.

Interestingly, Loomis's journal entry continues as follows:

Not much less wretched is the highest female in the nation, Kaahoomanoo, who having been ill several days was this morning apprehended to be at the

Queen Ka'ahumanu. Source: Hawai'i State Archives. Digital Collection. https:// digitalarchives.hawaii.gov/item/ark:70111/1Dwh

point of death, assiduously attended by the two Russian Physicians, but with little hope of her continuing through the day.

This juxtaposition of the lascars with the Queen Kaʻahumanu in the missionary journal, the commonness of their "wretchedness" in the eyes of Loomis, is shocking. However, the mention of the Queen Kaʻahumanu gives us an important temporal marker in Lani's life. Two days later, the Queen requested Mrs. Bingham to pray for her. Mrs. Bingham

> sat down by her & kindly applied camphor to her aching head, which she gratefully acknowledged gave her some little comfort, desiring that the phial might be left with her, which of course was most cheerfully granted. As Br. B. rose to take leave, K. made a request that he should pray with her before he left her, requiring the company to suspend their conversation, & be still. There was a profound silence, which we seldom witness among them. The season was solemn & interesting, while a minister of Christ, the representative of his church, kneeled by the couch of the afflicted queen at her special request, imploring divine grace to send light & health to her soul, & to raise her up in newness of life, to lead the way for her countrymen to the Kingdom of righteousness & the mansions of glory.

Queen Kaʻahumanu, the favorite wife of King Kamehameha I, was one of the most powerful rulers of the Hawaiian Islands. After the death of the king, she shared the throne with Liholiho, Kamehameha II, the king's son. At first she opposed the missionaries, but after a series of tragic deaths—of her second husband, the king of Kauaʻi, Kaumualiʻi, in 1824, followed by the young Liholiho, also in 1824, the queen turned to Christianity. Loomis's journal entry quoted above highlights the time in the queen's life when she was most physically and spiritually vulnerable. She fell sick, and upon recovering, converted to Christianity and acknowledged it publicly in 1824. She took on the name Elizabeth and was baptized in 1825 at the site where the Kawaiahaʻo Church now stands. Other chiefs on Maui, Kauaʻi and Hawaiʻi followed her lead (Speakman 60–66).

Like Queen Kaʻahumanu, Lani too recovers. Unlike the queen, however, his medicine is not the Christian faith, but work. At some point in the early 1820s, Lani, adept at sniffing good business, valuable opportunities, and a good welcome, makes his way from Honolulu to Lahaina, the once capital of the Hawaiian Kingdom.

VI. Receiving the Generosity of the Kama'āina

The archives are silent as to which ship and business opportunity took Lani from Honolulu to Lahaina. But soon after Lani landed in Lahaina, we know that he became domesticated. He took up residence with a woman named Puipui. We can understand domestication to mean living together, sharing meals, income, and chores. Domestication need not necessarily mean official marriage complete with a marriage certificate. Still, Puipui is mentioned as Lani's wife, i.e., a close female companion in the foreign testimony attached to Lani's claim for the Māhele lands awarded to him. The testimony claims that Lani received a piece of land "from his wife Puipui, in the days of King Liholiho." This temporal marker is important and signifies that Lani was able to get domesticated with Puipui by 1824, before King Liholiho passed away.

Puipui appears many times as a landlord in numerous native and foreign testimonies attached to land claims during the Māhele. She is likely a relative of Solomon Laahili, another konohiki who obtained LCA 581 during the Māhele. Puipui is described as a luna, a landowner under Laahili. Puipui had several pieces of land under her control and shared it with other Kānaka for cultivation.

It is important to note that like the Queen Ka'ahumanu, native Hawaiian women enjoyed a great degree of freedom and equality with men. Kamakau reported that "on Maui and Hawaii the women worked outside as hard as the men, often cooking, tilling the ground, and performing the duties in the house as well," (Kamakau quoted in Van Dyke 23). Puipui was just one of thousands of native Hawaiian women who acted as konohiki and luna on lands before the Māhele.

Puipui not only welcomed Lani into her 'ohana, she also shared with him land that he used for cultivation. Other native and foreign testimonies given in favor of his land claims stated that Lani had been cultivating several pieces of land. In one testimony, a Kanaka named Kaauwai cited other Kānaka who occupied Lani's land: Kalaukumuole, Nakapa, Kauhihope, and Kapule. All these men are described as husbandmen on Lani's land, i.e., they were cultivating the lands under his supervision. What we can glean from this detail is that Lani obtained some lands from Puipui, a luna, with whom he became domesticated, and he used these lands, like the other Kānaka, for cultivation. This is before the days of sugar, so we know that on these fertile Lahaina lands the Kānaka cultivated taro, breadfruit, coconuts, and later, after the introduction of the non-native species by the merchants and missionaries, sweet potatoes, squash, pumpkins, potatoes, and onions.

Another reason to believe that Lani's lands were being cultivated is that in one of the testimonies, one of his lands is described as a moʻo, which is a strip of land between two irrigated lands, or "raised surface extending lengthwise between irrigation streamlets" (wehewehe.com). Chinen describes a moʻo as: "arable portions of an ʻili . . . further subdivided into smaller tracts . . . the moo was next in size to an ʻili and was set aside for the purposes of cultivation only" (5).

Kaauwai's testimony describes the relationship between the Kānaka and Lani. Their relationship is one of mutual trust and cooperation. In another one of the testimonies related to Lani's land claims, Kaoo-wahine swears that her neighbor, a man named Kuihelani, did not wish to fence the land returned to him prior to the Māhele because a portion of it had been occupied by Lani's moʻo, and he wished for Lani's land to be returned to him. Based on what is described in the foreign and native testimonies of the Māhele land commission awards, the relationship between Lani and his neighbors, between Lani and Puipui, and between Lani and the Kanaka men described as farmers on his land, can be interpreted as one of cooperation and deep appreciation.

Not only did Lani receive lands from the kamaʻāina, he was placed in the position of giving lands too. In the foreign testimony for LCA 6874, Kaulahea testifies that Kahuena received land from Lani in 1840. We can safely assume this Lani is our Serang because the land lies in Alio, Lahaina, and Kaulahea is a neighbor of Lani. Kaulahea's land borders the first piece of Lani's Alio land. Kaulahea himself received land from Lani before 1839, in the days of Hoapili. Pakala is another kamaʻāina who receives land from Lani before 1839. Nakapa is yet another. Some of these lands are kalo lands and kula lands, which again suggests that Lani was cultivating taro or acting as a konohiki headman on these lands—a position he came into soon after his domestication with Puipui. In fact, Kooka claims a loʻi of Lani in 1848, another proof that the lands Lani in receipt of had been cultivated lands.

```
No. 352 - Lani

Kaoo-wahine sworn:

    When the council had returned your place which was in Lani's moo there,
the place was returned with the fence down.  Then I said to Kuihelani, "Shall
we fence this place?"  Kuihelani answered negatively and said, "Lani's place
is in here; therefore, Lani's place should be returned [to him].
                                               Cont'd pg. 10, Vol. 10
```

Native testimony in favor of Lani. Māhele Award Book Volume 10:114; Source: Hawaiʻi State Archives

The fact that a destitute lascar could so quickly rise to the position of a small konohiki, tilling land alongside native Hawaiians, is proof not only of the generosity of the native Hawaiians, but a testament to the traditional Hawaiian practice of land tenureship that came to an end following the Māhele. The legislative acts enacted during 1845–1855 wrestled the power to grant lands away from the king, the aliʻi and the landowners, and introduced the Western concepts of private land ownership and the purchasing of land with money. Following the Māhele, the makaʻainana, or the common public, could acquire titles to lands they had cultivated or lived on, and purchase other lands from the government. Too, naturalized foreign residents could purchase land (Moffat 11).

Cultivation and longevity of land use are the basis for many of the land claims. These claims, known as kuleana claims, allowed native tenants, after an act of 1850, to claim lands they had cultivated and improved. It is important to note that Lani applied for land not as a naturalized foreign resident, but on the basis of his longevity of land cultivation and use, and most importantly, on the basis of a grant from an aliʻi.

It is safe to assume that Lani lived away from the watchful eyes of the missionaries, not willing to receive the gospel. As a prior resident of Bombay, Lani undoubtedly had exposure to the proselytizing culture of the missionaries, who had been active in Western India since the fifteenth century. In place of the Christian missionaries, Lani found the companionship, welcome, and aloha of the makaʻainana far more acceptable. He lived with them as Lani, cultivating land like them, eating what they ate.

Foreign testimony in favor of Lani. Source: Māhele Award Book Volume 7:328; Hawaiʻi State Archives

Foreign testimony in favor of Lani. Source: Māhele Award Book Volume 7:328; Hawaiʻi State Archives

Why did Lani choose not to return to Bombay? Had he left a wife or children behind? We can assume that the hardships he experienced in his previous voyages caused him not to want to board another long-distance ship. The weather of Lahaina likely soothed his homesick soul. The skin color and appearance of the makaʻāinana likely reminded him of the family and friends he left behind in Bombay. The home he made among the makaʻāinana was warm and comforting enough for Lani to resist the urge to return to his native land.

And what of his many names? It is significant that Serang is referred to as Lani in many of the native and foreign testimonies. While some of the makaʻāinana were acquiring (or were forced to acquire) Christian names, Lani had acquired a native Hawaiian name. Who had bequeathed him the name Lani, meaning "heavenly," and why? Was it an aliʻi? Or was it Puipui or the many kamaʻāina he worked and lived with? Names are never without significance, and each of Lani's names tells a story about a different aspect of his life and his aspiration: Serang, his occupation that brought him to the Hawaiian Islands; Sheikh, a king, hinting to his ambitious leadership; Mahomet, a testament to his faith, which led him away from the missionaries and toward the native Hawaiians; and finally Lani, that highlights his aloha and kinship with the kama'āina, who no doubt heard of his exploits at sea and considered his knowledge of ship navigation as something to be prized (interesting, too, that in Polynesian culture, the navigation of ships required constant consultation of the heavens). Out of all his names, Lani appears to be the only appropriate name by which this man ought to be addressed: the rest are titles, while "Lani" is bequeathed to him after a bout of familiarity and love.

The fact that Lani disappeared from the pages of the missionary journals is more proof that he lived close to the maka'āinana—like them, respecting the ali'i: receiving, granting and tilling land in the manner of other luna such as Puipui and Iano Pi'ikoi, who befriended him and welcomed him into their 'ohana.

Another proof that Lani had blended in with the maka'āinana is the fact that he began the process of applying for land grants before the July 10, 1850 act that authorized the sale of lands in fee simple to resident aliens. Lani's LCAs and royal patents aren't awarded to him until 1852, but he begins the process of application in 1846, before the law permitted resident aliens to do so. Might Lani have achieved a harmonious working and living situation with Kānaka enough to pass as a foreigner they'd adopted as their own? Lani's name is the only foreign one in the list of Kanaka names in the testimonies collected on his behalf. No other foreign or non-native name is present. This causes us to conjecture that given his appearance as a dark-skinned native of Bombay, he was accepted into the 'ohana of the kama'āina, and he lived with them, separate from the European sailors and missionaries.

On Lahaina, Lani negotiated a liminal position, living between the maka'āinana and the European and American merchants and visitors. Unlike the white settlers, Lani appeared on the Hawaiian shores a refugee. As such, Lani was one of the first South Asian transplants. His neighbors knew he was foreign; he was called "Serang" by the non-natives who knew very well what vital work the boatswains did. In fact, a survey of Lahaina shops published in the newspapers lists his retail shop as owned by "a Lascar." Given the constant flow of lascars from South Asia into the Hawaiian ports, the maka'āinana became aware of India. The lascars were among the first immigrant-refugees to land on Hawaiian shores—lascars were in Hawai'i long before laborers arrived from China in 1852 to work on the sugar mills.

VII. Receiving the Generosity of the Aliʻi

The strongest reason for Lani's claim to his little house lot in Kainehe is that the aliʻi Kaikioʻewa gave him the land in 1837. His testimony states: "this is the right—the aliʻi Kaikioewa gave me the land." Again and again, the generosity of the aliʻi to Lani is cited as his claim to his piece of land. In keeping with the traditions of land tenure prior to the Māhele, the authority of the aliʻi over land was second only to the king. This testimony forms Lani's strongest claim—stronger than his claims of cultivation and long-term residence. Indeed, a kanaka named Kaauwai confirms this gift from the aliʻi Kaikioʻewa as Lani's strongest claim in his testimony.

Interestingly, Lani's testimony notes that the land given to him by the aliʻi Kaikioʻewa was later taken away and given to Princess Nāhiʻenaʻena, a granddaughter of Kaikioʻewa who gave it to her husband, Prince Leleiohoku. Upon petition from Kaoo, a wahine, another kamaʻāinana, and a neighbor of Lani's, the lands were returned. Lani's testimony is in keeping with the land tenure traditions of Hawaiʻi before the Māhele. After King Kamehameha I united the Hawaiian Islands under his control, all land on all the islands belonged, first and foremost, to the king. After the king set aside certain pieces of land for his use, he "divided the rest among his principal warrior chiefs for distribution to the lesser chiefs and, down the scale, to the tenant-commoners" (Chinen 6). Every person possessing land paid King Kamehameha I in services, a land tax, and a portion of the products they grew on the land. But these gifts of land weren't irrevocable. The king, the chiefs, and even the lesser landlords could take their gifts back and render the tenant dispossessed—hence Lani's testimony that the aliʻi Kaikioʻewa had given him the land, but the land was then taken away and given to the family of the aliʻi for their use.

Yet again, the story of Hawaiian royalty intersects with Lani's story as a testament to the uncontested power of the aliʻi that formed the basis of numerous claims to the Land Commission.

Aliʻi Kaikioʻewa was a cousin of King Kamehameha I, as well as a warrior chief in the king's army. A chief of second rank, Kaikio/ewa served as the governor of Kauaʻi from 1835 until his death in 1839. He also acted as the guardian of the young Prince Kauikeaouli, whom he had raised since birth, and who was nine years old in 1823. Having been introduced to Christianity by the missionaries, Kaikioʻewa is described in the missionary journals as pious and "consistent with Christian propriety" (Stewart 247). Stewart describes the residence of Kaikioʻewa and his wife Keaweamahi as "neat and ornamental," with "a Chinese sofa…a very large mahogany dining table, two circular tables…an elegant escritoire…a handsome card table…a dressing case, and a large expensive mirror" (246). Stewart finds that Kaikioʻewaʻs house "exhibited a degree of neatness, comfort, and convenience, not often found in the dwellings even of the highest chiefs" (246). Kaikioʻewa and his wife wore "loose dresses made in the European fashion." Stewart notes that "their persons, more than the furniture of their apartment, presented a strong contrast to the appearance they made but a year or two since, when seen only in unblushing nakedness; and when they knew no higher subjects of thought or occupation, than to ʻeat, drink, and be merry'" (247).

This rapid transformation in the clothing, furnishings, and thinking of such an important chief indicates the profound and rapid influence of both the foreign missionaries and merchants on the society, culture, and economy of Lahaina. That Kaikioʻewaʻs house is fitted with Chinese couches and European furnishings is indicative of his constant dealings with the merchants who provided the chiefs and the kings of Hawaiʻi with European goods in exchange for sandalwood. Kaikioʻewa and his wife, along with Hawaiian royalty, opened their hearts to the message of the gospel, which indicates a remarkable open-mindedness—a quality we can't quite credit all the missionaries with.

Kaikioewaʻs European deportment also indicates that he was friendly to foreigners in Lahaina, as were many other Hawaiian royalty and chiefs. He frequently sailed to the neighboring islands for various councils, to advise King Kamehameha II, and for the purchase of goods such as schooners (Chamberlain 10).

Not all missionaries looked upon Kaikioʻewa favorably. In his 1827 journal, Levi Chamberlain describes the aliʻi as "a great villain," due to the abundance of kapu on the island of Kauaʻi. Chamberlain writes: "The island is the very worst in the group of things there are in a dreadful state, every thing is kapu, not a potatoe from the land, not a fish from the ponds, nor from the sea can be procured—the people are exceedingly oppressed" (6–7). We can take this as proof that Kaikioʻewa commanded great authority over the island of Kauaʻi. The missionary journals trace his taking up new residences, indicating that as a high-ranking chief, a guardian of a prince, and an advisor to the king, he had ultimate access to the land and could move about and use the lands as he saw fit.

Stories abound of Kaikioʻewaʻs generosity. In a letter dated 10 July 1832, E. W. Clark and A. Thurston write to Rev. Anderson about Kaikioʻewaʻs gift of a piece of land on Kauaʻi for the mission, calling it "a valuable piece of land, from which an abundant supply of fresh meat, poultry & other kinds of native food could be obtained for a family" (1116). Kaikioʻewa also gave land to a Maj. William R. Warren, on which Warren built the Warren Hotel and the Canton Hotel on Hotel Street in downtown Honolulu (LCA 790, Greer 54). Another foreign resident to receive the gift of land from Kaikioʻewa was a shipwright named Henry Farmer (Greer, "Notes on Early Land Titles and Tenure in Hawaii," 36).

When it came to trading with the foreign merchants, native Hawaiians, be they chiefs and royalty or the makaʻāinana, were put at a great disadvantage. In one historical account of early trading in Hawaiʻi by W. D. Alexander, King Kamehameha is said to have purchased two shirts in 1819 with a boatload of vegetables. He also purchased $8,000 worth of guns with over 113,000 pounds of sandalwood. In the same account, Kaikioʻewa is said to have purchased a shirt in exchange for a hog (Alexander 23–24). By any account, these were never fair trades.

Yet, the aliʻi's authority over the makaʻāinana reigned supreme, and Lani's testimony regarding his land claims is proof. For Lani to claim that an aliʻi of Kaikioʻewa's stature—the very cousin of King Kamehameha I—gave him his land, carries a lot of weight. While Lani's neighbors submitted longevity claims and kuleana claims, he was able to submit an even more exclusive and sacred claim.

VIII. Lands Awarded to Serang, AKA Lani

Under Royal Patent No. 409, Land Commission Award No. 352, Lani secured five pieces of land totaling 3.085 acres, situated in the Alio ahupuaʻa of Lahaina. For these pieces, Lani paid $12 for the documents, $100 as fee simple, and $75 for the survey. He began the process of applying for these lands in January 1847; the survey and witness testimonies continued to be submitted on his behalf until December 1851. The basis of Lani's claim on his Alio lands is that the aliʻi Kaikioʻewa gave them to him.

Under Royal Patent No. 1174, Land Commission Award No. 352, Lani secured another plot of land in the Kainehe ahupuaʻa of Lahaina. He paid $12.50 in fee simple and $50 for the appraisal of this land. The basis of Lani's claim on his Kainehe house lot is that he had uncontested possession of it for twenty-five years. Witnesses testified that he had obtained this land from Puipui, his wife, in the days of King Liholiho. A witness, 36 years of age, also claimed that he knew Lani since he (the witness) was a child. Lani began to petition for possession of this land in December 1846, and the paperwork for this land was completed in November 1852.

Area of 1st Piece — 1.079
2 — .875
3 — .405
4 — .595
5 — .130
Total acres 3.085

Honolulu Augt 1st 1851 —

His Highness John Young.
Minister of the Interior

Sir

I am desirous of obtaining a Royal Patent for the several lots of land Situated in Lahaina Awarded to me by Award no 352 and am willing to pay the Sum of $75 Seventy five dollars as Commutation of the same —

Your Obt Servt
Serang by
his Attorney
A. W. Brown

The Board of Land Commissioners having this day 15th April 1851 adjudicated Claim No. 352 (Lahaina Maui)

Serang estimate, and awarded to him a portion of land, less than allodial, subject to his decision to commutation, as the law permits, for a fee simple, or for a grant of thirty years: This instrument will become a valid voucher of the same, when payment of the costs incurred in said claim is made, and becomes acknowledged therein by the Board or its Secretary, amounting to _____ dollars unto A. F. Turner's bill of accompanying survey and diagram, of fairs pieces _____ dollars _____ cents; inclusive, Twelve dollars _____ cents: When, whatever documents may have been filed with the Board, annexed with the above claim, will be returned to the claiming party or his representative, who may also claim, upon application, a copy of the entire award verbatim, if desired, on payment of the usual charge of stamp and engraving.

By order of the Board of Commissioners to quiet Land Titles.
J. N. Price Secretary.

Halé Hána, Honolulu,
15th April 1851

Received the above sum of $12
W. P. Alexander

No. 352. Laui alias Serang
Lahaina.
5 Pieces of Land

1st Piece contains 1.079 acres.
Beginning at West angle and running
S. 40° E. 31 links along land belonging to Kailione
N. 9° E. 84 " " " "
S. 10° E. 17 " " " Paaua
N. 53° E. 123 " " " "
S. 26° E. 122 " " " "
N. 62° E. 538 " " " Kaluhea
N. 34° W. 203 " " " Kikoot
S. 80° W. 17 " " " Yooka
S. 55° W. 792 " " "
to point of commencement

2nd Piece contains 0.875 acre.
Beginning at the West angle and running
Kakihaliu, and running
S. 85° E. 203 links, along the Manukai
N. 47° E. 407 " " " Kikahi
N. 55° E. 165 " " "
N. 26° W. 203 " " " Kapule
S. 60° E. 230 " " " Kakapa
S. 67° W. 377 " " " Paaua & Pihana
to the point of commencement

3rd Piece contains 0.405 acre.
Beginning at West angle adjoining the old Road and running
S. 63° E. 126 links along the old Road
N. 68° E. 200 " " Kauluhu
N. 29° W. 153 " " "
S. 54° W. 330 " " Kahuiluhupe
to the point of commencement

4th Piece contains 0.595 acre.
Beginning at South angle and running
N. 61° E. 550 links along Kapule's lots
S. 60° E. 118 " " Kauluhu's "
S. 60° W. 451 " " "
S. 54° W. 142 " " "
to the point of commencement

5th Piece contains 0.15 acre.
Beginning at South west angle and running
N. 68° E. 136 links, along Kahuiluhupe
S. 20° E. 9 " " "
N. 67° E. 225 " " "
N. 62° W. 115 " " Yooka
S. 53° W. 293 " " "
to the point of commencement
A. F. Turner
Commissioner &c.

Papers from Lani's LCA Award # 352 File; Source: Hawai'i State Archives

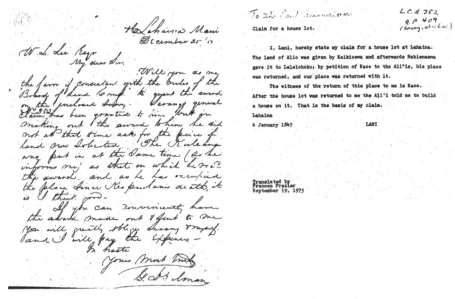

Papers from Lani's LCA Award # 352 File; Source: Hawai'i State Archives

IX. Love and Marriage

Over the course of his long and adventurous life, Lani had a few love interests. Three are chronicled in the archives. The first was Puipui, with whom he became domesticated, and who gave him lands for cultivation and overseeing. Their not-so-casual cohabitation is observed by one witness as marriage, who calls Puipui Lani's wife (the testimony is in English; therefore, the word is not a translation of *wahine,* which could also mean female companion). There is no mention of Puipui in Lani's will, which means that their companionship might have been of a casual nature, and that their relationship might have been more of a landlord-tenant or landlord-sub-landlord nature. The second woman in Lani's life, as per the archives, is Naomi, sometimes spelled Naaomi. Their companionship began sometime in the late 1840s and lasted only a few short years. Their relationship was clearly healthy and strong enough for Lani to leave his house lot and shop in Kainehe to Naaomi in his 1854 will. After his relationship with Naomi ended, Serang met another woman named Haulewahine. He married Haulewahine on December 17, 1852. Their relationship may or may not have lasted amicably until his death—there is evidence supporting both possible outcomes.

X. OTHER VENTURES

By the late 1840s, the money Lani made cultivating and acting as interim konokihi or luna on his lands and the lands of Puipui had stopped after the lands were redistributed in the Māhele. The 1840s were a period of great upheaval in Lahaina. More and more whalers and foreign merchant ships continued to arrive on Lahaina shores. The first two of these ships arrived in 1819. Their numbers quickly increased to a hundred by 1824—just five years. The number doubled between 1829–1849, and doubled again (Speakman 78). At its peak in 1846, 429 whale ships arrived in Lahaina. Lahaina town became a recruitment ground for Hawaiian seamen, who "began signing up as whalers or able seamen on the many ships coming in" (Speakman 78).

The Lahaina shore offered the whalers ten miles of anchorage. After paying the harbormaster a sum of ten dollars, the ships' captains could purchase refreshments for their crew: potatoes, water, hogs, goats, bananas, melons, pumpkins, onions, squash, turkeys, ducks, fowl, and beef (Speakman 78–9). The whalers also promoted and funded brothels—a point of contention between them and the missionaries, who fought the whalers tooth and nail on the matter of smuggling maka'āinana wahine onboard their ships.

Sometimes bloody fights broke out between the missionaries and the whalers on the matter of prostitution. In 1825 and in 1827, the crews of English whalers threatened the lives of the local missionaries, who were believed to instigate the law prohibiting maka'āinana wahine boarding the whalers. The sale of liquor was another point of contention between the whalers and the missionaries.

Lani, being a Muslim, very likely did not participate in the sale of alcohol. Still, he conducted a lucrative retail business as per the archival evidence and his obituaries. Starting in 1847, he applied for a license for his retail store each year until at least 1855-1856. From E. & H. Grimes, a major merchant who had a retail store on the corner of Broadway and Fort Street in Honolulu, he likely obtained the following items: beef, casks, barrels, shooks, whale boats, sperm candles, whale oil, spades, lances, whale irons, peas, beans, sad irons, arrowroot, crosscut and pit saws, coffee, vinegar, dried apples, whale lines, bedsteads, work tables, chairs, sarsaparilla syrup, rice, soap, syrup, molasses, sugar, pineapples, ginger, etc. From Stephen Reynolds he likely obtained farming implements, needlework, knitwork, leather, lampshades, iron castings, etc. From Pierce & Brewer he likely obtained sugar and molasses. From O. P. Ricker he likely obtained cedar, lumber, pepper, olives, cologne, walnuts, almonds, linen, thread, mackerel, codfish, souchong tea, Cuban cigars, and hats. Lani did not advertise his store in the newspapers. It was likely a modest retail store that ran on word of mouth—no advertising was necessary. Still, for many years, his store did well enough for him to leave the land and its assets to his previous companion Naomi and his wife Haulewahine. The store also became collateral when times suddenly became hard for Lani near the end of his life.

XI. A Moment of Adversity

Lani's obituaries state that he "became reduced in circumstances," and "became poor." A proof of these hard times is a sale Lani made to G. D. Gilman dated 19 January 1856, two years after he made his will. In the 1856 deed, Lani conveyed all his lands—the parcels described in RP 409 as well as those described in RP 1174—to G. D. Gilman for the amount of $624. As well as his lands, Lani sold all the merchandise in his store. As per a clause in the deed, the lands and property could be returned to Lani if he, his heirs, his executors, or his administrators pay Gilman $624 within six months from the date of the deed with interest at the rate of one percent per month. Interestingly, Lani's wife's signature and her name are completely missing from this deed. This omission raises some flags about both Lani's mental state and the state of his marriage. As per the laws and the customs of the time, the name of both husband and wife are usually present in all sale of land and property. Seeing as how Haulewahine's name is absent from this deed in which Lani sells all his property in one fell swoop for $624, one wonders if he was at odds with Haulewahine at this time. Had they separated? Why wasn't she consulted about this sale? Why is her name and signature absent?

What caused Lani to sell all his parcels of land as well as the items inside his store? We know that he did business with Stephen Reynolds. In 1854, Reynolds' Kahului store burned with a $7,000 loss. Could Lani have suffered the consequences of Reynolds' loss? It is also likely that Lani made a few bad business investments. In the mid-1800s, a lot of scoundrels could be found in Lahaina, offering dubious schemes and bad credit.

In a letter dated December 13, 1855, the sheriff of Maui, W. C. Parks, writes to the Marshall's Office alerting them about a "scamp" named Lewis who had diddled a few creditors out of money. The sheriff writes many more letters about confiscating Lewis's property to recover his debts. In a letter dated November 1856, Parks writes about yet another scoundrel named E. Jones, "walking about with large sums of money from men that he ships at the consulate." Parks says: "When he is paid the advances for the men that are owing him, you must attach

Lani sells his lands to G. D. Gilman for $1. Source: Bureau of Conveyances it in his hands; or if you see him in the streets with large sums of money in his pockets, why stop him and make him shell over. He is a d___d [damned?] scoundrel...." It is likely that Lani invested in one of these dubious schemes that quickly fell through.

It is important to remember that money was a fairly new concept in Hawai'i in the 1850s. Within Lani's own lifetime, the ali'i and the king transitioned from bartering goods—sandalwood in exchange for guns, shirts, furniture—to paper money. By the late 1840s and early 1850s, during the time of the Māhele, the sale of land for a fee simple allowed cash to flow between the maka'āinana and the Hawaiian government, and between the maka'āinana and the foreign whalers and missionaries. Lani would have been slightly more familiar with the concept of a currency, having received a salary for his work as a boatswain from the ship owner. Still, for the purposes of a small business of the kind Lani maintained, the credit system was still rudimentary, fledgling, and community-based. No banks existed in Lahaina at that time. In the words of Tilton: "Credit was extended for friendship" (Tilton 14). The captains of ships, transporting goods from port to port, acted as bankers and financiers, and their strongboxes were never safe from arson or theft. Writes Tilton:

> Getting new wares was accomplished by partial barter...and by partial payment of actual coin. Exchange was carried out in the [1820s] and [1830s] and [1840s] in many ways, none of which were very free from hazard. If the cargoes were entrusted to the captain's judgment, it meant that he was to be a banker. It was common procedure for a ship captain to have instructions from one merchant to take a given sum for the purchase of a cargo in one port, to sell the same at a "good market," and to bring back the profit. [...] Money was sent from place to place by the captain's strong box, the ship's chest for valuables which were mostly coin and bullion. But the dangers of mutiny and arson were evident to these early "financeers" so that men frequently requested their friends or at times total strangers to deliver money and letters to parties who by chance lived in the direction of the voyager's destination. [...] Even though the captain's strong box was protected well or the stranger honest, risks prevailed. Dishonest men were not entirely off the seas—a fact which proved unfortunate often. The actual sinking and destroying of a vessel, however, was by far the most disastrous feature for any person entrusted with treasure. Should robbery or a similar incident occur, the amount or very shipment might be recovered, but once it sank, permanent loss was the result (14–15).

It is very likely that Lani entrusted a large purchase and/or the cost of that purchase to a stranger who turned out to be a crook. The Lahaina of his times, as we have read before, was overrun by a constant barrage of whaling ships in need of native labor and refreshments. The constant flux of foreigners, while keeping Lani's store in business, likely also caused it to suffer a bout of bad credit.

Lani likely also suffered mentally from this sudden fall into economic hardship, because after selling all his land in one fell swoop to Gilman on 19 January 1856, he sold one-half of his Kainehe lot (LCA 352) to Gilman yet again for the amount of one dollar on 3 July 1856. We can imagine the conversation that might have transpired between the shrewd lawyer and merchant Gilman (who himself had a retail store in Lahaina), who chased the California Gold Rush and ended up a senator in Massachusetts: Gilman insisting that the old fool Lani had already sold him all his lands for $624, and Lani claiming old age, forgetfulness and insisting on selling the land again. For the last five years of his life, Lani might have lived under the care of his wife Haulewahine, or lived on in his land leasing it from Gilman. The archives are silent on the matter of these last years.

XII. Death and Legacy

Lani died on February 11, 1861. There is no mention of where he is buried. He is not mentioned in any of the Maui cemetery indexes at the Hawai'i State Archives. He did not have any children—or none that could be located in the archives. Interestingly, a lot of drama involving his properties ensued after his death. On 16 April 1861, two months after Lani's demise, G. D. Gilman issued a release of mortgage to Lani for both RPs 409 & 1174. A day later, a woman by the name of Naomi surfaced to reclaim a portion of Lani's Kainehe lands from G. D. Gilman. Naomi purchased half an interest in RP 1174 for $1, the same amount for which Lani had sold the land/shop, for the second time, to Gilman in July 1856. It is likely that Gilman prepared the release of mortgage after Naomi came knocking on his door. The document does not mention who, if anyone, supplied Gilman with the $624 that Lani sold him his lands for, along with the interest. Who bought Lani's lands back from Gilman? Was it Haulewahine? Or was it Lani himself?

Interestingly, there is some speculation in the archives that the Naomi who claimed Lani's Kainehe land after his death might not have been his ex-wife, the woman named in his will. In fact, there was heated debate as to whether this Naomi was Lani's companion or simply another woman by the name of Naomi who happened to know about Lani's land and death. Within the 28 March 1876 will of a woman named Naomi is proof of court debates about Naomi's identity. Witnesses are called in to testify. The case goes all the way up to the Supreme Court of Hawai'i. Among the witnesses is Haulewahine, who testifies that Lani's ex-wife is Naomi Poepoe, and that she is still alive, while the other Naomi died in 1859, and that her funeral was attended by Lani. A different witness testifies that the deceased Naomi is in fact Naomi Poepoe, Lani's ex-wife.

The reason for this debate is Lani's Kainehe lot, which lot a Naomi, claiming to be Lani's wife, sold to Jokua in October 1875. This property came to be contested by Kamale, the sister and only living relative of Naomi, with the 1876 will. Eventually, the court rules in against Kamale, and Jokua is able to hold on to the Kainehe lot. This property then passes from Jokua to Poepoe Pacheco (not to be confused with, and of likely no relation to, Naomi Poepoe). Poepoe Pacheco then sells Lani's little house lot and store in Kainehe to the Pioneer Mill Company in 1899, which by then commands vast acreage for its sugar mills in Lahaina.

And what of Lani's other lands in Alio? It isn't clear who owns the lands described in RP 409, after Gilman prepares documents on April 16, 1861, releasing all of Lani's lands to him. In fact, there is no sale of these lands for the next three decades. Then, in 1895, one acre of Lani's Alio land comes into possession of Joseph Ricard, who enters it into a leasehold agreement with Pioneer Mill. The other two acres of Lani's Alio land are mysteriously conveyed to Paul Nahaolelua, the governor of Maui from 1852 to 1874; there is no mention of this conveyance in the archives. Kia Nahaolelua, the adopted son of the governor, then sells these two acres of land to Pioneer Mill Co. in January 1899. The deed of this sale states: "All that certain parcel of land situated in Alio, containing an area of 2'70/100 acres, and being a portion of the land described in Royal Patent Number 409, LCA 352 to Serang aka Lani, and by the said Serang conveyed to P. Nahaolelua." As there was no official sale between Serang and P. Nahaolelua or between G. D. Gilman and P. Nahaolelua, we can suppose that a portion of Lani's Alio lands fell into the governor's lap, having been unclaimed by anyone.

And what of Haulewahine? Did she get a portion of Lani's lands as promised to her in his will? It doesn't look so in the archives. According to a division deed between Kamaika and Haulewahine, Haulewahine married Kamakauhaole (date of marriage unknown). She and Kamaika, a stepmother of Kamakauhaole, enter into an agreement to divide Kamakauhaole's property equally between each other. They entered into this agreement in 1872, 11 years after the death of Lani. Upon Lani's death, Haulewahine remarried. There is no other reference to

P. Pacheco et al.   To   Pioneer Mill Co.
Stamped ⅘¢°   Deed

Know all men by these presents: That we, Poepoe Pacheco wife of Manuel Pacheco, of Kailua, Kona, Hawaii and Kaeheikai Miki (w) unmarried, of Honolulu, Oahu, and Hattie Nu wife of John Namus Nu, of Waipio, Ewa, Oahu for and in consideration of the sum of Four Hundred and Fifty Dollars gold coin to us in hand paid by the Pioneer Mill Company a corporation duly organized, acting and existing under and by virtue of the laws of the Hawaiian Islands, doing business and having its principal place of business at Lahaina, Island of Maui, the receipt whereof is hereby acknowledged, do hereby give, grant, bargain, sell, convey and confirm unto the said the Pioneer Mill Company, its successors and assigns, all of our and each of our undivided three-fourths interest in and to the following described lots, tracts, pieces or parcels of land situate in Lahaina, Island of Maui, Hawaiian Islands, bounded and described as follows to wit: First All that certain parcel of land situate in Kainehe, Lahaina aforesaid, described in Royal Patent 1174, Land Commission Award 352 to Serang Lani. Second. All that certain parcel of land situate at Waianae, Lahaina aforesaid, described as Apana 3 of Land Commission Award 3424 to Kaleleiki. The first described parcel of land having been conveyed to Mrs. Iouea and Iouea (w) by deed of Naomi, dated October 25th, 1873, and recorded in the Registry Office in Liber 45, page 205, and the second above described parcel having been conveyed to Pokii (w) and Iokua by deed of Campbell and Turton, dated October 6th, 1876 and recorded in Liber 76, page 274, and both of said above described parcels of land having been conveyed to Kamoohila (w), Hattie (w), Poepoe (w), Kehukai (w) by deed of Pokii (w) and Iokua (w) dated October 7th, 1887, and recorded in Liber 148, page 171. To have and to hold the said granted premises together with all the rights, easements, privileges and appurtenances thereunto belonging unto the said the Pioneer Mill Company, its successors and assigns forever. And we do hereby for ourselves, our and each of our heirs, executors, administrators and assigns covenant with the said the Pioneer Mill Company its successors and assigns, that we are lawfully seized in fee simple of said granted premises, that they are free and clear of all incumbrances; that we will, and our and each of our heirs, executors, administrators and assigns shall warrant and defend the same unto the said the Pioneer Mill Company its successors and assigns forever, against the lawful claims and demands of all persons. And for the consideration aforesaid we, Manuel Pacheco husband of the said Poepoe Pacheco, and John Namus Nu, husband of the said Hattie Nu do hereby consent and agree to the foregoing conveyance and all of the terms and conditions thereof. In witness whereof, We, the said Poepoe Pacheco, Manuel Pacheco, Hattie Nu, John Namus Nu and

Deed of sale of Lani's lands between P. Pacheco & Pioneer Mill. Source: Bureau of Conveyances

Haulewahine in the early grantor-grantee registers. Haulewahine had to forfeit her claim to Lani's Alio lands, which he sold to Gilman without her signature. Lani's Alio lands ended up with Gilman, were mysteriously released back to Lani (after his death), and then were mysteriously conveyed to Paul Nahaole-lua, whose adopted son sold them to Pioneer Mill.

From 1899 until the dissolution of the Pioneer Mill, Lani's lands went to the service of the sugar industry. Those lands have again been redistributed. A road runs through one parcel. Many houses stand on others. Today, the total value of the lands awarded to Lani in 1852 stands at around $10 million dollars.

Still, Lani's name continues to live on in the pages of history as one of the first South Asian refugee-settlers on the Hawaiian Islands—long before the migration of the Chinese, the Japanese, the Koreans, the Filipinos, and the Portuguese laborers to the sugar mills. His many names—Serang, Lani, Sheik Mahomet—bear witness to the myriad journeys of seamen like him and the intercontinental lives they lived during the heyday of the British Empire from the early 1800s to the 1850s.

Works Cited

Accounts and Papers: Shipping; Mercantile Marine Committee. Vol. LXII. 1903.

Alexander, W. D. "Early Trading in Hawai'i," *Papers of the Hawaiian Historical Society,* No. 11, The Bulletin Publishing Company, 1904.

Anonymous. "Indian Lascars Fight the War at Sea," *Life,* 1944.

Bean, Susan S. "The American Market for Indian Textiles, 17851820: In the Twilight of Traditional Cloth Manufacture." *Textile Society of America Symposium Proceedings,* 1990.

Behal, Rana P. & Marcel van der Linden (eds.) *Coolies, Capital and Colonialism: Studies in Indian Labour History.* University Press Cambridge, 2006.

Chamberlain, Levi. *Journal,* vol. 19. The Hawaiian Mission Houses. Digital Archive.

Chinen, Jon J. The Great Māhele: Hawai'i's Land Divisions of 1848. University of Hawai'i Press, 1958.

Clark, E. W. & A. Thurston, "Letter to the Rev. R. Anderson," July 10, 1832. The Hawaiian Mission Houses. Digital Archive.

Fisher, Michael H. *Counterflows to Colonialism: Indian Travellers and Settlers in Britain 1600–1857.* Permanent Black, 2006.

Forbes, Cochran. Journal of Cochran Forbes. Voyage on "Averick" New Bedford to the Sandwich Islands: 1831–1832. The Hawaiian Mission Houses. Digital Archive.

A Glossary of Castes, Tribes and Races in the Baroda State. Compiled by Rao Bahadur. 1912.

Greer, Richard A. "Grog Shops and Hotels: Bending the Elbow in Old Honolulu," *Hawaiian Journal of History,* vol. 28, 1994.

Greer, Richard A. "Notes on Early Land Titles and Tenure in Hawai'i," *The Hawaiian Journal of History,* vol. 30, 1996.

Hackman, Rowan. *Ships of the East India Company.* World Ship Society, 2001.

Hood, W. H. Captain. *The Blight of Insubordination: The Lascar Question and Rights and Wrongs of the British Shipmaster.* London, 1903.

Loomis, Elisha. "Journal of the Sandwich I. Mission," in *The Missionary Herald, for the Year 1823,* vol. 19. The Hawaiian Mission Houses. Digital Archive.

Moffat, Riley, M. & Gary Fitzpatrick, *Surveying the Māhele: Mapping the Hawaiian Land Revolution,* Editions Limited, 1995.

Naval Documents Related to the Quasi-war Between the United States and France: Naval Operations February 1797–December 1801. United States, U.S. Government Printing Office, 1938.

Polynesian. (Honolulu [Oahu], Hawaii), 05 Feb. 1848. *Chronicling America: Historic American Newspapers.* Lib. of Congress. https://chroniclingamerica.loc.gov/.

Report of the Committee Appointed by the Board of Trade to Inquire into Certain Questions Affecting the Mercantile Marine with Minutes of Evidence. 1903.

Speakman, Cummins E. Jr. *Maui: A History.* United States, Mutual Publishing LLC, 2014.

Stewart, C. S. *Journal of a Residence in the Sandwich Islands During the Years 1823, 1824, and 1825.* H. Fisher, Son, and Jackson, 1828.

Tilton, Cecil. *The History of Banking in Hawaii.* University of Hawai'i, 1927.

Visram, Rozina. *Ayahs, Lascars and Princes: Indians in Britain 1700–1947.* Pluto Press, 1986.

Whitehill, Walter Muir. *The East India Marine Society and the Peabody Museum of Salem: A Sesquicentennial History.* Salem, Mass.: Peabody Museum, 1949.

KA MOʻOLELO O KE KŪLANAKAUHALE ʻO LAHAINA

I kākau ʻia e Hon. Daniel Kahāʻulelio,
KA LUNA [KĀNĀWAI] O LAHAINA.[1]
HE KEIKI PAPA A LĀLĀWAI NO KA MALU ʻULU O LELE.

NĀ MĀHELE

1. Ke kūlana a me ka hiʻohiʻona o ke kūlanakauhale ʻo Lahaina.
2. Ke ʻano nui o ka noho ʻana o nā kānaka.
3. Nā [aliʻi] hānau o ka ʻāina.[2]
4. Nā kaukaualiʻi.
5. Nā kānaka koʻikoʻi a naʻauao o ka ʻāina.
6. Nā makaʻāinana e noho ana ma luna o ua kūlanakauhale kaulana lā o ka laʻi o Lele, e hoʻomaka ana mai ka M.H. 1820 a hiki i kēia makahiki e neʻe mālie nei.
[7.][3] Nā hana ʻano nui i loko o ka ʻāina.

E Mr. Luna Hoʻoponopono o ka *Lei [Rose] o Hawaii,*[4] aloha ʻoe.
E ʻoluʻolu mai ʻoe iaʻu, e hōʻike aku i ke ʻano o ke kūlanakauhale ʻo Lahaina nei, kahi a ka nani a me ke [onaona] i noho ai,[5] ka Mōʻī Wahine hoʻi o nā kūlanakauhale i loko o ka pae moku kaulana ʻo Hawaiʻi nei; i haiamū ʻia e ka nani a me ka hiehie, ke kiʻekiʻe o ke ʻala a me ke onaona. Ua kīkīkōʻele wale nō a pau i laila, ʻaʻohe āu mea e hoʻohalahala ai, no laila [e] hōʻike mua aku ana au i ke kūlana o ke kūlanakauhale ʻo Lahaina nei,[6] mai ka M.H. 1820 mai a hiki i kēia makahiki (ʻauhuhu-paʻina) 1898 e neʻe nei—Aloha ʻoukou.

ʻO ke kūlanakauhale ʻo Lahaina nei, eia ʻo ia ke waiho ʻĀkau-Komohana nei a hiki i ka uluniu o Māla, kona palena, a ka uluniu hoʻi a ke aliʻi Kaleikoa i

kanu ai. E moe Hema-Hikina ana a hiki kona palena i ka pōhaku nui a Kaukuna
i manaʻo ai e hiki i kona ikaika ke hoʻoneʻe iā ia mai kona kahua e waiho ana a
i kahi ʻokoʻa aku, akā, ʻaʻole naʻe pēlā, a na ke diana pauda maoli ʻo ia i hoʻoneʻe
a hoʻopuehu aku iā ia a lilo i mea ʻole.

No laila, ʻo ka loa o ke kūlanakauhale ponoʻī ʻo Lahaina, ua like me 3 mile,
a he 2 ½ mile laulā mai ke kai a hiki i loko o ka hale o Rev. Debela, ʻo kekahi o nā
kumu kula o Lahainaluna; a me ka hale lāʻau nani o L. Kapokahi [Kapōkahi?],
aikāne a mī nei, a me ka Luna Hoʻoponopono o ka *Lei Rose o Hawaii*, a ma
kaʻu manaʻo koho, ua like paha me 10 [mile] ke anapuni o ke kūlanakauhale
ʻo Lahaina.[7] Ua hoʻonohonoho ʻia ʻo Lahaina nei i nā [ʻōlelo] kaulana a ka poʻe
kahiko,[8] ma muli o kona ʻano he Paredaiso no ka pae moku ʻo Hawaiʻi i loko o
ia au o ka nani a me ka hiehie e haiamū ana; a ʻo ia mau ʻōlelo lā e hoʻonani ana
iā Lahaina i loko o ia mau lā, e kū ana i luna o ke kūlana o Wahinekapu kona
nani a me ka hiehie.

1. Huaʻi ka ʻulu o Lele i ka mālie.[9]
2. E aha ana ka ulu kaulana o Lele e lohi nei?
3. Ka pohu laʻi o Hauola.[10]
4. Ka ua Paʻūpili o Lahaina.[11]
5. Ke aheahe makani i ka Maʻaʻa i ka laʻi.

A na ka poʻe haku mele hoʻi ia e pūneʻe hou aʻe ma ke ʻano hoʻohanohano iā
Lahaina, e like me kēia ʻala kiele:

Hālau Lahaina mōlale malu i ka ʻulu
Malu mai ka peʻa laulā o ka ʻāina,
Kiʻekiʻe Lahaina i ka ua Paʻūpili
Pili aloha Maunahoʻomaha me Kekaʻa
ʻAuʻau i ka wai hoʻolana kino.

MĀHELE I

Ke au o ka ʻāina mai ka makahiki 1820 a hiki i ka makahiki 1830. E hoʻomanaʻo,
e ka mea heluhelu, ʻo ka M.H. 1820, ʻo ia ka wā i ʻō mai ai nā kukuna ʻōlinolino o
ka mālamalama Christiano a Binamu a me Kakina mā i lawe mai ai, ʻaʻole i hala
ʻelima māhina ma ia hope iho, ua mālama ʻia he hōʻike kula ma Honolulu. [I] ia
wā pū nō hoʻi, he mau kula nō ma Lahaina nei i kapa ʻia "He kula pīʻāpā walu,"
ʻo ia hoʻi ka—ʻĀhē, ʻĀhā, ʻAha, Hana, Hāna, a pēlā wale aku a lehulehu maoli nō.

Ma ka hōʻike a koʻu makua kāne, ke hui pū lā nō ka naʻaupō me ke au kahiko, e laʻa ka pūhenehene, ke kōnane, ka heʻe nalu, ka hōlua, ka ʻūmaika ʻana,[12] ke keʻa pua, ka hoʻolele lupe, a pēlā wale aku o nā ʻano hana like a pau. [I] ia [wā] pū nō ke aʻo pū ʻia lā no ka pīʻāpā walu ma ka pualu a puana like ʻana,[13] a kohu hula maoli nō ka leʻaleʻa ma muli o ke olowalu like ʻana o nā leo pualu o nā mea a pau. Ua lilo ia i mea makemake loa ʻia e nā poʻe kamaʻāina o kēia kūlanakauhale, mai nā [aliʻi] a nā makaʻāinana, a ua poina mai hoʻi nā leʻaleʻa ʻano nui i maʻa [i] ia wā. A i mea e maopopo ai ka holo mua o kēia kūlanakauhale ma kēia lālā nui ʻo ka pono, ua hoʻāla aʻela ʻo Hoapili (k) a me Hoapili (w) ma ke kūkā ʻana me ke Kuhina Nui Kaʻahumanu a me nā [aliʻi] nō a pau, e kūkulu i pāpū, i mea e pale aku ai i ka ʻenemi. I loko o kēia māhele, ua paʻa ka hale pule o Waineʻe i ka makahiki o ka Haku 1828.

E hoʻi hou ana kākou i hope i ke kūlana o Lahaina i loko o kēia māhele, no nā mea e pili ana i ka pono kino o ka noho ʻana o nā kānaka e like me ka moʻolelo a koʻu mau mākua i kamaʻilio ai iaʻu. I kona hiki mua ʻana mai i kēia wahi ʻo Lahaina i kona mau lā ʻōpio wale nō, he 19 makahiki, ma ke ʻano mākaʻikaʻi iā Lahaina mai Honuaʻula aku nei, no ka ʻāina kaulana i ka maikaʻi a me ka momona ʻo Lahaina.

KA MOʻOLELO O KE KŪLANAKAUHALE ʻO LAHAINA

I kākau ʻia e Hon. Daniel Kahāʻulelio,

KA LUNA KĀNĀWAI O LAHAINA.

A i kona ʻike pono ʻana i ka momona o ka ʻāina, ua loaʻa ihola nā hale aikāne a me nā hale hoʻowahine, ua huli hoʻi koke akula ʻo ia i kona ʻāina hānau, iā Keoneʻōʻio, a lawe maila i kona makua kāne, nā kaikuaʻana, kaikaina, a me ka ʻohana a pau, he 10 ka nui, ma luna o nā waʻa, a noho malihini ihola ma kahi nō o ka Mea Hanohano, ka Luna Kānāwai D. Kahāʻulelio e noho nei, ma kahi i kapa ʻia ʻo Mākila.

Ua noho a hoʻokamaʻāina ihola lākou ma ia wahi i ka M.H. 1824, ua like me 74 makahiki i hala aʻe nei. E nā makamaka heluhelu o Lahaina, ka ʻāina momona hoʻokahi aʻu i lohe [ai],[14] a aʻu hoʻi e hōʻike aku nei i hui pū ʻia me koʻu ʻike maka no nā makahiki he 50 a ʻoi i hala aʻe nei. A penei e maopopo ai, ʻaʻole e ʻekolu kaulahao mai kahakai mai, e ulu ana nā loʻi kalo nunui. E hele ʻoe mai kēlā peʻa a kēia peʻa o Lahaina, aia nā loʻi kalo e ulu ana ma mua a ma hope o kauhale, he ulukō hoʻi me ka maiʻa, nā māla ʻuala, nā māla uhi pālau, nā māla ipu haole, ipu pū, kūlina, ʻakaʻakai, kaʻukama, pine, papapa, ipu pū, ʻōhiʻa, a pēlā aku, e uhi paʻapū ʻia ana hoʻi ka ʻāina e nā kumu ʻulu, e ka uluniu, nā kō 'aki o ka wā kahiko o kēlā a me kēia 'ano. Mai kēia wā a hiki i ka wā 'eono, 'o ia mau nō ka momona o ka 'āina, e piha ana nō me kēia mau hua 'ai i ha'i 'ia a'ela ma luna. 'A'ole au i lohe iki, he mau hua 'ōlelo no ka [auē],[15] e 'ī ana lā ho'i, "Ua wī 'o Lahaina," 'a'ole loa! 'O ka 'oi loa aku o ka puni a nā malihini, 'o ke kukui inamona waipahē a momona ke miki iho 'oe me kou mau manamana lima waliwali a palanehe, he keu aku a ke kuhikuhinia.

'O ka Luna Ho'oponopono o kēia nūpepa kekahi o nā keiki lālāwai a kupa o ua kūlanakauhale nei a mākou i holoholo pū iho ai i ko mākou mau lā 'ōpio, me nā keiki lālāwai 'ē a'e o ua 'āina lā, i pau aku i ka hala ma kēlā 'ao'ao, he 40 makahiki i hala aku nei ma hope. 'O ia kekahi hō'ike 'oia'i'o o kēia, a me nā kama'āina kahiko 'ē a'e a pau e ola nei o ka 'āina. 'A'ole 'o ia wale nō, 'o ku'u mau kaikua'ana a me ku'u mau kaikaina, i komo i ke Kulanui o Lahainaluna mai ka makahiki A.D. 1840 mai a i ka makahiki A.D. 1863; 'o lākou kekahi po'e nāna e hō'oia'i'o mai i ke kūlana momona o ka 'āina o ke kūlanakauhale 'o Lahaina.[16]

He 2 mau mea nāna e hō'ike maopopo aku i mua o nā malihini i kipa mai e 'ike i ka nani a me ka momona o Lahaina [i] ia au o ka 'āina i hala aku. 1. Aia ma uka iho o ka hale mākeke kū'ai i'a, e pili pū ala me ka hale ipu kukui, he lo'i kalo nui no nā [ali'i], 'o Apukaiao [Apukaiao?] kona inoa, a ma uka aku o nā hale inu tī, he lo'i kalo no ka Mō'ī Lunalilo i hala, 'o Lo'inui ka inoa a 'o ka 'oi paha kēia o ka lo'i kalo nui ho'okahi o Hawai'i nei. A he lo'i kalo iho na ke [ali'i] Lahilahi, e pili pū ana ma kahi noho o ko 'oukou mea kākau, i like nō ka nui me Apukaiao, he mau kapua'i wale nō ke ka'awale mai ke kai mai, a kahi a kēia mau lo'i kalo i kū ai. Aia nō ho'i nā 'ama'ama a me nā 'anae, nā awa, nā āholehole, nā 'o'opu, a me nā 'ōpae ['ula] e holo ana i loko o kēia lo'i kalo, ua hele a momona.[17]

I ke o'o 'ana o ka 'ai, a mana'o e hō'ā imu, ua mākaukau nō ka i'a, eia nō i mua o ka 'īpuka hale. Māhele 2. He māhele 'ano nui loa kēia o ke kūlanakauhale 'o Lahaina.

'A'ole i pau.

KA MO'OLELO O KE KŪLANAKAUHALE 'O LAHAINA

I kākau 'ia e Hon. Daniel Kahā'ulelio,
KA LUNA KĀNĀWAI O KA MALU 'ULU O LELE.

He 'elua mea nāna e hō'ike maopopo aku i mua o nā malihini i kipa mai e 'ike i ka nani a me ka momona o Lahaina [i] ia au o ka 'āina i hala aku, aia ma uka iho o ka hale mākeke kū'ai i'a e pili pū lā me ka hale ipukukui, he lo'i kalo nui no nā [ali'i] 'o Apukaiao ka inoa, a ma uka o nā hale inu kī, he lo'i kalo nui no ka Mōʻī Lunalilo i hala, ʻo Loʻinui ka inoa, a ʻo ka ʻoi paha kēia o ka loʻi kalo nui hoʻokahi o Hawaiʻi nei; he loʻi kalo iho nō na ke [aliʻi] Lahilahi i pili pū me kahi noho o ko ʻoukou mea kākau. Ua like ka nui me Opukaiao [Apukaiao] he mau kapuaʻi mai ke kai mai, aia nō hoʻi nā ʻamaʻama me nā ʻanae, nā awa, nā āholehole, nā ʻoʻopu me nā ʻōpae e holo ana i loko o kēia mau loʻi, ua hele a momona. I ke oʻo ʻana o ka ʻai a manaʻo e hōʻā imu, ua mākaukau nō ka iʻa, eia i mua o ka ʻīpuka hale.[18]

MĀHELE 2

He māhele ʻano nui kēia o ke kūlanakauhale ʻo Lahaina. 1—ma ka makahiki 1830, ua paʻa ka pāpū kaua o Lahaina. 2—kūkulu ʻia ke Kulanui o Lahainaluna, 1831. 3—ʻo ka wā kēia i pae nui mai ai nā misionari i Hawaiʻi nei. 4—ʻo kēia ka wā i ninini nui ʻia mai ai ka ʻUhane Maikaʻi ma luna o kēia kūlanakauhale a hoʻohuli nui ʻia nā [aliʻi], nā poʻe koʻikoʻi a me nā makaʻāinana, e huli i ka pono o Iēhova ke Akua nāna i hana i ka lani a me ka honua.

Māhele 1—Ka Paʻa ʻAna o ka Pāpū

I ka paʻa ʻana o ka pāpū kaua, ua hoʻonoho ʻia kekahi kanaka [aliʻi] o ka ʻāina, ʻo Kalaikoa [Kālaikoa?] kona inoa i Luna Nui no ka pāpū,[19] a ʻo kēia ke kupuna kāne o ke [aliʻi] Albert Kūnuiākea Kaleiopapa, ma ka ʻaoʻao o ka makua kāne, ʻo Kaeo [Kāʻeo?], ke kāne mare a Lahilahi, kaikaina o Kekelaokalani, ka makuahine o Kaleleonālani, a ʻo Unele [Unele?] (k) a me koʻu makua kāne nā kānaka lawelawe a noho paʻa ma loko o ka pāpū no ke kiaʻi i ka maluhia me ka hale pauda, a me ka hoʻomaʻemaʻe i nā pū kuni ahi e kau ana.

Mai ka paʻa ʻana o ka pāpū a hiki i ke kau ʻana o nā pū kuni ahi, ʻo ia ka 1830, ʻaʻole i hoʻohana iki ʻia nā pū kuni ahi me ka lohe ʻole ʻia o ko lākou mau leo nākolokolo e hoʻopaʻiakuli ana i nā pepeiao, he oki loa nō.

Aia ma ka wehena o ke alaula o ke ao o ka lā 12 o Feb 1837, ʻo ia ka manawa i lohe mua loa ʻia ai ka leo nākolokolo kuʻilua o ua mau pū kuni ahi nei, e hōʻike mai ana i kēlā me kēia peʻa o ke kūlanakauhale nani ʻo Lahaina, aia ma luna o ka moku aliʻi *"Kai"* ke kino wailua o ka Lani [Nāhiʻenaʻena],[20] kaikuahine o Kauikeaouli Kamehameha III Kaleiopapa, no ka hoʻihoʻi ʻana mai no ka hoʻolewa.

Ma kēia wahi, e ka mea heluhelu, e kala mai no ka loaʻa ʻana o ke kauoha i koʻu makua kāne, no ka hoʻomākaukau koke ʻana e hoʻohana i nā pū kuni ahi, ua haʻalele ʻia ihola koʻu māmā me ka wahine a kona kōkoʻolua, a Unele.

ʻO ka leo mua o ka pū kuni ahi a koʻu makua kāne i kuni aku ai a kani, na ia leo nō i ho'oku'u maika'i mai ia'u mai ka pūhaka mai o ko'u makuahine a hanu i nā ea hu'ihu'i o ka Malu 'Ulu o Lele i ka mālie.

Ma ka ha'i mai a ko'u lūau'i makua kāne, 'oiai ka ho'oku'u 'ia 'ana mai o ka wa'apā e waiho ana ke kino o ke [ali'i], me ka Mō'ī Kauikeaouli a me nā [ali'i], ua puni ke kūlanakauhale i nā leo uē[21] kanikau me ka hea inoa, a ua lawe loa 'ia ke kino make a [*Hawai'i Kaku*],[22] he hālau nui. Aia kona kahua i kū ai ma ka lihi kahakai, kokoke nō i kahi noho o ka Luna Ho'oponopono o kēia pepa, ma kai iho o kahi o J. B. Jones (Keonikikane), ma laila kahi i ho'opae 'ia ai.

'A'ole i pau.

KA MO'OLELO O KE KŪLANAKAUHALE 'O LAHAINA[23]
I haku 'ia e Hon. D. Kahā'ulelio.
KA LUNA KĀNĀWAI O KA MALU 'ULU O LELE.

Ma laila kahi i ho'opae 'ia aku ai ka heana makamae a ka lāhui o ia au i hala, 'a'ole ia hale i kēia wā, ua pau aku i ke kai ka hapanui o ke kahua i kū ai, a he wahi 'āpana 'u'uku loa koe, 'a'ole nō i 'ike nā haumāna hou o Lahaina, a me ka Luna Ho'oponopono o kēia pepa. 'O ko 'oukou mea kākau kai 'ike, i ke au o Timoteo Keaweiwi. I ka ho'olewa 'i'o 'ana o ke kino wailua o Ka Lani Nāhi'ena'ena, ua hāli'i 'ia ke alanui i ka moena mai kēia hālau nui aku a hiki i ka luakini 'o Waine'e, 'a'ole na'e ma ke alanui aupuni, he wahi alanui kēia ma uka, 'o ia ka Helu 2 o nā alanui, a ma uka o ia alanui pi'i i uka o Lahaina, [pili] aku 'oe mai ke alanui pili kahakai aku,[24] a laila, a loa'a nō iā 'oe ua wahi alanui lā, e hele ana mai laila aku a hiki i ka luakini pōhaku 'o Waine'e. 'O ka ho'omaka 'ana o ka huaka'i ho'olewa kai hiki i ka luakini, aia nō ka lehulehu i hope, kahi i ho'onohonoho ai. I ka pau 'ana o ka hapa nui o ka ho'olewa i loko o ka luakini, 'akahi nō a hele mai ka hope, hewa i ka wai ka nui o nā kānaka. 'O Rev. W. Rikeke (Richard) ka mea nāna i mālama ke anaina haipule kāhoahoa o Ka Lani Nāhi'ena'ena.

Wahi a kekahi kanaka ko'iko'i a makua o ka pono, o Akulamoku [Akulamoku?] kona inoa i kāna ha'i 'ana mai ia'u, he kū i ke anoano a me ka walohia nā ha'i 'ōlelo, a wahi hou nō āna, he nui Kona aloha i Kāna hānai (Nāhi'ena'ena) a me ka minamina nō ho'i. I ka pau 'ana o ke anaina pule, ua [ho'olewa] hou 'ia kona kino kupapa'u a ma ke kahua o Mokuola,[25] ka home noho o nā ali'i 'ai moku mai ke au mai o Kamehameha I a hiki iā Kamehameha III, pau. Aia nō ka hale kupapa'u ke waiho lā nō ma kahi i waiho 'ia ai nā iwi ali'i o ua lani lā, a ke 'ole au e kuhihewa, i ka makahiki 1885 paha ia, i ka wā e noho kia'āina ana ka Luna Ho'oponopono o ka *Lei Rose o Hawaii,* ka hiki kino 'ana mai o ke aliʻi Pauahi Bishop i Lahaina nei, a lawe ʻia ai nā iwi aliʻi a pau i ka pā ilina o ka [luakini] ʻo Waineʻe e pili ana ma nā hē kupapaʻu o Hoapili kāne a me Hoapili wahine.[26]

Māhele 2

ʻO ia ke kūkulu ʻia ʻana o ka hale kula ʻo Lahainaluna, makahiki 1831. ʻO ke Kulanui ʻo Lahainaluna, ʻo ia kekahi mea nāna i hoʻohanohano i ke kūlanakauhale ʻo Lahaina, a i kapa ʻia hoʻi kona inoa ʻo ke kūlana poʻokela o ka naʻauao, nona ka ʻōlelo ʻana, "ka ipu kukui pio ʻole i ka makani Kauaʻula." Inā e piʻi ka malihini a hiki i Lahainaluna a nānā mai i ke kaona o Lahaina, he laulā a he nani maoli nō ʻoe ke nānā aku, a no ka lilo ʻana o Lahaina i kahua nāna e hāpai i ke kaona o Lahaina a kiʻekiʻe, no laila i kapa ʻia ai ʻo [Lahainaluna],[27] ua kapa ʻia hoʻi i kekahi wā "ka hōkū mālamalama o ka moana Pākīpika," a pēlā i kapa ʻia ai ke kaona o Lahaina, ʻo Lahainalalo, ʻo kēia nā māhele mua ʻelua o Lahaina.

Eia hoʻi kekahi, i ka wā e kū ana kēlā kula kiʻekiʻe mua i kūkulu ʻia i loko nei o ke aupuni Hawaiʻi, ʻo ia hoʻi ka hale kula i pau i ke ahi i ka M.H. 1860, a me nā hale lepo e moe ai nā haumāna, i kūkulu ʻia ma ka ʻaoʻao Hema Hikina o ua hale kula lā, he nui ʻokoʻa nō ia ke nānā aku ʻoe mai ke kaona aku i ka pō, i ka hulili mai o nā kukui, a pēlā nō hoʻi me ka hale noho o nā kumu, a he uluwehiwehi hoʻi i nā ulukukui i kapa ʻia e nā haumāna "ka ulukukui ʻo [Kaukaweli],[28] ka ipu kukui pio ʻole i ka makani Kauaʻula." A mai loko mai o kēia hale kula i puka mai ai nā kānaka kaulana i ka naʻauao, a ua ʻike ka lehulehu mai Hawaiʻi a Niʻihau [i] ia poʻe. A ʻo ko Lahainaluna kaulana loa i loko o kēia māhele ʻelua, ʻo S. P. Kalama Waiawaawa [Waiʻawaʻawa?], ma ke ana ʻāina, ka holomoku, penei kahi moʻolelo e pili ana iā ia a me kona kūlana [i] ia mau lā.

No kahi wā aku.

KA MOʻOLELO O KE KŪLANAKAUHALE LAHAINA
I haku ʻia e ka Hon. D. Kahāʻulelio
KA LUNA KĀNĀWAI O KA MALU ʻULU O LELE

S. P. KALAMA WAIʻAWAʻAWA

Penei kahi moʻolelo e pili ana nona ma kēia helu:

E holo ana ka Mōʻī Kamehameha III ma luna o kekahi moku kaua ʻAmerika no ka ua Kanilehua o Hilo, aia pū nō hoʻi ʻo G. P. Kauka, makua kāne o ka Luna Kānāwai Kiʻekiʻe A. F. Kauka me ia, he punahele a māhele ʻōlelo na ke aliʻi ma luna o ka moku. Ua makemake ke kāpena i kona mau aliʻi moku e hoʻomaopopo i ka lōʻihi o ka manawa a me ka ihu, a ʻoiai e mākaukau ana kēlā poʻe aliʻi moku i kā lākou, ua nīnau akula ʻo S. P. Kalama Waiʻawaʻawa i ka Mōʻī, "He aha kā kēlā poʻe e hana maila?"

Ua nīnau aku ka Mōʻī iā Kauka, a haʻi ʻia maila, "E ʻimi ana lākou i ka lakitū me ka lonitū e holo ana a kū ka moku i ke awa o Hilo."

[I] ia manawa, ua kiʻi akula ʻo S. P. Kalama i kāna puke huihui helu holomoku e huli a e ʻimi i ka nīnau. I ka ʻimi ʻana a loaʻa ka nīnau, [i] ia wā nō i ninau aku ai ke kāpena i ka hāʻina a kona poʻe aliʻi moku, a pane maila ka mea nāna i hōʻike mua mai:

"Inā e mau ana ka ihu o ka moku i ka holo ʻana pēlā, a laila, he 60 lā, kū kākou i Kaleponi."

Nīnau maila ka Mōʻī iā Kalama, "Pehea hoʻi kāu, e ka Lahainaluna, no kēia ihu?"

Ua pane akula ʻo Kalama i mua o ka Mōʻī, "Inā ʻo ka ihu kēia o ka moku e holo ai, a pēlā ke ʻano o ka makani e pā mau ai, a laila, he ʻekolu lā i koe, komo kākou a kū i Hilo."

[I] ia wā i unuhi aku ai ʻo G. P. Kauka i ke kāpena o ka [manuā] ʻAmerika,[29] a huli maila ʻo ia a nīnau iā Kauka, "Ma hea kahi i hoʻonaʻauao ʻia ai ʻo kēia kanaka?"

Ua haʻi aku ʻo Kauka, "Ma ke Kulanui ʻo Lahainaluna."

Ua pane mai ke kāpena, "Ua pololei maoli kāna hāʻina. ʻEkolu ʻiʻo nō lā, komo kākou i Hilo, me kēia makani mau e pā nei a ma lalo o kēia ihu.

[I] ia manawa i wehe koke aʻe ai ke kāpena i kāna [uaki] gula e lei ana a hāʻawi makana akula iā S. P. Kalama Waiʻawaʻawa,[30] ua hoʻohanohano ʻia ʻo Lahainaluna, a ua hoʻokiʻekiʻe ʻia hoʻi ʻo Lahaina a me ka lāhui Hawaiʻi ma ka naʻauao.

Ma ke kau ʻAha ʻŌlelo o ka makahiki 1870, koʻu ʻike pono ʻana i ua [uaki][31] gula lā i makana ai iā S. P. Kalama.

MANAʻO 3

Ma lalo o kēia māhele manaʻo no kēia helu aʻe, e hoʻopuka aku ai mākou no ka pae nui ʻana mai o nā Misionari, &c., a ʻo kekahi hapa hoʻi ia o kēia moʻolelo.

ʻAʻole i pau.

NOTES

1.   Original Document (OD) = Ka Luna Lanawai.
2.   OD = Na'lii. As this is an extremely common spelling convention in the newspapers, all subsequent changes of "na'lii" to "nā ali'i" will not be identified.
3.   OD = No number.
4.   OD = "Ka Lei Lose o Hawaii." Although the writer used the Hawaiian letter "L" instead of "R," this editor has chosen to keep the official name of the newspaper, *Ka Lei Rose o Hawaii*.
5.   OD = onana.
6.   OD = . . . no laila e e hoike mua aku ana au . . .
7.   OD = meli.
8.   OD = oleio.
9.   See "Hua'i ka 'ulu o Lele i ka makani Kona" (Pukui 1983:119:1117).
10. See "Ka la'i o Hauola" (Pukui 1983:154:1425).
11. See "Ka ua Pa'ūpili o Lele" (Pukui 1983:172:1594).
12. OD = kau-maika ana. " 'ūmaika" here is most likely a shortened version of " 'ulu maika," a game in which a bowler attempts to roll a stone disc through a target. This word is not found in any of the current dictionaries.
13. OD = wu.
14. OD = "ka 'aina momona hookahi a'u i lohe,".
15. OD = "auwe"
16. OD = . . . e hooiaio mai i mai i ke kulana momona . . .
17. OD = "opae ua"
18. Text of first paragraph is a reprint from the second issue of the series with minor differences.
19. OD = "kekahi kanaka alii"
20. OD = Naahienaena
21. OD = "uwe"
22. The editor was unable to find more information on "Hawaii Kaku." It may be a misprint of "Hawaii Haku," but as there is not enough information to make the change, it has been left as "Hawai'i Kaku."
23. In this issue, the newspaper name changes to *Ka Malamalama Hawaii.*"However, *Ka Lei Loke o Hawaii* or *Ka Lei Rose o Hawaii* is still used in reference to it.
24. OD = pli
25. OD = honlewa.
26. OD = "Luaeni."
27. OD = "Lahainaluua."
28. OD = "Kankaweli."
29. OD = "manuwa"
30. OD = "wati"
31. OD = "uwati"

CHAPTER 4

AN ACCOUNT OF
THE CITY OF LAHAINA

Written by Hon. Daniel Kahā'ulelio,

MAGISTRATE OF LAHAINA.

A NATIVE-BORN SON OF THE BREADFRUIT-SHELTERED LAND OF LELE.

Translated by Frank Ezra Ka'iuokalani Damas

SECTIONS

1. The conditions and features of the city of Lahaina.
2. The typical way of life.
3. Royalty born of this land.
4. Lower-ranking chiefs.
5. Prominent and knowledgeable people of this place.
6. The common folk who reside within this famous city in the calm of Lele, from 1820 until now [1898].
7. The main events of this land.

To the Editor of the *Lei Rose o Hawaii,* greetings to you.

Please allow me the opportunity to explain some things about the city of Lahaina, where beauty and poise makes its home, the Queen of cities here in our famed Hawaiian islands; where beauty and grace meet, exalted by fragrance and sweetness. A land at its absolute peak, one cannot find flaw, and so I begin by explaining the nature of Lahaina, from the year 1820 until this year (in the month of 'Auhuhu-Pa'ina) 1898—greetings to you all.[1]

Lahaina town stretches from North to West, from the coconut grove of Māla, to the coconut grove planted by the chief Kaleikoa. It stretches South-East to the great stone that Kaukuna thought himself strong enough to relocate, and when he could not, used dynamite to blow it up, leaving nothing left.

Lahaina, then, has a length of about three miles and stretches up from the sea for about two and a half miles until the home of Rev. Dibble, one of Lahainaluna's teachers, as well as the beautiful wooden home of L. Kapokahi [Kapōkahi?]—a personal friend, and the Editor of *Lei Rose o Hawaii*—and by my estimation, the city about ten miles in circumference. Lahaina has been classified by the people of old with famous sayings because it was a paradise in the Hawaiian islands in those times where beauty and grace were ever present; such sayings glorifying Lahaina in those days may even rival the beauty and poise of Wahinekapu.[2]

1. The breadfruit of Lele is exposed in the calm.[3]
2. What is to become the famous breadfruit of Lele, shining forth?
3. The calm tranquility of Hauola.[4]
4. The Paʻūpili rain of Lahaina.[5]
5. The cool Maʻaʻa breeze in the calm.

There is also the composers who had come forth to exalt Lahaina, as seen in the fragrance of this gardenia:

Lahaina is sheltered, clearly visible in the shade of the breadfruit
Sheltered from all boundaries of this land,
She is made majestic by the Paʻūpili rain,
Lovingly embraced by Maunahoʻomaha and Kekaʻa,
Bathing in the waters on which its people float

SECTION I

The nature of the land from 1820 to 1830. Remember, dear readers, 1820 was the time in which the brilliant rays of Christianity flashed forth, brought by Bingham, Thurston, and others; and not five months later, a school exam was held in Honolulu. During that same time, some schools were set up in Lahaina, known as "English Primer School," learning pronunciation: "Ah," "Ah-Ah," "Ha-na," "Hā-na," and so on and so forth.

When my father took his exams, they mixed in some of the ignorant activities of old times, such as pūhenehene [stone hiding], kōnane [checkers], surfing, sledding, stone-bowling, dart-throwing, kite-flying, and other such activities. It really seemed like a dance, the gaiety from everyone reciting everything in unison. This became something so enjoyed by the locals of this town, both royal and common, that the major games of those times were forgotten. In order to make apparent the progress of this city in terms of morality, Hoapili (m) and Hoapili (f) spoke with Kaʻahumanu, the Royal Premier, as well as all the other chiefs, in regards to establishing a fort to protect against enemies. Waineʻe Church was also built in this time period, in 1828.

Let us relook at the state of Lahaina in this time as it relates to the necessities of those who lived there, as explained to me by my parents. When [my father] first came to this area of Lahaina in his youth, around 19 years old, he was visiting from Honuaʻula, as Lahaina was the famous land of wellness and prosperity.

AN ACCOUNT OF THE CITY OF LAHAINA
Written by Hon. Daniel Kahāʻulelio,
MAGISTRATE OF LAHAINA.

When he saw for himself the abundance in this land, having befriended men and women with whom he stayed, he returned to his homeland and brought back with him his father, his older and younger brothers, and the rest of his family. There were 10 of them that came by canoe, making their new home in the same place where the Hon. Judge D. Kahāʻulelio currently lives, an area known as Mākila.

They made their permanent home here in 1824, about 74 years ago. O readers, Lahaina is the only fertile land I have known, and I present it to you as I have seen it with my own eyes for over 50 years. Here is something of note, not three chain-lengths from the shore, enormous taro are growing. Should one walk from one end of Lahaina to the other, taro patches are found on either side of the homes, as well as a sugar cane grove, bananas, sweet-potato gardens, yams, watermelons, pumpkins, corn, onions, cucumbers, pine, beans, squash, tomatoes, and more.[6] The land is completely covered in a breadfruit grove, a coconut grove, and various old kinds of kō ʻaki. From this time until the 6th section,[7] the production of the land was the same, filled with those fruits that I have mentioned previously. I have never heard any bemoaning saying that Lahaina was struck by famine. Not in the slightest! The favorite dish of its visitors is the kukui nut relish, simply delicious and juicy as one eats delicately with the fingers. It is an absolute delicacy.

The Editor of this newspaper is also a native born son of this city, with whom we explored in our youth, along with the other well-to-do boys of this land, some of which have passed on to the other side some 40 years ago. That is more proof [of Lahaina's prosperity], along with the old folks of this place still living. And there is more, my older and younger brothers attended Lahaina-luna Seminary from 1840 to 1863, and they also serve as proof of the productive nature of the city of Lahaina.

Here are two things to make the glory of Lahaina apparent to visitors who come to to experience its beauty and fruitfulness. 1. Just inland of the fish market, next to the lighthouse, was a large taro patch for the chiefs, named Apukaiao, and just above the tea house was a taro patch for King Lunalilo, who has since passed, named Lo'inui; this may have been the largest taro patch in Hawai'i. There was another taro patch that belonged to Chief Lahilahi near the home of your author, which was about the size of Apukaiao, just a few feet from the sea. Due to the location of these taro patches, there was 'ama'ama, 'anae, awa, āholehole, 'o'opu, and 'ōpae 'ula swimming in them; it was incredibly fertile.

When the food was mature, and an underground oven was to be prepared, the fish was also prepared, as it was done in of the home. Section 2. This is a large period of Lahaina town.[8]

To be continued.

AN ACCOUNT OF THE CITY OF LAHAINA

Written by Hon. Daniel Kahā'ulelio,

MAGISTRATE OF LAHAINA.

Here are two things to make the glory of Lahaina apparent to visitors who come to to experience its beauty and fruitfulness. 1. Just inland of the fish market, next to the lighthouse, was a large taro patch for the chiefs, named Apukaiao, and just above the tea house was a taro patch for King Lunalilo, who has since passed, named Lo'inui; this may have been the largest taro patch in Hawai'i. There was another taro patch that belonged to Chief Lahilahi near the home of your author, which was about the size of Apukaiao, just a few feet from the sea. Due to the location of these taro patches, there was 'ama'ama, 'anae, awa, āholehole, 'o'opu, and 'ōpae 'ula swimming in them; it was incredibly fertile.[9]

SECTION 2

This is a large period of Lahaina town. 1. Lahaina Fort was completed in 1830. 2. Lahainaluna Seminary was built in 1831. 3. Many missionaries arrived in Hawai'i during this time. 4. The Good Spirit poured many blessings upon this town, and many of the chiefs, important folks, and commoners converted to the ways of Jehovah God, who created the heavens and the earth.

Part 1—The completion of the Fort

When the fort was completed, Kālaikoa, a chief of this land, was appointed as its overseer. He was the paternal grandfather of Albert Kūnuiākea Kaleiopapa, whose father was Kāʻeo, husband of Lahilahi, who was the younger sister of Kekelaokalani, the mother of Kaleleonālani. Unele and my father were the ones who lived at the fort, kept the peace, guarded the powder room, and cleaned the cannons that had been set up.

From its completion until the time when the cannons were put in place, which was in 1830, the roaring voices of the cannons, which would undoubtably deafen the ears of all who heard them, were not experienced.

That is, until dawn on Feb. 12, 1837. That was the first time this resounding roar of the cannon was heard as it announced, throughout all of Lahaina, that the deceased Chiefess Nāhiʻenaʻena, sister of Kauikeaouli Kamehameha III Kaleiopapa, was aboard the ship the *Kai,* being returned for her funeral procession.

At that time, o readers, if you would indulge me, my father received word that he was to rush and prepare the cannons for use. My mother was left with the wife of his friend, Unele.

The sound of the first shot lit by my father was actually what caused my birth, allowing me to breathe the cool air of the "Breadfruit Shade of Lele in the calm."

As my father recalled it, when the skiff carrying the body of chiefess, King Kauikeaouli, and the chiefs was lowered [from the ship], the entire town was filled with laments and name songs. The deceased was brought all the way to *Hawaiʻi Kaku,* which was a long house that stood just along the shore, near the home of the Editor of this paper, just below the home of J. B. Jones (Keonikāne), and that is where they came ashore.

To be continued.

AN ACCOUNT OF THE CITY OF LAHAINA

Written by Hon. Daniel Kahāʻulelio,

MAGISTRATE OF LAHAINA.

There, the remains of one of the nation's most cherished chiefesses of that time came ashore. That building [Hawaiʻi Kaku] is no longer there; most of its foundations have been taken by the sea, and only a tiny portion remains. The newer students of Lahaina, and possibly even by the Editor of this paper, have not seen it. Your author is one that has seen it, in the time of Timoteo Keaweiwi. When the actual funeral procession for the body of Chiefess Nāhiʻenaʻena was held, the streets were covered with mats from this large long house all the way to Waineʻe Church. This was not, however, along the government road, but on a second, inland road. Travel inland from the seaside road and you will reach this one, which laid out from there to the stone church of Waineʻe. When the beginning of the funeral procession reached the church, the masses were situated in the rear. By the time most of the people had gone into the church, and the last ones had finally arrived, people could barely fit inside.[10] Rev. W. Richard presided over the services for Her Royal Highness Nāhiʻenaʻena.

Akulamoku, a prominent elder of the church, told me that the speeches given were awe-inspiring and full of emotion. He also said that He [God] loved his child (Nāhiʻenaʻena) and cherished her. When the services were through, her body was carried in procession on to Mokuola, the home of royals from the time of Kamehameha I to Kamehameha III. The mausoleum in which her body lay was still there in 1885, if I am not mistaken, when the editor of the *Lei Rose o Hawaii* was governor, when Princess Pauahi Bishop came to Lahaina, which was when all the royal remains were moved to Waineʻe Church, near the graves of Hoapilikāne and Hoapiliwahine.

SECTION 2

Lahainaluna School was built in 1831. Lahainaluna Seminary was something that uplifted the city of Lahaina, and it was referred to as the champion of wisdom, who begot the phrase, "the lantern that would not go out in the Kauaʻula wind." If a visitor were to go up to Lahainaluna and look down at Lahaina Town, they would see its vast beauty. And since Lahaina[luna] became a something that raised the status of Lahaina Town up high, it was called Lahainaluna, and was sometimes referred to as "the bright star of the Pacific Ocean," and so the town was referred to as Lahainalalo, which gives us the two sections of Lahaina.

Here is another thing, when the first school house that was built here in the Kingdom of Hawaiʻi—which had burned up in a fire in 1860—and the brick houses the students lived in on the South-Eastern side of the school house were still standing, it all seemed enormous from the town: the lights all ablaze along with the teachers homes, as well as a kukui grove that was referred to by the students as "the kukui grove of Kaukaweli, the lantern that would not go out in the Kauaʻula wind." Many famous scholars came out of this school, and people from Hawaiʻi to Niʻihau knew their names. Lahainaluna's most famous student during this time was S. P. Kalama Waiʻawaʻawa; a land surveyor and a sailor. Here is a small story about him and his regard in those days.

For another time.

AN ACCOUNT OF THE CITY OF LAHAINA

Written by Hon. Daniel Kahāʻulelio,

MAGISTRATE OF LAHAINA.

S. P. KALAMA WAIʻAWAʻAWA

Here is a short story about him.

King Kamehameha III was sailing on an American warship for the Kanilehua rains of Hilo. With him was the father of High Judge A. F. Kauka, G. P. Kauka, who was a favorite of the king's and his translator onboard. The captain wanted his ship leads to inform him of the length of the trip and the heading. As they were carrying on with their responsibilities, S. P. Kalama Waiʻawaʻawa asked the king, "What are those folks doing there?"

The king asked Kauka, who said, "They are figuring out the latitude and longitude the ship needs to travel along to arrive in Hilo Bay."

At that time, S. P. Kalama grabbed his sailing charts book to search for the information. As he was determining the answer, the captain asked his ship's leads for the information and the first one who answered said, "If the ship continues on in that direction, then we will reach California in 60 days."

The king asked Kalama, "What do you think, Lahainaluna, about the heading?"

Kalama responded to the king, "If the ship continues in this direction, and if the wind stays the same as it is now, then we will reach Hilo in three days."

G. P. Kauka translated for the American warship captain, at which time he turned to Kauka and asked, "Where was this man educated?"

Kauka responded, "At Lahainaluna Seminary."

The captain responded, "He is exactly correct. In three days, we will reach Hilo, based on these winds and this heading."

At that time, the captain took out his gold watch he had on and gifted it to S. P. Kalama Waiʻawaʻawa. Lahainaluna was given distinction in this act, and Lahaina [Town], along with the Hawaiian people, were seen as being elevated in wisdom.

During the Legislative Session of 1870, I got to see this gold watch that was gifted to S. P. Kalama.

SECTION 3

In this time period, we will explain the arrival of the many missionaries, which is another part of this story.

Unfinished.

NOTES

1. "'Auhuhu-pa'ina" is a Maui term for the month of Makali'i, which is often equated to February. It was so called because the 'auhuhu fruit would make a popping sound (pa'ina) when picked during this time ("Ka Malama o Feberuari" 6 Feb. 1892; S.W.K 1890).
2. Wahinekapu is a reference to Pele, goddess of Hawai'i's volcanoes.
3. See "Hua'i ka 'ulu o Lele i ka makani Kona" (Pukui 1983:119:1117).
4. See "Ka la'i o Hauola" (Pukui 1983:154:1425).
5. See "Ka ua Pa'ūpili o Lele" (Pukui 1983:172:1594).
6. "ipu pū" are listed twice in the original. This could be a misprint, but the translator has left both in, one as pumpkin, and the second as squash.
7. The "6th section" is most likely refering to the list in the first issue of things to discuss about Lahaina. Unfortunately, the author does not complete his series.
8. This last sentence is reorganized in the following issue.
9. Since this is a reprint of the last major paragraph of issue 2, and since the information in issue 2 is more complete, the translator has chosen to use that paragraph again here.
10. "Hewa i ka wai ka nui o nā kānaka." This is an idiom that compares the number of something to that of water, something uncountable.

CHAPTER 5

PANE AKU KŌ MAUI KOMOHANA

Nā Poʻe ʻIlihune, Nā Poʻe Waiwai, Nā Aliʻi, Nā Kānaka, Nā Makaʻāinana[1]

Ronald Williams Jr.

Hoʻolauna—Introduction

During the early to mid-nineteenth century, in the center of the Pacific Ocean, far from the nearest continental land mass, a prescient and dedicated Native sovereign, with the assistance of a few dozen American Protestant missionaries and thousands of his loyal subjects, realized one of the most incredible educational achievements in the history of the world. Following the organized introduction of the written word in 1820, the Hawaiian Kingdom, under Mōʻī (King) Kauikeaouli (Kamehameha III), transformed from a wholly oral society to a near-fully literate one in the matter of a few decades—in the process, becoming of the most literate nations on earth.[2] A master narrative, founded on non-Native sources and centered on foreign action, has posited the idea that this extraordinary achievement was due to the efforts of American Protestant missionaries who delivered literacy to Hawaiʻi's shores. While significant credit is certainly due those few dozen committed foreign agents, the bold proclamations of a near-deific Kanaka ʻŌiwi (Native Hawaiian) ruler—" ʻO koʻu aupuni, he aupuni palapala koʻu" (Mine shall be a nation of literacy)[3]—coupled with the implementation of instruction by dozens of aliʻi (chiefs) and thousands of Kānaka ʻŌiwi across the pae ʻāina (archipelago), enabled this incredible feat. Throughout the reigns of Mōʻī Kauikeaouli and his successors to the throne, the project of a broad and inclusive education for all the nation's subjects took a central role in domestic affairs.[4]

One of the great ironies within the current master narrative regarding the history of the Hawaiian Islands and its people is the blatant discrepancy between that narrative's characterization of the seizure of the Islands by the United States in 1898 as having delivered education and enlightenment to the Hawaiian people, and an actual primary-source record that reveals the near opposite. The source of this historical incongruity lies within the plan and actions of the minority, white oligarchy that dethroned the rightful sovereign of the Hawaiian constitutional monarchy in 1893.

A plan to hand over a stolen, independent nation to the United States of America faced a major obstacle. Organized and prolific calls by Kānaka ʻŌiwi for the American government to adhere to its foundational democratic principles directly challenged the idea of minority white rule in Hawaiʻi. Faced with demands for a vote of the people on the proposed annexation—a vote that all sides agreed would be handily defeated—the ruling oligarchy flailed about trying to avoid the question until they could no more. In late 1896, with Her Majesty Queen Liliʻuokalani having left the Islands to take the story of her nation directly to the American people, the Rev. Sereno Edwards Bishop, missionary's son and staunch advocate of annexation, penned a column for the *Washington Evening Star* titled "Hawaii for Us":

> This takes us back to the point first made, that the ʻpeople of Hawaiiʼ must be a party to the contract for annexation. Here is the very question to be settled. Who are the real people of Hawaii? Are they the decadent and dwindling race of aboriginal Hawaiians who still linger in the land, a feeble and inefficient people, pushed aside from active life by the swarming Asiatics and the vigorous whites? Or are they not rather the fresh, active, brainy white race, who have by their skill and energy created the great wealth and the thriving commerce of the islands, who own what they have thus created, and who are manifestly the heirs of the future of Hawaii, rather than the weak native race? Whites Must Govern. By reason of their superior capacity and force the whites of Hawaii have become the real people of Hawaii.[5]

In 1863, Rev. Rufus Anderson, the Boston-based architect of the American Protestant Mission, had written to Mōʻī Alexander Liholiho (Kamehameha IV) praising the Hawaiian Kingdom under Native rule as a "fully Christian nation" and declaring, "In no nation in Christendom is there greater security of person and property, or more civil or religious liberty."[6] Now, three decades later, the Sons of the Mission were reintroducing century-old tropes of Kanaka ʻŌiwi savagery, incompetence, and corruption, and claiming its Native subjects were undeserving of any say in their nation's future. While their racist arguments promoting white rule in the Hawaiian Islands did not succeed, and an 1897 treaty of annexation failed to get the necessary votes in the United States Congress, military needs amidst an ongoing war between the United States and the Philippines meant that the Islands were eventually seized by America in 1898. Over the next near-century, the story of Kanaka ʻŌiwi brilliance, passion, and love of both land and nation was covered in a deluge of misinformation that rewrote the history of Hawaiʻi and its people.

Current-day historians, exploring both the English-language record and a massive and mostly untapped archive of Native-language primary sources, have accumulated a plethora of evidence that leaves no doubt that the nineteenth-century Hawaiian Kingdom under Native rule was one of the most literate and progressive nations on earth. Yet, after a century of American rule in the Islands, its Native people head lists of houselessness, impoverishment, and unequal education.

Education in the Hawaiian Islands did not, of course, begin with literacy and foreign structures of institutional education. A millennium-old system of learning that included focused training in fields mastered by generations was used to teach young haumāna who continued on this path long after becoming kāhuna (experts). Kānaka ʻŌiwi of ka wā ʻŌiwi Wale[7] (the Native-only Era) were trained in the fields of medicine, astronomy, math, geography, architecture, oceanography, carving and woodworking, literature, history, religion, oration, political science, law, and many more. The arrival of foreign methods and tools of education brought changes that can be argued as both beneficial and detrimental. What is beyond debate is that once a decision was made to engage with this new tool/technology, Kānaka ʻŌiwi mastered it.

The story of institutional education under the Hawaiian Kingdom—1840–1893—is complex, with threads of colonialism, patriarchy, and racism certainly present, but what is also clear is that Kānaka ʻŌiwi heeded the call of their Mōʻī to master and claimed this new tool of literacy and foreign education, and in doing so, enabled a nation of proud, engaged subjects to have their voices heard amidst a rapidly changing world and in ways that we are just now coming to hear and understand more fully.

This work is not a general history of education in Hawaiʻi—its aims are much more humble. More qualified scholars such as Maenette Benham, Jennifer Noelani Goodyear-Kaopua, and Umi Perkins have done significant work along those broader lines and in more focused portions of this piece. While this investigation will provide a moʻokūʻauhau (genealogy) of the structure of institutional education in the Hawaiian Kingdom, its relatively brief explorations of political, social, and legal themes will have a particular focus on "West Maui."[8] While it leaves many questions unanswered, it does offer significant new understandings of its own and provides a foundation from which remaining questions can be approached.

He Moʻokūʻauhau—A Genealogy of Educational Administration in the Hawaiian Kingdom

Prior to the 8 October 1840 creation of a constitutional monarchy in Hawaiʻi— with its codification and institutionalization of education—the acquisition of literacy was controlled by Mōʻī Kauikeaouli and ancillary Aliʻi Nui. American Protestant missionaries arriving in 1820 began, as prescribed, instructing the ruling Mōʻī and Aliʻi Nui. What happened next was fairly unique. Well aware of the power afforded those who possessed this new technology, Mōʻī Kauikeaouli eschewed a class-based monopoly on literacy and declared that it would be given to all those under his reign—ka poʻe ʻilihune (the poor) as well as ka poʻe waiwai (the rich). A later government report on education in Hawaiʻi explained, "Between the years of 1823 and 1827 a peculiar system of schools sprang up, which spread rapidly over the islands to the remotest villages."[9] By 1824, most of the Aliʻi Nui were not only supporting schools in their lands by sending out the Alo Aliʻi (court members) who had mastered literacy to teach, but they were also actively urging their people to attend classes and to "learn the pīʻāpā, or alphabet, for reading and writing."[10] The eagerness of the people to acquire the novel arts of reading and writing was intense, and almost the whole population of both sexes and all ages went to school."[11]

On 6 May 1825, Her Britannic Majesty's ship *Blonde* arrived in Honolulu with the bodies of Mōʻī Liholiho [Kamehameha II] and Mōʻīwahine Kamāmalu, revealing the passing of the ruling monarch. The young Kauikeaouli stepped into the role of mōʻī as Kamehameha III.[12] In a June 1863 speech offered at Lahainaluna School in 1868, T. Puuohau quoted a line from one of the new sovereign's first public pronouncements, "E naʻLii a me na Makaainana, e hoolohe mai oukou o koʻu manao. O koʻu Aupuni, he Aupuni Palapala."[13] (O chiefs and commoners, listen to my thoughts. Mine is a nation of learning.) The new Sovereign continued:

> He mea pono ia kakou e hooikaika me ke ao palapala. E hooikaika hoi oukou e na kumu i ke ao i na haumana. O koʻu makemake nui, e ike pono

ka poe ilihune, ka poe waiwai, na'Lii, na kanaka, na makaainana a me na kamalii a pau loa o ko kakou aupuni i ka ike a me ka heluhelu i ka olelo a ke Akua.[14]

> *It is right that we strive hard to learn letters. Those of you who are teachers, be faithful in teaching your pupils. It is my great desire that the poor, the rich, the chiefs, the men, the commoners, and all the children of our nation acquire knowledge and read the word of God.*

Powerful Aliʻi Nui such as Kalakua Kaheiheimālie—also known as Hoapili Wahine—were important advocates of this new learning. Kalakua, grandmother to nā Kamaliʻikāne (Princes) Alexander Liholiho and Lota Kapuāiwa—both who would later become sovereigns of the Hawaiian Kingdom—organized a school in Lahaina for the older female kaukualiʻi (class of chiefs of lesser rank than the high chief) and other influential people of the area.[15] There "ma ka hale pohaku o Wainee mawaho o ka lanai" (at the stone house of Wainéʻe [Church] outside on the lānai), the group read the bible and transcribed ecclesiastic lessons. In more evidence of the growing egalitarian nature of the spread of literacy, Kalakua also conducted similar women's meetings among the makaʻāinana (commoners) of nearby Kāʻanapali and Olowalu.[16]

In 1831, the American Protestant Mission founded a school in upper Lahaina under the name Lahainaluna Seminary with the mission of training chosen haumāna Kānaka ʻŌiwi to be leaders of their lāhui in the fields of teaching and religious ministry. Haumāna from throughout the nation were recommended by local officials, and those accepted boarded at the West Maui institution. The nation's first newspaper, the Hawaiian-language *Ka Lama* (The Torch), was published at the school beginning in February 1834, and its first written history, *Ka Moolelo Hawaii*—authored by select haumāna of the school and edited by one of the kumu—was published in 1838. The school quickly became thought of by the mission as the pinnacle of institutional education in Hawaiʻi.

In July 1840, in a move to formerly codify the education and training of the Keiki Aliʻi (Chief's Children), Mōʻī Kauikeaouli and Kuhina Nui Kekāuluohi signed into law "He Mau Kanawai No Ka Hale Kula No Na Keiki Alii (Laws for the Chiefs' Childrens' School).[17] Founded in 1839 near the royal palace, the school held the lofty kuleana (responsibility/privilege) of grooming the next generation of the highest-ranking chief's children that would govern the Hawaiian Kingdom as it moved through a quickly transforming future. Amos Starr Cooke and his wife, Juliette Montague Cook—recent arrivals as part of

the eighth company of missionaries from the American Protestant Mission—
were chosen to operate the school and teach the initial sixteen royal children.
The King's trusted advisor, Ioane Papa ʻĪʻī, was appointed kahu, or guardian
of the pupils.

EDUCATION UNDER A CONSTITUTIONAL MONARCHY, 1840–1893

On 8 Okakopa 1840, Mōʻī Kauikeaouli, along with His Kuhina Nui, Kekāuluohi, signed Ke Kumukānāwai o Ko Hawaiʻi Pae ʻĀina (The Constitution
of the Hawaiian Islands), transforming Hawaiʻi's former absolute monarchy
into a constitutional one. With the framework of a new government in place,
Mōʻī Kauikeaouli and his ʻAha Kūkākūkā Malu (Privy Council) established the
ʻOihana Aʻo Palapala (Department of Instruction/Education) to engage the
project of universal education in the Islands. Ka ʻOihana Aʻo Palapala was to
be led by a Superintendent of the Whole, later titled Minister of Public Education. On 15 October 1840, one week after enacting Hawaiʻi's first constitution,
the two signed "Kanawai Hooponopono Kula" (A Statute for the Regulation of
Schools).[18] The law opened by setting the context for the project: "O ka naauao,
a me ka ike, oia ke kumu e pono ai ke aupuni. Aole e malu maikai ka aina, aole
hoi e kuapapanui, ke ao ole ia na kanaka ma ka palapala, a me na mea e pono
ai."[19] (The basis on which the kingdom rests is wisdom and knowledge. Peace
and tranquility cannot well prevail in the land, unless the people are taught in
letters, and in that which constitutes prosperity.) This foundational education
law placed much of the kuleana of school formation and operation with the
parents.

> 1. Ina e noho ana kekahi poe kanaka mea keiki, ua umikumamalima keiki
> a keu aku paha, he poe keiki pono ke hele i ke kula, a ua noho lakou ma
> kahi kokoke, ma ke kulanakauhale hookahi paha, a i ole ia, ma ke ahupuaa
> hookahi paha, pono ia lakou e imi i kumu kula no lakou. Penei hoi lakou
> e hanaʻi. E akoakoa na makuakane o lakou, a e koho i mau, mea ekolu o
> lakou, i lunakula no ia wahi. Ina uuku iho na kamaliʻi o kekahi kulanakau-
> hale i ka umikumamalima, alaila, e hui ko lakou poe makua, me kekahi
> poe a ae e kokoke ana.[20]
>
> *1. Whenever there is any number of parents having fifteen or more children
> of suitable age to attend school, if they live near each other, in the same village,
> or in the same township, it shall be their duty to procure themselves a teacher,
> which they shall do in the following manner. The tax officer shall give notice by*

a crier of the time and place at which all the male parents of the township, district or village shall meet, and they shall choose three of their number as a school committee for that place. If the number of children in any village be less than fifteen, then their fathers shall unite with another company nearby.

2. Alaila, e hele kela poe luna i kekahi kumu misionari kokoke, a e imi pu lakou i kumu kula no ia wahi. Ina uuku na kamalii, hookahi na kumu, ina mahuahua na kamalii elua no kumu, a i nui loa na keiki, ekolu kumu a keu aku paha, aia no ia lakou, e like me ko lakou manao like ana.

2. Said school committee shall then apply to the general school agent, spoken of below, and they together shall look out a teacher for that place. If there are but few children, then there shall be but one teacher, if more, then two teachers, and if the children are very numerous, then there shall be three or more teachers as they shall think best.

3. A loaa ke kumu, alaila, e olelo pu lakou i ka uku, o ka misionari o ia wahi, o ke kumu, a me na lunakula, a holo ka olelo no ka uku, alaila, aia no i na lunakula ka auhau aku i na kanaka e like me ko lakou ike ana he mea e pono ai ke kumu, a o na kumu paha o ia wahi. Penei hoi e hana'i na lunakula. E huli lakou a pauku aina kaawale, aole i mahiia, a e hele lakou i ke konohiki o ia wahi, a hoike aku ia ia, alaila, e lilo ia wahi i ke alii, i mea e pono ai ke kumukula.

3. When the teacher is obtained, then the general agent, the teacher and the school committee shall agree as to the wages. If the teacher have no land and they shall agree in the opinion that it is important that he should have some, then the general school agent shall endeavor to secure some which is not occupied, and that land shall be given to the teacher, but not in perpetuity.[21]

The school law also prescribed kuleana to the haumāna, declaring, "O na keiki kane maloko o ke kula, o lakou kekahi e hana i ka hana a ke kumu, eono hora i ka hebedoma hookahi." (It shall be the duty of the children[22] to be generous to their teacher, and aid him by working his land, according as they shall agree, or according to their good will.) The law offered further rewards to those who committed to teaching school, such as freedom from all public labor for the chiefs and land agents, and that neither they nor their spouses had to pay any poll tax while they were employed as school teachers. A relatively organized system from the start, the law made clear, "Aole nae i kapaia kekahi i kumu ma keia kanawai, ke loaa ole ia ia ka palapala kumu (no person is by this law considered a teacher unless he have a teacher's certificate from the general school agent.)[23] The law allowed for discretion in teacher pay, declaring, "O ke kumu akamai loa a ikaika loa ka hana ana a nui kana poe haumana, pono e uku nui ia oia. A o ka mea i emi mai kona akamai, a me ka ikaika o kana hana ana, e emi pu no me kona uku." (A very wise teacher who is exceedingly laborious in his business and has many pupils should be paid a high price, while he who is less wise and less laborious in his business should be paid a lower price.) Existing schools incorporated the new mandates outlined in the initial law, and new schools were created around them.

Seven months later, on 21 May 1841, an extension of the school law, under the same title, expanded on the first law with five new sections.[24] These latest additions to Hawaiian Kingdom education made clear to everyone the seriousness with which Mōʻī Kauikeaouli took his 1825 proclamation. Of particular note, pauku 16 of the law mandated, "O na kanaka a pau i hanau, mai ke kau ia Liholiho mai, ina aole lakou ike i ka heluhelu, a me ke kakau lima a me ka palapala aina, a me ka helu, aole lakou e noho i kiaaina, aole luna i kanawai, aole i lunaauhau, aole noho konohiki, aole hoi noho i luna maluna o kekahi kanaka."[25] (No man born since the commencement of the reign of Liholiho [1819], who does not understand reading, writing, geography, and arithmetic shall hold the office of governor, judge, tax officer, nor land agent, nor hold any office over another man. [. . .]) In a final appplication of tremendous pressure to induce the plan, the 1841 law then declared, "A o ke kane ike ole i ka heluhelu, a me ke kakau lima, aole ia e mare i wahine a pela no hoi ka wahine i ike ole i ka heluhelu, a me ke kakau lima aole ia e mare i kane."[26] (nor shall a man who is unable to read and write marry a wife, nor a woman who is unable to read and write marry a husband.) A subject of the Hawaiian Kingdom who was illiterate, by law would not be granted a license of marriage.

Mōʻī Kauikeaouli took a direct interest in the process of educating the nation, keeping a keen eye on the progress of schools. A strongly supportive Hawaiian Kingdom legislature passed an additional school law that was signed on 13 May 1842. The new law explained, "In the estimation of the Nobles and Representative Body, schools for the instruction of children in letters are of vast importance. We are firmly determined to give protection to the schools, and also to treat with great severity all those who oppose schools or throw hindrances in the way of that business."[27] Looking to address specific issues, they then explained, "One great evil of the past year has been that the teachers have not been properly paid." The members of the legislature reminded all that it was the "duty of the Parents to aid in supporting the teacher in such a manner as shall be mutually agreeable," explaining, "It is important that parents should have so much sincere regard to the welfare of their children as to influence them to attend to instruction."[28] Haumāna did not escape criticism in this early assessment, with the statute declaring that "a school is of little value if the scholars are disorderly."[29]

THE ORGANIC ACTS OF 1845–1847

The creation of a constitutional monarchy in 1840 was a deeply transformational first step towards the codification of governance in Hawai'i. Soon after, the task of creating more definitive assignments of kuleana within this nascent constitutional monarchy was addressed. John Ricord, an Englishman and legal advisor to Mō'ī Kauikeaouli who had been named Attorney General of the Kingdom, took on the task. On 21 May 1845, Ricord read a draft of organization to the King and the Hawaiian Kingdom Legislature. The legislature responded by passing a resolution on 24 June 1845 officially assigning the Attorney General with the task. Kauikeaouli and Kekāuluohi signed it the same day. Over the course of the following two years, three organic acts were passed: *First Act of Kamehameha III to Organize the Executive Ministries,* the *Second Act of Kamehameha III to Organize the Executive Departments,* and the *Third Act of Kamehameha III to Organize the Judiciary Department.*[30]

The first of the organic acts, passed on 29 October 1845, created five positions of kuhina (minister) over various aspects of the executive branch with the mō'ī appointing those kuhina. Among the five was a Kuhina no ke A'o Palapala (Minister of Public Instruction.) The Kuhina no ke A'o Palapala was charged with the lofty kuleana of superintending "the moral and intellectual well being of all who reside within the jurisdiction of this kingdom, and in an especial manner of all children within the age of legal majority."[31] In 1855 the office of Minister of Education was replaced by a Board of Education whose members, including its president, were appointed by the mō'ī. The Board administered the educational system through local school agents, who, in 1855, were stationed in 24 school districts throughout Ko Hawai'i Pae 'Āina. School agents held kuleana to hire, pay, transfer, and evaluate kumu as well as build facilities, maintain school grounds, and provide regular reports and correspondence.

He Mau Kanawai Hou no na Kula (New Laws Concerning the schools) were passed and signed into law in 1849.[32] Paukū (Section) 1 of the new law addressed concerns about having enough lands set aside for the increasing number of schools and keeping those lands under the department's control. It declared, "O na kahua hale pule a me na kahuahale kula e noho nei, i pili ole i kekahi kanaka, no ke Aupuni no ia." (All sites for School Houses and Houses of Public Worship, not owned by private parties, now occupied and in use, shall be reserved as Government property).[33] Paukū ʻekolu (three)—offering another display of the Kingdom government's serious commitment to not only offering but requiring universal education—took an aggressive step towards addressing the issue of school truancy, declaring: "Na na Lunakanawai apana a pau, ke koiia mai lakou e na makua, e na kumu, a me na Lunakula paha, e kena i na makaie hopu i na keiki hele ole i ke kula i ka wa pono, a e lawe ia lakou i ko lakou hale kula, e hoopaiia malaila e ke Kumu e like me ke kanawai."[34] (All district justices, when applied to by the parents, teachers, or school trustees, are authorized to have truant children arrested, and taken to their respective schools, there to be punished by the teachers according to law.)

The most recent school law ordered the testing of "ka hana maoli oluolu" (a mild system of manual labor) in public schools, to be followed up by a report of the Kuhina no ke Aʻo Palapala. It also created more accounting for tax revenues set aside for education by offering more specific assignments for the gathering, handling, and spending of education funds. The final paukū of the law posited education as one way to treat vagrancy and criminality among young people. It empowered the island governors to "e haawi ma ka palapala hoohiki i na keikikane a me na kaikamahine aia wale, a me ke kolohe maoli, I hoopaiia e ka Luna kanawai, i kekahi kanaka ano pono, nana e ao ia lakou i ka palapala a me ka pono a me kekahi hana maikai" (bind out, under proper indentures, vagrants and vicious young people convicted of crime, to persons of good character, who shall teach them the rudiments of knowledge, guard their morals, and teach them trades or other useful employments).[35]

SIGNIFICANT LEGAL ADDITIONS/ALTERATIONS TO HAWAIIAN KINGDOM EDUCATION LAW, 1850–1893

1851 He Kanawai e Naauao ai Na Keiki a Na Haole, a me Na Mamo o Na Haole ma Honolulu nei, a me Na Wahi e ae ma keia Aupuni[36]
(An Act to Provide for the Education of the Children of Foreigners, and Those of Foreign Extraction in the City of Honolulu, and Other Places in the Kingdom)[37]

1854 He Kanawai e Hooulu ai e Kokua i Na Kula Beretania no Ko Hawaii Poe Opiopio[38]
(An Act for the Encouragement and Support of English Schools for Hawaiian Youth)[39]

1855 He Kanawai e Hoololi ae i ka Oihana Aopalapala[40]
(An Act to Remodel the Department of Instruction)[41]

1859 No ke Auhau Kula[42]
(The School Tax)[43]

1860 E kukulu i mau kula Ohana no na kaikamahine Hawai'i[44]
(Establishing family schools for the domestic training of Hawaiian girls)[45]

1862 He Kanawai no ka Hookaawale ana i na Keiki Kane a me na Kaikamahine iloko o na Kula Kumu Mua o ke Aupuni[46]
(An Act to Provide for the Separation of the Sexes in the Government Schools)[47]

1865 He Kanawai e Hoopau ai ka Mokuna 10 o ke Kanawai Kivila, a e Hooponopono ai ka Oihana Aopalapala o ke Aupuni[48]
(An Act to Repeal Chapter 10 of the Civil Code, and to Regulate the Bureau of Public Instruction)[49]

1874 He Kanawai e Kokua ai i ka Oihana Mahiai me ka Hanalima ma na Kula Aupuni o ka Pae Aina[50]
(An Act to Promote Agriculture and Industrial Pursuits in the Public Schools of the Kingdom)[51]

1880 Hoonauao ana o na opio Hawaii ma na Aina e, aole e Hooliloia no ka makaikai, aka, no ka Hoonaauao io ia[52]
(Education of Hawaiian Youths Abroad)[53]

1882 He Kanawai E Hooi ai i ka Maluhia o na Kula Hanai Kaikamahine[54]
(An Act to Provide More Efficient Protection of Female Boarding Schools)[55]

1892 He Kanawai e Pili Ana I ka O Lima[56]
(An Act Relating to Vaccination)[57]

Maui Komohana—West Maui

'Āpana 'Elua (District 2) of the Hawaiian Kingdom school system mimicked the tax division set out for the same area and stretched from Ukumehame at the south end to Kahakuloa at the north. An organized Department of Education kept quarterly reports that documented kula (schools), kumu, and haumāna. A look at "He Papa Hoike no na Kula Aupuni o ka Apana Elua Mokupuni o Maui No ka Hapaha o ka Makahiki 1863 ka la 1 o Aperila a hiki i ka la 1 o Julai" (Schedule concerning the government schools of the Second District Island of Maui for the quarter of the year 1863 April 1 until July 1) reveals that 'āpana 'elua was populated with twelve government schools at that time, and that all twelve were staffed by kumu Kānaka 'Ōiwi (Native Hawaiian teachers).

Na Kula Aupuni o Maui Komohana—July 1863

1. Kula Puehuehu—*Kahulanui*
2. Kula Waiokama—*Makekau*
3. Kula Puou—*Kapule ame Kalua*
4. Kula Puunoa—*Napeha*
5. Kula Papalaua—*Haro*
6. Lahaina Select School—*Kahaulelio*
7. Kula Olowalu—*Kawelo ame Nawahine*
8. Hakuole—*Kauaula*
9. Kula Honokowai—*Kauhi ame J. H. Moku*
10. Kula Honolua—*Nahaku*
11. Kula Honokohau—*Wahinehookae ame Luahine*
12. Kula Kahakuloa—*Kuamoo ame Hale*

These seventeen kumu Kānaka ʻŌiwi taught 497 haumāna—272 keiki kane and 225 kaikamahine—across these twelve West Maui schools.

LAHAINALUNA

The west Maui seaside town of Lahaina served as the capital of the Hawaiian Kingdom until 1850[58]; the site of the creation of the nation's first constitution[59]; and in the early years of institutionalized education, the site of the American Mission's most elite educational endeavor, Lahainaluna Seminary.[60] Aliʻi Nui Kalakua Kaheiheimālie was a strong supporter of the Mission, and as the project of national literacy was expanding in the early 1820s, this powerful and politically astute Aliʻi Wahine offered land mauka of ka Malu Ulu o Lele—an ancient name for Lahaina—for a select mission school to be built.[61] The "School on the Hill" opened on 25 September 1831 under the leadership of Rev. Lorrin Andrews. Five years later, in 1836, the Mission school began to take on boarders, welcoming haumāna from East Maui and the other islands throughout Ko Hawaiʻi Pae ʻĀina (The Hawaiian Archipelago). Perhaps the most well-known of the early haumāna of this important site was Davida Malo.

Born in Keauhou, Hawaiʻi Island, Davida Malo would serve in a plethora of different positions of import over his nearly sixty-year life. This intellectual, educator, writer, counselor to and confidant of the highest aliʻi, elected politician, and ordained minister arrived at the newly founded Mission school already equipped with a deep and broad knowledge of Hawaiian history, culture, religion, law, and politics. In locating Malo's place among his community, Kanaka ʻŌiwi Historian Noelani Arista explains, "Malo was trained aurally and orally, through a disciplined pedagogy of listening, retaining, and repetition. Experts (kāhuna) and elders (kūpuna) trained oral intellects like Malo from the age of four or five to practice and hone listening, reiterated speech, and memory."[62] She continues, "The world in which Malo was raised and trained held the authoritative speech of akua (gods), 'aumākua (gods belonging to certain lineages), ali'i (chiefs), kahuna (chiefly experts or experts in other fields of knowledge), and Kaula (seers), as indices of ancestral knowledge." Combining this foundation training with a newly mastered literacy and understanding of communication outside his own transformed Malo into a critical communicator of wisdoms both past and present to a transforming Hawai'i. Malo and others were not the "naked and chattering savages" described by some, but rather engaged, often brilliant, knowledgeable people who had chosen to be students of the new way.

Lahainaluna Structure and Purpose

The Mission launched their grand experiment unsure of how it would go, but as the inaugural class headed towards completion of their studies, the general assessment was that the young men had outperformed expectations. In June 1835, the Mission set down in writing their continuing mission, with its rules and policies, in a pamphlet titled, *He Mau Kanawai no ke Kulanui o Hawaii Nei, I Kauia e ka Poe Misionari, June 1835.*[63] The opening page offered a preamble:

Manaomua.

No ka lokomaikai mai o ke Akua, ua maopopo ka hiki pono o ke Kulanui o Hawaii nei I hoomakaia e ka poe misionari, i ka makahiki 1831, a no ka loaa ana o kekahi pono malaila e like me ka mea i manaoia mamua; a no ka mau ana o ka pono ma ia Kulanui: nolaila, ke hoikemai nei ka poe Kahu [o ua kula nei] i kekahi mau ano hou e pono ai, i akaka ai ka hana, a i mahuahua ai no hoi. No ka hana ana mamua, ua manaoia, ua hiki paha, a he mea hoi ia e pono nui ai ka noho ana o ko Hawaii nei poe kanaka, a me ka naauao, a me ka noho pono ana o ke kino, a me ka uhane.[64]

Preamble.

Whereas, in the good Providence of God, the experiement of High School established by the Mission in 1831, having proved successful and having accomplished all that could reasonably have been expected, and the neccessity of such an institution still continuing, the Directors now lay before the Mission a more definite and enlarged plan of operations such as they suppose from actual experiment to be practicable and of the highest interest to the moral social literary and spiritual condition of this people.[65]

The foundational purpose of the school for the Mission was stated in Mokuna (Section) 1: "oia keia o ana mai, a e hoomau hoi i ka pule oiaio a ko kakou Haku a Iesu Kristo...." (to introduce and perpetuate the religion of our Lord and Savior Jesus Christ....)[66] The thoughts that followed clarified a troubling dismissal of the aforementioned ʻike (wisdom/knowledge) brought to the new experiment by Kānaka ʻŌiwi by declaring that the institution's further purpose was, "ke hoalaʼe i ka manao o na kanaka, i pau ka naaupo a me ka noho hemahema ana, a e hoolilo ia lakou i poe noonoo, a i poe ike, a me ka hana maikai"[67] (to elevate the whole mass of the people from their present ignorance and degradation, and cause them to become a thinking, enlightened and virtuous people).[68] The section then offered specifics: "Eia hoi kekahi mea nui; o kea o pono aku, a ike loa, kekahi poe kumu ao kula, i akamai lakou ma ia hana."[69] (A more definite object of the High School is to train up and qualify teachers for their respective duties.) Also, "kekahi mea i oi aku" (another object still more definite and of equal or greater importance) was to train Kānaka ʻŌiwi to be ordained ministers of the gospel and "e kokua aku no hoi ma ka hai ana aku i ka olelo maikai a Iesu Kristo...."[70] (fellow laborers with us in disseminating the gospel of Jesus Christ....).[71]

Governance of the school was to be local with a seven-member Board of Directors comprising candidates from Maui and Molokaʻi. Kumu hired for the school were expected to be involved in all aspects of their students' lives with school laws declaring, "9. Na na kumu pakahi hoi e hele e nana i kela hale keia hale o na haumana, elua hebedoma, hookahi ia hele ana, i ka wa e kula ai wale no keia hana a na na Kumu e hooikaika i na haumana ma ka noho pono ana, ma ka maemae o ka hale, a e hooikaika hoi ma na mea e pono ai ka uhane." (It shall be the duty of all the Instructors to visit in rotation each of the houses of the scholars, at least once in two weeks during term time, to encourage improvement in domestic habits and character, and promote the spiritual welfare of the scholars as occassion may offer.)[72] Prospective students—between the ages of 12 and 25—were tested in reading, writing, mental arithmetic, and topographical geography. A total of fifty haumāna were to make up a class: from Hawaiʻi Island, 18; from Maui, 14; from Oʻahu 10 and from Kauai, 8.

Scholars accepted to the school were expected to read the students' pledge before an assembly of the entire school: "No koʻu makemake i ka ike a me ka naauao a me ka maikai o ia mau mea, nolaila, i hele mai nei au me ka manao e komo iloko o keia kula. Ke hai aku nei au i koʻu manao e malama loa i ke kanawai o ke kula. E hoikaika no au e ao i na mea a pau a na kumu e olelo mai ai."[73] (On account of my desire for knowledge and instruction and its benefits, therefore it is my wish to enter this school. I declare it to be my intention to obey the laws of the school. I will be diligent in my attention to all the instruction of the teachers.) Every scholar wore a uniform suit, and each received a copy of *He Mau Kanawai no ke Kulanui o Hawaii Nei.* Tuition was set at ten dollars a year, but could be paid in labor in support of the school.

Section 7 of the school laws described "Na Mea E Aoia (The Studies of the School)" with a regular course of study expected to be a full term of four years.

MAKAHIKI KAHI. O ka Helu, o ke Anahonua me ka Anahuina, o ka Hoikehonua no ka Palapala Hemolele o ka Piliolelo Hawaii, na olelo Kahiki i kekahi poe.

MAKAHIKI LUA. O ka Helu no, o ka Heluhua, o ka Holomoku, o ka Anaaina, o ka Mooolelo, na olelo Kahiki i kekahi papa.

MAKAHIKI KOLU. O ka Helu no, o ke Akeakamai, o ke Akeakamai kanaka, na olelo Kahiki i kekahi poe.

MAKAHIKI HA. O ke Aohoku, o ke Akeakamai kanaka, o ka Mooolelo no ka Ekalesia, na olelo Kahiki i kekahi poe.[74]

FIRST YEAR. Arithmetic, Geometry and Trigonometry, Sacred Geography, Hawaiian Grammar, Languages for a select class.

SECOND YEAR. Mathematics, embracing Algebra, Navigation and Surveying, History, Languages for a select class.

THIRD YEAR. Mathematics continued, Natural Philosophy, Moral Philosophy, Languages, for a select class.

FOURTH YEAR. Astronomy, Chemistry, Moral Philospohy continued, Church history, Languages, as above.[75]

The level of study at the school was elevated with the haumāna mastering high-level mathematics and English. In the preserved essay below, the 16-year-old haumāna Kanaka ʻŌiwi, Richard Pelekai of Waikapū, Maui, diagrams a sentence, using his second language [ʻŌlelo Haole]:

English
Richard Pelekai, age 16 yrs.   Lahainaluna Seminary
Born Waikapu.   January 21, 1889.
    As Egypt is annually overflowed by the Nile, it is a very rich country.

Analysis.—This is a complex declarative sentence, intransitive. The principal clause is "it is a very rich country" and the dependent clause is "Egypt is annually overflowed by the Nile." As is the connective.

The subject of the principal clause is it, unmodified. The predicate is "is a very rich country," is is the predicate verb and country is the predicate nominative, and country is modified by the indefinite adjective a and the adjective rich, and rich is modified by the adverb very.

Of the dependent clause Egypt is the subject, unmodified. Is overflowed is the predicate, transitive passive verb and modified (1) by the adverb annually, (2) by the simple prepositional phrase by the Nile, of which Nile is the principal part modified by the definite adjective the.

Lahainaluna Student Essay of Richard Pelekai, age 16, of Waikapū, page 1 of 2. Series 320 Volume 1, Student Papers, Lahainaluna, Hawai'i State Archives.

Parsing. <u>As</u> is a connective, and connects the two clauses "Egypt is annually overflowed by the Nile" and "it is a very rich country," according to Rule XI., which says, "Conjunctions connect words, phrases, or prepositions."

<u>Egypt</u> is a proper noun, neuter gender, third person, singular number, nominative case to the verb <u>is overflowed</u>, according to Rule I., which says, "The subject of a verb is in the nominative case."

<u>Is overflowed</u> is regular transitive verb, indicative mode, third person, singular number, and agrees with its subject <u>Egypt</u>, according to Rule II., which says, "A verb agrees with its subject in person and number."

<u>Annually</u> is an adverb and modifies the verb <u>is overflowed</u> according to

Lahainaluna Student Essay of Richard Pelekai, age 16, of Waikapū, page 2 of 2. Series 320 Volume 1, Student Papers, Lahainaluna, Hawai'i State Archives.

rule VIII., which says, "An adverb modifies a verb, an adjective, or another adverb."

<u>By</u> is a preposition and connects the noun Nile with the verb <u>is over-flowed</u>, according to Rule X., which says, "A preposition joins a noun or pronoun to some other word."

<u>The</u> is a definite adjective and limits the noun <u>Nile</u>, according to rule III., which says, "Adjectives and participles modify nouns or pronouns."

<u>Nile</u> is a proper noun, neuter gender, third person, singular number, objective case after the preposition <u>by</u> according to Rule X., which says, "A noun or pronoun depending on a preposition is in the objective case."

<u>It</u> is a simple person pronoun, neuter gender, third person, singular number, nominative case to the verb <u>is</u>, according to rule I., which says, "The subject of a verb is in the nominative case."

<u>Is</u> is an irregular intransitive verb, indicative mode, third person, singular number and agrees with its subject <u>it</u>, according to Rule II., which says, "A verb agrees with its subject in operson and number."

<u>A</u> is an indefinite adjective and limits the noun <u>country</u>, according to rule III., which says, Adjectives and participles modify nouns or pronouns.

<u>Very</u> is an adverb and modifies the adjective <u>rich</u>, according to rule VIII., which says, "An adverb modifies a verb, an adjective, or another adverb."

<u>Rich</u> is an adjective and limits the noun <u>country</u>, according to rule III., which says, "Adjectives and participles modify nouns or pronouns."

<u>Country</u> is a common noun, neuter gender, third person, singular number, nominative case after the intransitive verb is according to Rule VII., which says, "A noun or pronoun used as the complement of an intransitive or a passive verb is in the nominative case."[76]

In the work below, 16-year-old haumāna Kanaka ʻŌiwi, Joel Nakaleka, answers posed questions using his second language [ʻŌlelo Haole]:

Trigonometry and Surveying
Joel Nakaleka, age 16 yrs.   Lahainaluna Seminary
Senior Class   Jan. 25, 1889
    A straight line AB, at Lahaina, is 108.8 chs. [chains] long; the two angles between this line and the chuch L on Lanai are L AB = 96*.29′ and LBA = 75*.10′ What is the distance from Lahaina to Lanai church?
    From a station at Lahainaluna, the distance to the Mala church, Lahaina, is 116.9 chs. To the Wainee church. Lahaina, 124.4 chs. And the

angle subtended between the two churches is 44,* 48'. What is the distance between the two churches?

At each end of a straight line at Lahainaluna, 8.28 chs. Long, the angles between the line and the centre of Mt Ball are 49*. .26' and 127* . .31'. The angle of elevation to the top of Mt Ball is 15*. .4'. What is the height of Mt Ball?

A base line AB at Lahainaluna is 8.42 chs. Long. The angles between this line and the centre of the Pioneer Mill chimney at Lahaina are, at A 87* . .53', at B 87*. .26'. The angle of depression from Lahainaluna are, to the bottom of the chimney 4* . .46'; to the top of the chimney 3*. .56'. What is the height of the chimney?[77]

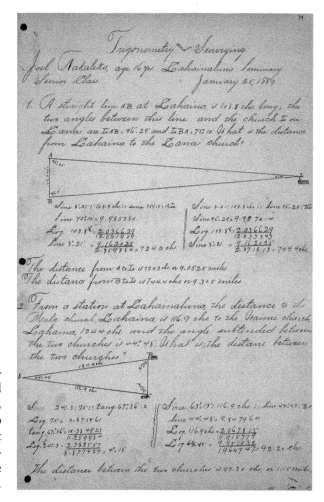

Lahainaluna Arithmetic Paper of Joel Nakaleka, age 16, page 1 of 2. Series 320 Volume 1, Student Papers, Lahainaluna, Hawai'i State Archives.

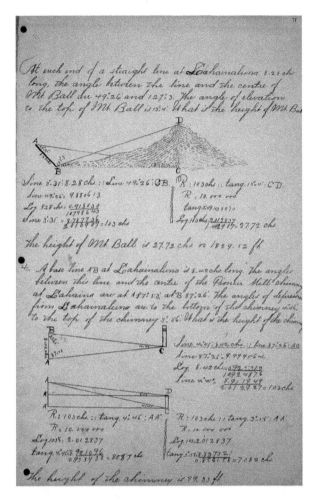

Lahainaluna Arithmetic Paper of Joel Nakaleka, age 16, page 2 of 2. Series 320 Volume 1, Student Papers, Lahainaluna, Hawai'i State Archives.

Haumāna, who completed the course of study, recieved a diploma that read,

> Kaulanui, Lahaianluna
>
> Ua noho mai nei o _____ ma keia Kulanui i keia mau makahiki eha i hala iho nei, ua malama no oia i na Kanawai o ke Kula, ua ao no hoi oia i na mea i aoia'i ma ke Kula, a e hiki no ia ia ke ao aku ia hai, aole hoi i ikeia kona hewa, a ke hoi aku nei no ia me ke aloha ia mai e na Kumu.[78]
>
> *High School, Lahainaluna*
>
> *This letter certifies, That _____ has resided these four years past at the High School, has obeyed its Laws, attended to all branches*

taught, and is competent to instruct others. His moral character has not been impeached, and he leaves with the respect of the Teachers.[79]

KE KULA LUAʻEHU

The position of Lahainaluna Seminary as the premier instituion of learning for haumāna Kānaka ʻŌiwi did not go unchallenged. Neither did the related ongoing rise of the American Protestant mission's influence in the Islands. In 1859, Mōʻīwahine Emma Naʻea Rooke and her husband, Mōʻī Alexander Liholiho (Kamehameha IV), petitioned Queen Victoria of Great Britain to send a mission of the Church of England to the Hawaiian Islands. Following the organizing of such a mission in London by the Society for the Propagation of the Gospel in 1861, Rev. Thomas Nettleship Staley was ordained as the first bishop of the British "Hawaiian mission."[80] "A farewell service for the missionaries was celebrated in Westminster Abbey on 23 July 1862 and the party left England aboard the *Tasmanian* on 18 August. Bishop Staley, accompanied by Rev. G. Mason and Rev. E. Ibbotson, arrived in Honolulu on 11 Novmber. Rev. Mason wrote of the "unflagging zeal" of both of their Majesties for the promotion of the Anglican Church in the Islands, saying, "The King said to me, 'You must apply at once for a charter of incorporation, that you may be able to receive endowments of land for the Church by the Crown.'"[81] Queen Emma envisioned schools for Kānaka ʻŌiwi led by the royal church. Within weeks, the British party had indeed incorporated under Hawaiian Kingdom law—with Hawaiian Kingdom Kuhina Nui Mataio Kekūanaōʻa and future Sovereign, Kamaliʻikāne Kalākaua, as founding trustees—with the name "Synod of the Hawaiian Reformed Catholic Church," renamed in 1873 as the "Anglican Church in Hawaiʻi."[82]

This Royal contestation of the American Protestant mission in the Islands was made more evident when its first school, tasked with training up future Kanaka ʻŌiwi leaders of the Hawaiian Kingdom, opened in Lahaina. Ke Kula Luaʻehu was named for both the site of the construction of the nation's first constitution and the home of the akua moʻo, Kihawahine. The Anglican Mission leased a building near the shore formerly used by the U.S. consul as a hospital for seamen. The school, often referred to as "Lahainalalo College," was a "college for boys of superior classes."[83] In its second year of operation, Luaʻehu had 56 pupils, and a female boarding school, St. Cross, was opened and taught by Mrs. Mason.[84] The Mōʻī himself paid to erect the new school building, which Rev. Mason noted in a report home, saying, "The Government has spared no expense to foster the education of the people. [...]"[85] The current governor of Maui, Paul Nahaolelua, was appointed to a committee that governed the school. Speaking of the close support he and the English mission to Hawai'i received from the Hawaiian monarchy, Bishop Staley wrote, "Often were the King and Queen seen standing side by side at the font, to answer for the little ones whom they brought to receive Holy Baptism, and for whose proper training and instruction they made themselves responsible."[86] The project of Mō'ī Alexander Lihiliho and Mō'īwahine Emma in training future leaders of the Hawaiian Kingdom under British mission guidance at Ke Kula Lua'ehu in Lahaina and other Anglican schools increased the ties between these two constitutional monarchies to the detriment to the American relationship to the Hawaiian Crown. After obtaining a hand printing press in early 1868 and being trained in its use, the haumāna of Lua'ehu took up a project of printing a new anthem for the Hawaiian nation, written by Rev. Mason and modeled after the official national anthem of the United Kingdom. It was reproduced in the *Hawaiian Gazette* of 16 September 1868:

> God save our gracious King,
> Long may we see him reign;
> God save the King!
> Send him prosperity,
> And may no enemy
> O'erthrow his dynasty;
> God save the King!
> Thy choicest gifts in store,
> On him be pleased to pour;
> God save the King!
> May he defend our laws,
> And ever give us cause
> To sing with heart and voice
> God save the king![87]

GENDER, RACE, AND AGENCY
The Case of Maria Karua

The project of national, institutionalized education in the Hawaiian Kingdom was mandated, launched, and enabled by Kanaka 'Ōiwi leaders who recognized the significant power present in the technology of literacy. It succeeded because of the dedicated participation of Kanaka ʻŌiwi kumu, haumāna, and ʻohana throughout the nation who sought to add this new tool to a foundation of ʻāina-based ʻike founded upon more than a millennium of living in these Hawaiian Islands. This noted, agency is of course not a binary. Despite the fact that Kānaka ʻŌiwi were both central and majority agents within the system of institutional education in the Hawaiian Kingdom, critical points of power within the system were often held by non-Kānaka ʻŌiwi promoting sometimes different values. The evils of racism and sexism, prominent in American society of the era, appeared in the educational system of the Hawaiian Kingdom.

On 14 September 1888, a young Kanaka ʻŌiwi woman living in Pāʻia, Maui composed a letter, in English—a second language in which she had worked to become fluent—to the most powerful man within the Hawaiian Kingdom's educational system: President of the Board of Education, Mr. Charles Reed Bishop.[88] Miss Maria Karua, excited about the opportunity to help support her family by obtaining a government job, had recently attended the teacher certification examinations held in Lahaina, Maui. She reported her experience to the board president:

> Mr. C. R. Bishop,
> Dear sir:—Knowing you to be a friend to the natives I open my mind to you freely. It is a very important thing to me. I am a girl of good character and try to do what is right and nothing wrong. I went to Lahaina to stand the teachers examination conducted by Mr. Moore. The last day of examination which was 31 of August a Friday, Mr. Moore handed me a note saying thus:—"Maria Karua, if you want me to help you, you must do something good to please me, that is you must come down stairs in a little room I want to meet you there and you must not show this to any body; if you do you'll be sorry after."[89]

The young woman went on to explain that she "did not quite understand what he meant" and had therefore shown it to her friend Mrs. Noah, who had also come from Pāʻia to take the teacher exam and was sitting at the desk beside hers. Mrs. Noah clarified to Miss Karua the proposition made by Moore and added, "He ought not to write such things to you."[90] Karua explained to Bishop that Moore had noticed the two of them talking, hurried their work, and within a short period of time closed the examination. She explained further that on the way to the launch that was prepared to take her and the other outer district applicants home, Moore had approached her and asked why she had shown the note to others, saying, " 'Why didn't you do as I told you to? You'll be sorry for what you have done; you can't have any certificate or a place to teach.' " Maria continued, "I told him, 'I did not care,' though I am a poor girl and my father is very old."[91]

Miss Karua's lengthy correspondence continued, reporting what followed in the aftermath of the initial incident: "A few days after I arrived home from Lahaina he [Moore] came over to stay with Mr. C. H. Dickey at Haiku. Sunday morning, Sept. 9, he came to my house. I was not at home." Miss Karua reported that when she did return home, accompanied by Henry Long, the Captain of Police at Pāʻia, and his wife, they found Mr. Moore standing on her veranda. Moore announced that he had come to speak to Mr. Noah and his wife and inquired as to which house they lived in. Miss Karua pointed it out. Moore met with Mrs. Noah at her home and then had her call Miss Karua inside. The letter continued, "He said to me 'Now if you just do what I want you to, you'll get a good place to teach.' What he want me to do was so dirty and nasty that I am ashamed to write it on the paper. I told him I did not want a certificate or position from him. Mrs. Noah heard him said [*sic*] this to me." Miss Karua closed her missive to Bishop with apologies and a plea: "I am sorry I have to write but I felt it is my duty. I want to know if he can keep my certificate from me if I really earned it. I remain, your obedient servant, Maria Karua."[92]

The day after receiving the letter, Bishop wrote Dickey—school agent district and member of the Hawaiian Kingdom House of Representatives—enclosing Maria's letter and noting that it "troubles me very much."[93] Bishop included a copy of his reply to Miss Karua and explained,

> Mr. Damon and Mr. Atkinson are the only persons to whom I have shown the letter, which is only one side of the story. Trusting in your discretion and disposition to do what is right, I refer the young woman to you, wishing to get at the truth. Can it be that she has misunderstood Mr. Moore's note and what he said to her...? The note and what Mrs. Noah may have heard are important. Her statement is...and she appears to understand English so well that it seems truthful, and yet it seems hard to believe that Mr. Moore would be such an extreme fool as she makes him appear to be. If Miss Karua is honest and what she claims to be, she deserves protection and the consideration of the board and should have an appointment. I shall be anxious to hear from you.
>
> Yours truly Chas r Bishop
> P. S. Return Miss Karua's letter to me. CRB

Bishop then wrote to Miss Karua on the same day, explaining to her that in reviewing her examination, she had scored just below a full pass and saying, "If you are the kind of girl you claim to be, and that I hope you are, the Board of Education will be [able] to give you a school to teach and give you a provisional certificate." He encouraged her to continue to study "so that you may fit yourself to pass at a future date."[94] He asked why she hadn't sent him Mr. Moore's letter, and ended by explaining that he had asked Mr. Dickey to look into the matter: "Mr. C. H. Dickey is the Agent of the board of Education in your district and is worthy of your confidence. Go to him and tell him the whole truth of the matter...."[95] Maria answered the letter of President Bishop on 21 September, thanking him for his kindness and explaining that she had not kept the note and that the most vulgar of the talk came when he visited Pāʻia. "I will say, if you think I am telling you a lie, I am willing to stand before you and Mr. Moore to explain what he said to me and Mrs. Noah."[96]

The results of the investigation of C. H. Dickey backed up Maria's claims. Peter Noah reported that his wife had stated to him the same facts as reported to Bishop by Maria, and the young woman's pastor, Father James at Kūʻau, had strongly vouched for her integrity, saying he had always known her to be an honest and sincere young woman. Yet, Moore continued to swear that he was innocent of anything other than perhaps letting himself get too familiar in his speech and actions with Miss Karua and Mrs. Noah, which allowed him to get ensnared in this current trap. In early December, C. R. Bishop made the decision to appoint another investigator. In an official letter of 8 December 1888, President Bishop explained to the board secretary that the Rev. Sereno Edwards Bishop "has lately had a confidential conversation with Mr. John A. Moore at Lahainaluna" and instructed the secretary to "please place in Rev. Bishop's hands for perusal all correspondence relating thereto."[97] To any Kanaka ʻŌiwi familiar with the political machinations of the day at this time, the choice of agent could not have been more problematic.

The Rev. Bishop was an intensely polarizing figure whose public racism extended far beyond the bounds of most of the era. In the year prior to his appointment as investigator of the Karua case, he had taken over the editorship of the monthly mission publication *The Friend*. Under its previous and founding editor, the Rev. Samuel Chenery Damon, the publication offered shipping news, temperance advocation, and reports from the churches of the Hawaiian Mission/AEH around the islands—but no overtly polemic political advocation. Newspaper historian Helen Chapin has written, "Damon held independent, progressive views and editorialized for women's rights, a more humane whaling industry, and health services for Native Hawaiians."[98] Rev. Sereno Bishop took over editorship of the paper immediately following the July 1887 political coup that imposed the hated "Bayonet Constitution" on the nation. Rev. Bishop made clear his joy and commented, "The politics of the country are fast ranging themselves in Anglo-Saxon line...." and explained the recent events by saying that "the resistless tide of Anglo-Saxon principles of government suddenly overtopped the frail 'palace' dykes, and swept away all that retrograde rubbish."[99]

On 10 December 1888, only two days after C. R. Bishop's order to turn over all relative correspondence to Sereno Bishop and without talking to Miss Karua, the reverend submitted a five-page letter defending Mr. Moore, declaring he suspected no abuse had taken place, and viciously attacking Miss Karua and Mrs. Noah. Rev. Bishop opened his correspondence by saying that while he was not "sufficiently intimate" with Mr. Moore, "He has impressed me as a man of excellent aims and intentions and of much candor."[100] He dismissed the claim that Moore had propositioned Miss Karua near her home with Mr. Long and others in the vicinity, saying, "He is charged with addressing the [...] solicitation to her in her own house and close to her white protectors!" He also characterized the claim that Mr. Moore asked Maria to meet him in a room downstairs at the exam "absurd!" Rev. Bishop then moved to his central point, assuring President Bishop:

> I have had considerable private knowledge of the history of a large number of the best-trained and best-protected Hawaiian girls, as well as of the higher classes of native women in our schools and churches. I feel prepared to say that we cannot believe it probable that one in ten of them would repel such advances as Moore is charged with, under such peculiar advantages as he had for making them. If Mrs. Noah and Maria Kalua did as they say, they are a very rare pair of Hawaiian females. It is to be considered that neither of them would have lost much, or anything of respectability among their own people by yielding.[101]

Rev. Bishop closed by asking to make one final point. It would be one thing if he were newly applying for his important position as principal of the most important school, but "being now successful at work, the evident evils of his removal should forbid its being made, until positive evidence of the truth of those charges is afforded. I think that in the interests of the school, taken alone should secure to him the fullest benefit of the doubt. Myself—[Rev. Bishop was former principal of Lahainaluna and still had strong connections to the institution]—as well as Mr. Moore's family, have a strong personal interest in the result."[102] Mr. Moore remained at Lahainaluna as principal, and Miss Karua did not appear on the list of Maui schoolteachers moving forward.

CONCLUSION

The Native-led Hawaiian Kingdom of the mid-late-nineteenth century was one of the most literate nations on earth. It comprised an engaged and enlightened populace that both demanded much of its leaders and supported the nation itself with an unyielding devotion. This progressive character of the lāhui (nation/people) challenged ascendent ideas of white superiority and frustrated calls for annexation to the United States from 1893 to 1898. The failure of a second treaty of annexation in the fall of 1898 was followed by a seizure of the Islands by a United States eager to use the islands in the center of the Pacific for a military base in their ongoing war against Filipino independence fighters. This seizure of control of Hawaiʻi by the United States in 1898 was followed by an indoctrination and Americanization program that at its foundation could not accept Kanaka ʻŌiwi intelligence, opinion, and independence. Moving forward, Kānaka ʻŌiwi would be recharacterized as unintelligent, inept, and incapable of leadership.

Definitions of "education" are diverse, with some more narrowly focused on institutional learning—"the process of receiving or giving systematic instruction, especially at a school or university"[103]—and others offering a more broad characterization—"the act or process of imparting or acquiring general knowledge, developing the powers of reasoning and judgment, and generally of preparing oneself or others intellectually for mature life."[104] Under any rubric, and acknowledging all its complexity, the national project launched by Mōʻī Kauikeaouli in the 1830s was extraordinary.

His acceptance of the missionaries and the tool of literacy does not equate with a wholesale acceptance of the mission. It is important to remember Hawaiian monarchs had witnessed the power of the written word for decades prior to the arrival of the American missionaries in 1820. While the Mission saw literacy as a way to get to religion, some Aliʻi Kanaka ʻŌiwi certainly saw the new religion as a way to get to literacy. Throughout this difficult and complex time, in looking to the future of his people, Mōʻī Kauikeaouli saw a rapidly changing world that required difficult decisions and determined action. In response, he made his decisions and called for the support of his people:

E hooikaika kakou. E na kanaka, e na kamalii, a me na wahine, e hooikaika oukou. E hooikaika hoi oukou e na kumu i ke ao i na haumana. O ko'u makemake nui, e ike pono ka poe ilihune, ka poe waiwai, na'Lii, na kanaka, na makaainana a me na kamalii a pau loa o ko kakou aupuni, i ka ike a me ka heluhelu i ka olelo a ke Akua...."[105]

(Let us be diligent, men, children, women; let us be strong. Those of you who are teachers, be faithful in teaching your pupils. It is my great desire that the poor, the rich, the chiefs, the men, the commoners, and all the children of our nation acquire knowledge and know how to read the Word of God....)

The people of Maui Komohana heeded his call.

NOTES

1. The chapter title references an 1825 speech of Mōʻī Kauikeaouli (Kamehameha III). An oft-cited phrase within the speech declares, " 'O ko'u aupuni, he aupuni palapala ko'u" (Mine Kingdom shall be a Kingdom of literacy). The Mōʻī continues on in the speech to issue a call for all of his people "Na Poe Ilihune, Na Poe Waiwai, Na Alii, Na Kanaka, Na Makaainana" to take up his bold challenge to become a literate nation. The title "PANE AKU KO MAUI KOMOHANA" reveals that the people of West Maui answered his call.

2. The move from a wholly oral society to a near-fully literate one had a range of effects on society that are seen as both positive and negative by many Kānaka 'Ōiwi, and the use of the word "achievement" is not meant to imply judgment but rather simply the success of a stated task.

3. Samuel Manaiakalani Kamakau, "Ka Moolelo o Na Kamehameha." *Ka Nupepa Kuokoa*, 3 Okatoba 1868, 'ao'ao 1.

4. The section HE MOʻOKŪʻAUHAU: A Genealogy of Educational Administration in the Hawaiian Kingdom within this chapter documents some of the many educational policies signed into law by successive monarchs of the Hawaiian Kingdom.

5. "Hawaii For Us," *Washington Evening Star*, 17 December 1896, page 7.

6. Rev. Rufus Anderson to Alexander Liholiho, letter of 6 July 1863, FOEx Chronological Files, 1863, Hawaiʻi State Archives.

7. 'Ōiwi wale was a term coined by Kanaka 'Ōiwi historian Kanalu Young circa 1990s that was meant to replace "contact" and de-center Captain James Cook in histories of Hawaiʻi.

8. For the purposes of defining that geographical term, the work turns to the designated school district covering that area during the Kingdom era, Apana 'Elua (District 2).

9. Report of the Governor of the Territory of Hawaii: To the Secretary of the Interior. United States: U.S. Government Printing Office, 1902.

10. M. Puakea Nogelmeier, *Mai Pa'a i Ka Leo: Historical Voice in Hawaiian Primary Materials, Looking Forward and Listening Back* (Honolulu: Bishop Museum Press, 2010), page 68.

11. Report of the Governor of the Territory of Hawaii: To the Secretary of the Interior. United States: U.S. Government Printing Office, 1902.

12. As Kauikeaouli was only 11 years old at the time, his Kuhina Nui, Ka'ahumanu ruled as regent until his coming of age.

13. T. Puuohau, "Ka Haiolelo a T. Puuohau o Lahainaluna ma Wainee," *Ka Nupepa Kuokoa,* 23 Mei 1868, 'ao'ao 1. Samuel Manaiakalani Kamakau recounts this event several months after Puuohau with different wording quoting Kauikeaouli: "Ka Moolelo o Na Kamehameha." *Ka Nupepa Kuokoa,* 3 Okatoba 1868, 'ao'ao 1.

14. Samuel Manaiakalani Kamakau, "Ka Moolelo o Na Kamehameha," *Ka Nupepa Kuokoa,* 3 Okatoba 1868, 'ao'ao 1.

15. Samuel Manaiakalani Kamakau, *Ke Au Okoa,* 17 June 1869.

16. Ibid.

17. FOEx Series 418, Box 1, Folder 7, Pre Constitutional Laws and Regulations, 1840, Hawai'i State Archives.

18. "Na Kanawai o Ko Hawaii Pae Aina" in *Kumu Kanawai, a me Na Kanawai o Ko Hawaii Pae Aina. Ua kauia I ke ka[u] ia Kamehameha III.* Honolulu, 1841, 'ao'ao 47–52.

19. "Kanawai Hooponopono Kula," in *Kumu Kanawai, a me Na Kanawai o Ko Hawaii Pae Aina. Ua kauia I ke ka[u] ia Kamehameha III.* Honolulu, 1841, 'ao'ao 62–67.

20. "Kanawai Hooponopono Kula," in *Kumu Kanawai, a me Na Kanawai o Ko Hawaii Pae Aina. Ua kauia I ke ka[u] ia Kamehameha III.* Honolulu, 1841.

21. Ibid.

22. The English-language version of this law, published in 1842, says "children," while the original Hawaiian-language law, published in 1841, says "na keiki kane" (boys).

23. "Kanawai Hooponopono Kula," in *Kumu Kanawai, a me Na Kanawai o Ko Hawaii Pae Aina. Ua kauia I ke ka[u] ia Kamehameha III.* Honolulu, 1841.

24. Ibid.

25. Ibid.

26. Series 263, Laws 1840–1842, Box INT 1, Hawai'i State Archives.

27. Ibid.

28. Ibid.

29. Ibid.

30. The third and final organic act was completed by the new Attorney General, William Little Lee.

31. *First Act of Kamehameha III to Organize the Executive Ministries.*

32. FOEx Series 418 Box 1 Folder 8, Rules and Regulations of the King in council, "He Mau Kanawai hou no ke kula" 8 Novemapa 1849.

33. Ibid.

34. Ibid.

35. Ibid.

36. "He Kanawai e Naauao ai Na Keiki a Na Haole, a me Na Mamo o Na Haole ma Honolulu, a me Na Wahi e ae ma Keia Aupuni" in *Kanawai o ka Moi, Kamehameha III., KE Alii o ko Hawaii Pae Aina, i Kauia e n aAlii Ahaolelo, a me ka Poeikohoia, iloko o ka Ahaolelo o ka Makahiki 1851.*

37. "An Act to Provide for the Education of the Children of Foreigners, and Those of Foreign Extraction in the City of Honolulu, and Other Places in the Kingdom," in *Laws of His Majesty Kamehameha III., King of the Hawaiian Islands, Passed by the Nobles and Representatives at thier Session, 1851,* pages 84–86.

38. "He Kanawai e Hooulu ai e Kokua i na Kula Beretania no ko Hawaii Poe Opiopio," in *Kanawai o ka Moi, Kamehameha III., Ke Alii o ko Hawaii Pae Aina I Kauia e na Alii Ahaolelo a me ka Poekohoia, iloko o ka Ahaolelo o ka Makahiki 1854,* 'ao'ao 10–11.

39. "An Act for the Encouragement and Support of English Schools for Hawaiian Youth," in *Laws of His Majesty Kamehameha III., King of the Hawaiian Islands, Passed by the Nobles and Representatives at Their Session, 1854,* pages 18–20.

40. "He Kanawai e Hoololi ae i ka Oihana Aopalapala," in *Kanawai o ka Moi Kamehameha IV., Ke Alii o ko Hawaii Pae Aina, I Kaula e na Alii Ahaolelo a me ka Poeikohoia, iloko o ka Ahaolelo o ka Makahiki 1855,* 'ao'ao 6.

41. "An Act to Remodel the Department of Public Instruction," in *Laws of His Majesty Kamehameha IV., King of the Hawaiian Islands, Passed by the Nobles and Representatives, at Their Session,* 1855, page 9.

42. "No ke Auhau Kula" pauku 486 of *Kanawai Kivila o ko Hawaii Pae Aina, Hooholoia i ka Makahiki 1859,* 'ao'ao 79. In part, "E uku no kela kane keia kane e noho ana maloko o keia Aupuni, i kela makahiki keia makahiki, i ka auhau no na kula, elua dala pakahi, o na kane hoi ia mawaena o na makahiki he iwakalua a me kanaono, ina he kanaka kupa Hawaii, a ina paha he haole i hookupu oleia. . . ."

43. "The School Tax" Section 486 of Civil Code of the Hawaiian Islands In part, "an annual tax of two dollars, for the support of public schools, shall be paid by every male inhabitant of the Kingdom between the ages of twenty-one and sixty [. . .] every male 21–60 years, whether a Hawaiian subject, or an alien. . . ."

44. "He Kanawai e Hoololi ai i Na Pauku 742, 743, a me 744, o ke Kanawai Kivila," in *Kanawai o ka Moi Kamehameha IV., Ke Alii o ko Hawaii Pae Aina, i Kauia e Na Alii Ahaolelo a me ka Poekohoia, iloko o ka Ahaolelo o ka Makahiki 1860,* 'ao'ao 10–12.

45. "To Amend Sections 742, 743, and 744 of the Civil Code," in *Laws of His Majesty*

Kamehameha IV., King of the Hawaiian Islands, Passed by the Nobles and Representatives, at their Session, 1860, pages 9–11.

46. "He Kanawai no ka Hookaawale ana i na Keiki Kane a me na Kaikamahine iloko o na Kula Kumu Mua o ke Aupuni," in *O na Kanawai o ka Moi Kamehameha IV., ke Alii o ko Hawaii Pae Aina. I Kauia e na Alii Ahaolelo a me ka Poekohoia, iloko o ka Ahaolelo o ka Makahiki 1862,* page 11. Approved 25 Iulai 1862.

47. "An Act to Provide for the Separation of the Sexes in the Governmnet Schools," in *Laws of His Majesty Kamehameha IV., King of the Hawaiian Islands, passed by the Legislative Assembly, at its Session, 1862,* page 11.

48. He Kanawai e Hoopau ai ka Mokuna 10 o ke Kanawai Kivila, a e Hooponopono ai ka Oihana Aopalapala o ke Aupuni.

49. An Act to Repeal Chapter 10 of the Civil Code, and to Regulate the Bureau of Public Instruction.

50. 1874 He Kanawai e Kokua ai i ka Oihana Mahiai me ka Hanalima ma na Kula Aupuni o ka Pae Aina.

51. "An Act to Promote Agriculture and Industrial Pursuits in the Public Schools of the Kingdom," in *Laws of His Majesty Kalakaua King of the Hawaiian Islands, passed by the Legislative Assembly, at its Session, 1874,* page 13.

52. Hoonauao ana o na opio Hawaii ma na Aina e, aole e Hooliloia no ka makaikai, aka, no ka Hoonaauao io ia

53. Education of Hawaiian Youths Abroad.

54. "He Kanawai E Hooi ai i ka Maluhia o na Kula Hanai Kaikamahine" in *Na Kanawai o ka Moi Kalakaua Ke Alii o Ko Hawaii Pae Aina, i Kauia e ka Hale Ahaolelo, i loko o ka Ahaolelo o ka Makahiki 1882,* 'ao'ao 62.

55. "An Act to Provide More Efficient Protection of Female Boarding Schools," in *Laws of His Majesty Kalakaua I., King of the Hawaiian Islands, Passed by the Assembly, at its Session 1882,* page 60.

56. "He Kanawai e Pili ana I ka O Lima," in *Na Kanawai o ka Moi Liliuokalani, Ke Alii o ko Hawaii Pae Aina, I Kau ia e ka Hale Ahaolelo kau Kanawai, I ke Kau o 1892,* 'ao'ao 181–182.

57. "An Act Relating to Vaccination," in *Laws of Her Majesty Liliuokalani Queen of the Hawaiian Islands, Passed by the Legislative Assembly at its session 1892,* pages 165–166. [No child to be admitted to any school in the Kingdom without vaccination.]

58. Privy Council Meeting Minutes, 30 August 1850, Hawai'i State Archives.

59. The 1840 Luaehu Constitution was drafted, edited, and signed into law at Luaehu, Lahaina, Maui.

60. The Lahainaluna Seminary opened on 25 September 1831 under the leadership of Reverend Lorrin Andrews.

61. Kalakua Kaheiheimālie, also known as Hoapili Wahine, was wife of Maui's governor, Hoapili, at the time of the founding of Lahainaluna Seminary. She was

also grandmother to two future mōʻī, Alexander Liholiho (Kamehameha IV) and Lota Kapuaiwa (Kamehameha V).

62. Noelani Arista, "Davida Malo, a Hawaiian Life," in "The Moʻolelo Hawaiʻi" by Davida Malo (Honolulu: UH Press, 2020) page 23.

63. *He Mau Kanawai no ke Kulanui o Hawaii Nei, I Kauia e ka Poe Misionari,* Iune, 1835.

64. "Mamaomua," I loko o *He Mau Kanawai no ke Kulanui o Hawaii Nei, I Kauia e ka Poe Misionari,* Iune, 1835, ʻaoʻao 5.

65. "Preamble," in *Laws of the High School, as Amended and Adopted by the Mission,* June, 1835, page 4.

66. *He Mau Kanawai no ke Kulanui o Hawaii Nei, I Kauia e ka Poe Misionari,* Iune, 1835.

67. *He Mau Kanawai no ke Kulanui o Hawaii Nei, I Kauia e ka Poe Misionari,* Iune, 1835, pages 6–7.

68. Ibid.

69. Ibid.

70. Ibid.

71. Ibid.

72. *He Mau Kanawai no ke Kulanui o Hawaii Nei, I Kauia e ka Poe Misionari,* Iune, 1835, pages 12–13.

73. Ibid.

74. "No Na Mea e Aoia," i loko o *He Mau Kanawai no ke Kulanui o Hawaii Nei, I Kauia e ka Poe Misionari,* Iune, 1835, ʻaoʻao 17–19.

75. "Of the Studies of the School," in *Laws of the High School, as Amended and Adopted by the Mission,* June, 1835, pages 16–18.

76. Department of Education, Student Essays, Series 320, Box 2, Folder 1, Hawaiʻi State Archives.

77. Ibid.

78. *He Mau Kanawai no ke Kulanui o Hawaii Nei, I Kauia e ka Poe Misionari,* Iune, 1835, pages 16–17.

79. Ibid.

80. *Five Years' Church Work in the Kingdom of Hawaii.* By Thomas Nettleship Staley, Bishop of Honolulu. London, Oxford and Cambridge: Rivingtons, 1868.

81. Sandwich Islands, Extracts from Journal of the Bishop of Honolulu, September to November, 1862, London, 1862, page 10.

82. Articles of Incorporation, 1862, Commerce and Consumer Affairs, Hawaiʻi State Archives. Bishop Staley and Reverend Mason were tutored in ʻōlelo Hawaiʻi by Kalākaua.

83. Annual Report of the Minister of Education of the Hawaiian Kingdom, 1864, Hawaiʻi State Archives.

84. Ibid.

85. *Five Years' Church Work in the Kingdom of Hawaii.* By Thomas Nettleship Staley, Bishop of Honolulu. London, Oxford and Cambridge: Rivingtons, 1868.

86. Ibid.

87. *Hawaiian Gazette,* 16 September 1868, page 3.

88. Maria Karua to C. R. Bishop, letter of 14 September 1888, Series 261–21–10 General Correspondence, Incoming Letters of the Board of Education, 1888, Maui, August–December, Hawai'i State Archives.

89. Ibid.

90. Ibid.

91. Ibid.

92. Ibid.

93. C. R. Bishop to C. H. Dickey, letter of 15 September 1888, General Correspondence, Department of Education, Series 261-Box 21-Folder 2, Hawai'i State Archives.

94. C. R. Bishop to Miss Maria Karua, letter of 15 September 1888, General Correspondence, Department of Education, Series 261-Box 21-Folder 2, Hawai'i State Archives.

95. Ibid.

96. Maria Karua to C. R. Bishop, letter of 21 September 1888, Series 261–21–10 General Correspondence, Incoming Letters of the Board of Education, 1888, Maui, August-December, Hawai'i State Archives.

97. C. R. Bishop to W. J. Smith, letter of 8 December 1887, General Correspondence, Department of Education, Series 261-Box 21-Folder 2, Hawai'i State Archives.

98. Helen Chapin, *Guide to Newspapers of Hawai'i, 1834–2000.*

99. "Anglo-Saxonizing Machines," *Friend,* August 1887.

100. Sereno E. Bishop to Charles Reed Bishop, letter of 10 December 1888, General Correspondence, Department of Education, Series 261-Box 21-Folder 2, Hawai'i State Archives.

101. Ibid.

102. Ibid.

103. Cambridge English Dictionary, 2019.

104. Dictionary.com, 2023.

105. Samuel Manaiakalani Kamakau, "Ka Moolelo o Na Kamehameha," *Ka Nupepa Kuokoa,* 3 okakopa 1868 'ao'ao 1.

CHAPTER 6

NO KA WI O LAHAINA NEI
On the Lahaina Famine

Bianca K. Isaki and Kahealani Lono

I. No ka wi o Lahaina Nei

No ka wi o Lahaina nei.[1]

Iloko o keia makahiki e hele nei, a mamua aku nei hoi, ua hoomaka na kane, a me na wahine o Lahaina nei e mahi ai ko, ua huli a mahi ka hapa nui ma ia hana, a ua paa pono ka aina i ke kanu ia, a ua haalele na kanaka i ke kanu ana i ke kalo, a me ka uala, a ua komo aku nei na kane, na wahine i ka hana mahu wili ko, ekolu hapawalu no ka la, a ua lilo loa ma ia hana, a ke waiho wale nei na aina kalo o Kauaula, aohe mahi ia, ke pii nei ka nahelehele a ke uhi paapu nei i na loi, ke lanakila nei na opala, a me na mea e ae, ke hehi nei na lio, a me na bibi ke kua ia nei na ulu, a me na kuikui i paila wahie, i mea e loaa ai o na dala, i loaa ona wahi pai ai o Molokai mai.

Within this current year and just before, men and women here in Lahaina began to farm sugar cane, and the majority shifted and farmed this work; the land was well planted and the people abandoned planting taro and sweet potato, and both men and women began to tend to sugar cane and ⅜ for the day, and they became absorbed in this work. Taro farms in Kauaula just sit unattended, and weeds are growing and covering the taro patches; the rubbish is taking over and everything else; the horses and cattle are stepping on it; whatever grows is being cut and logs are burned to produce an income so that one would have some undiluted taro from Molokai.[2]

Ina oe e naue iho e makaikai ma ka malu ulu o Lele nei, aole e halawai iki kou mau onohi me kekahi mau loi kalo i hele a po-ka-ki-manu, aole no hoi me kekahi mau mala uala, aole hoi e like me ka wa o ke alo o ka aina, ina e kilohi

164

aku oe ma ke kahawai o Lahainaluna, aole oe e ike aku ua alima loi i pokeokeo ma kahi hookahi elike me na kipuka kolea pela ka waiho, ke ike aku nei au i ka lehulehu i ka hele ae, no ka mea, eia koʻu hale ma kapa alanui, e ninau ana, aohe ai o keia wahi ea? E hahai hele ana i Olowalu, a me Ukumehame, e aumeume ana ka loaa aku kekahi maauauwa, i na e nele mai, a laila hoi aela lakou me ka olelo iho, pilikia loa keia la, aole paha e moe iki ana ka po, no ka houpo lewalewa kekahi poe aʻu e ike aku nei, o ke ala wale aela no i ka wa kakahiaka, a hele no i ka hana mahu a wili ko hoi, a komo akula kahi wai ko hala ka la, a ahiahi hoi maila pupuu hiamoe, a pela aku.

Should you pass by and take a look at the shady areas here in Lele, your eyes will not see taro patches that weren't ravaged by birds, and it's the same for potato patches—certainly not like how one would pass by these lands before. If you glance over by the Lahainaluna river, you won't see those five taro patches that were healthy and lush near the place where the Pacific golden plovers gathered and stayed. I see the majority going about because my house is at one end of the road and I'm wondering: is there no food here? People are following the journey to Olowalu and Ukumehame; it's a struggle to obtain something to trade, and if there is nothing, they return saying it was a terrible day, won't be able to sleep tonight. This is due to hunger, is what I've noticed. Wake in the morning, go and tend to steaming and milling sugar cane, have a little sweet water. Then the day is done, evening comes, return home to curl up and sleep.

A ina e ohi mai kahi dala i ka Poaono, i ka aie akula no i kahi o ka Pake, a koe iho he wahi hapalua paha, he hapaha i kahi ia, he hapaha i kahi pola poi, o ka pau no ia, ina aohe poi, o ka hele no ia i ka inu ki i kahi o ka Pake, o ka wai holoi no o ka lima o ke ki ihola no ia e inu ai, aohe e hiki ke haalele ae aia ka pono o ke kamau o ka ea.

And if money is collected on Saturday, it goes to the debt with a Chinese [person]. Perhaps you will only have half left; a quarter will go to fish and a quarter to a bowl of poi, and then the money is gone. If there isn't any poi, it goes to drinking tea with the Chinese—tea is good for cleansing and for drinking; it's impossible to dodge this as it's something that keeps us going.

Ke pii nei ke kumukuai o ke pai ai ma Lahaina nei, elima hapawalu a oi ae, a ina hoi i kuai nui ia e kekahi kanaka, hoowali ia maila hoi kakale me he lepe palahu la, i loko no oia kakale aole he haalele aku, i koʻu nana maoli aku i ka waiho a ka aina o Lahaina nei, aole e hoohalahala ka maka no ka uliuli launa ole o ke ko, ua paa pono na makalua, na niu, na wahi pupu, na olaelae, na auwaialoi maloo, na auwaha, a pela aku, o ka hua ole no i ka okioki ia i wahie, a e lilo aku ana paha ka ulu o Lele nei i mea ole, pela io no, o ka poe hoonawale no ma na wahi kihapai, paapaahana no, mikimiki no, ola no i kahi ku o-o, a i kahi onihinihi, a oweowene. A o ka nui ihola he ola i ka makani, eia nae ina e ku mai na kalepa hali ai i Lahaina nei, hoahu ia he pale uhauha paha.

The price of undiluted taro is increasing here in Lahaina, 5/8 and a little more—and if a lot is purchased by one person, it is mixed 'til it is very watered down, but even with it watered down, no one leaves. When I carefully observe how the Lahaina area currently stands, no one ridicules the discoloration of the sugar cane, unkept planting areas, coconuts, blocked areas, land coming out in wet areas, dried up taro patch canals, ditches and so forth. If there was no fruit it was chopped for firewood, and thus Lele turned into nothing.[3] *It is true. Only people who quietly tend to this land division are there, very busy, working diligently, surviving due to small taro shoots and small taro.*

E na makamaka, ua haule na kuaua mua, malama ua waele e ke-pulu, kanu ia aku ka lau, hou ia aku ka huli, eli ia ae ka lua, a ho-o ia aku na pohuli maia, onou ia aku na [illegible] aku na mea kanu, hawele ia aku na hua momona, a pela aku: E aloha ae i.

To our friends, the fertilizing rains are no longer, weeds thrive because of satu-ration, greens are planted, stems are pierced, a pit is made, banana shoots are planted for food—forcefully given out, [illegible] the plants, fruits are bundled and so forth.[4]

* * *

W. Sebena penned this article in 1866, when famine had taken Lahaina. Famine in Lahaina spanned Hawaiian-language newspaper pages through at least 1866–1867, reoccurring in 1877. This specifically Hawaiian public vigorously discussed Lahaina famine. The discussions are descriptive and prescriptive, urging wide-spread socioeconomic changes as well as shifts in cultural values, and personal comportment—how, what, and when to eat.

Yet, little was said of the issue in English language sources of the time. This disjointed attention may proceed from the concerns constellated by the famine—that traditional systems of social reproduction were no longer working. And they no longer worked for all of the settler-colonial and genocidal reasons that came to characterize Hawai'i's interactions with the U.S.

This chapter considers the Lahaina famine, and the then-contemporaneous reporting of it, within that longer historical context of settler colonialism: exploitation of Kānaka Maoli under sugar industrial agriculture, the Pacific Decadal Oscillation, and Kanaka Maoli resilience and resistance, and in the further context of the public assembled by various Hawaiian-language nūpepa (newspapers).

II. Settler Media was Fascinated by Famines Across the World, but Silent on Local Famine in Hawaiʻi

"No Ka Wi o Lahaina Nei" was one of many analyses of famine in Lahaina in the 1860s and 1870s in various Hawaiian-language newspapers. Together, these analyses found Lahaina's famine a clear consequence of Kānaka Maoli moving from traditional farming and other subsistence economies into exploitative commercial agriculture. No English language sources reviewed registered famine in Lahaina between 1865–1868. Twentieth-century settler historians have asserted: "The last recorded famine in Hawaiian history occurred in Kau, Hawaiʻi in 1845–46."[5] The 1866 Lahaina famine was not recorded in settler histories of Hawaiʻi.

English-language newspapers in Hawaiʻi described few "famines" in Hawaiʻi, but registered the many occurring in America, India, Russia, Sweden and elsewhere in the world in grisly detail.

- "The pressure of famine is so terrible in Tunis and other parts of the coast of Africa that mothers have been found eating the flesh of their own children. The Irish famine was nothing compared to the horrors of this now prevailing at Tunis. We do not hear much just now from the famine in Finland, but it has been fearful there, and in the north of Sweden. In Russia we learn that the famine is spreading far and wide and pestilence is apprehended to follow in its wake."[6]
- "The late extensive commercial disasters in India have been followed by a famine among a different class of the population of the country. The wealthy have had their dark day, and now, in turn, the poor have theirs. India seems fated."[7]
- "The Russians divided their rations with the Coreans as far as possible, but hundreds of natives perished from starvation and cold. Upwards of 500 dead bodies of men, women, and children were seen in a ride of 14 miles lying in the snow."[8]
- "From the north of Europe, especially Sweden and Finland, we have heart-rending reports of famine, and multitudes are perishing. From Algeria and Tunis, warm climates, we have even worse accounts—the dead and dying laying by the wayside."[9]
- "In Algiers the famine is terrible. An Arab woman recently killed her daughter, twelve years of age, and gave the flesh to her other children and partook of it herself."[10]

- "The late drought, or famine, in India was alarming in its aspect. More than thirteen millions [*sic*] of people were affected by the famine. Of these four and a half millions [*sic*] suffered cruelly, and half a million died."[11]
- "There is a famine at the Cape of Good Hope."[12]
- "The official report of the famine in Eastern India shows one million deaths from starvation!"[13]
- "Look, for an illustration, at the Cape de Verde Islands. Since the destruction of the woods, they have experienced all the miseries of famine and disease."[14]
- "Burmah is said to be still threatened by famine, and the King is buying up grain [for] his troops."[15]
- "From the latest reports it would seem that something like 2,000,000 people have died of famine on the shores of the Bay of Bengal. It is too fearful and painful a subject to dwell on."[16]
- "The famine in Norrland, in the northern part of Sweden, has reached its climax. Nearly 300,000 people are wasting away and actually dying from starvation."[17]
- "All persons who desire to subscribe to the fund for alleviating the fearful distress and famine now reigning in the Eastern provinces of Germany, will please add their names to the subscription list opened in this Consulate."[18]
- "The society for relief of the East Prussians, founded by the Crown Prince on December 20, 1867, terminated as the famine ceased. The private subscriptions amounted to about 2,000,000 thalers."[19]

Certainly, a famine on the scale of mass death of millions in India does not describe the same food shortage in Lahaina in the late 1860s. None of the articles about the Lahaina famine of 1867 refer to deaths. The difference in attention is not only one of scale or extremity. All of these famines, including those across Hawai'i, were caused by, amongst other things, shifts towards industrial agriculture and displacement of traditional labor economies and subsistence structures.

Though Mike Davis credited economic historian Karl Polanyi as the "only twentieth-century economic historian who seems to have clearly understood that the great Victorian famines (at least, in the Indian case) were integral chapters in the history of capitalist modernity," many Hawaiian writers, including those transcribed here, reported the relationship between the Lahaina famine and capitalist modernity in Hawai'i.[20]

Polanyi located the source of famine in Europe and Asia with "the free marketing of grain combined with local failure of incomes," discounting thereby the primacy of drought and crop failure.[21] Railroads and shipping had made it possible to send food to famine areas, but affected communities were unable to afford food at famine prices—prices set under a free market. Further, because larger markets swept up surpluses that would otherwise have remained in local stores set against harvest failure, impacts of famine were more swift and acute.[22] Polanyi concluded, the famines that "decimated India under British rule since the Rebellion were thus neither a consequence of the elements, nor of exploitation, but simply of the new market organization of labor and land which broke up the old village without actually resolving its problems."[23]

Mike Davis' *Late Victorian Holocausts* built on Polanyi's analyses, noting the insane faith of various East India Company operatives and British bureaucrats in Western macroeconomic theories, particularly those of Malthus and Adam Smith.[24] In the 1870s, "[b]y official dictate, India like Ireland before it had become a Utilitarian laboratory where millions of lives were wagered against dogmatic faith in omnipotent markets overcoming the 'inconvenience of death.' Grain merchants, in fact, preferred to export a record 6.4 million cwt. of wheat to Europe in 1877–'78 rather than relieve starvation in India."[25] Davis, commenting on famine in India, called the displacement of subsistence farming by industrial, export-oriented agriculture, the "personification of free market economics as a mask for colonial genocide."[26] Lahaina's 1867 famine too, as its contemporary analysts surmised, was not caused by an overall lack of food, but rather the "arrival of numerous sugar mills in Hawai'i."[27]

The famine would continue throughout 1867. Yet, news from Lahaina continued to include references to elite gatherings and feasts, including upon the arrival of Queen Emma:

A Party.—On the evening of Thursday, Reverend G. Mason held a party to honor the Queen, and those who were instructed, and everything carried out at the party was gracious, and the tables were laden with things of all sorts, and we ate until satiated, and most was leftover.[28]

As in other colonies, famine did not mean foremost a shortage of food but a different structure of food distribution. Economic inequality, labor exploitation, and a relentless narrowing of options for safeguarding traditional life in Lahaina continued in many forms, including in a famine that would last through 1867 and reoccur in 1877.

III. THE 1867 COMMITTEE

In 1867, Lahaina's Honorable Daniel Kahaulelio, and S. W. Nailiili, M. Ihihi, and D. Baldwin, were appointed to investigate and report on the causes of diminishing food supplies in Lahaina.[29] Their report, "No Ka Wi" (About the Famine), as well as Kahaulelio's further analysis and advice was published in *Ka Nupepa Kuokoa*. English translations are included in italics at intervals below.

* * *

NO KA WI.
Concerning Famine.
E na hoa aloha:—Mamuli o ka olelo i hooholoia ma ka halawai o ka la 12 o Maraki, no ke kuka ana a noonoo i na kumu i wi ai ka apana o Lahaina, a ma ia halawai, ua kono ia mai au i mea haiolelo no keia la, no laila, ua hooili ia mai keia hana maluna iho o'u a na keia hana i hoohanohano mai ia'u i keia la.

Greetings friends:—Due to what was decided at the meeting on the 12th of March, regarding the discussions and thoughts about the reasons Lahaina is experiencing a famine, and it was at this meeting that I was invited as a speaker for the day, therefore, this work was bestowed upon me and it is this work that has elevated me today.

Ua lana kuu manao me ka olioli pu, e hoike aku i kekahi mau kumu i wi ai ka apana o Lahaina nei, mahope iho o kuu hai ana 'ku i ka manao o ke komite i koho pu ia'i ma ua halawai ana la, oia hoi ka'u e hoike pu aku nei. Ua ike pinepine ia keia mea he wi, mai ka hoomaka ana o keia honua a hiki i keia la. Ua ike ia ma ka Baibala ka wi a me ka pilikia o ko Aigupika poe, i na makahiki ehiku, i ka wa o Parao ke alii a o Iosepa hoi ke kauwa a ke Akua, ka mea nana i hoike maopopo i keia wi. A pela no i ka wa o Elia ke kaula, ua nui ka wi o ka aina i manawa, no ka ua ole i na makahiki ekolu me na malama eono, nolaila, ua hele wale lakou e imi i na lau ulu o kela ano keia ano, a kupa lakou ia mau mea i loko o na ipuhao, a olelo lakou, he mea make ka i loko o ka ipuhao! A pela no ka neenee ana mai o ka wi i keia apana Lahaina. A ke lohe mai nei kakou, a ke ike nei hoi ma na nupepa i ka wi ana o kela apana keia apana o keia mau Mokupuni. A ikaika loa no hoi ka wi ana o kekahi mau Aupuni Europa, Asia, Aferika, Amerika Hema, Amerika Akau, a ma kekahi mau Mokupuni o na Aina Moana, a hiki loa mai i Hawaii nei.

I have thoughts, with pleasure, to show some reasons for the hard times here in the Lahaina area, and after I share the thoughts of the committee that was selected at the meeting, that is, I will also share mine. This famine is often seen, from the beginning of this earth until today. It was seen in the bible, the famine and the struggles of the Egyptian people, in seven years, in the times of Farroh the king and Joseph, the servant of God, the one who knowingly exhibits this famine. And it was the same for the time of Elijah the prophet, the famine was extreme at this time because there was no rain for three years and six months, so, they went in search of plants of different kinds, and they would boil them inside of a pot, and they would say, there is something in the pot! And that is how this famine came to this area in Lahaina. And we are hearing and seeing in the newspaper of the famine of every land division on the island. And this famine is stealth in the Kingdom of Europe, Asia, Africa, South America, North America and other islands of the great ocean and all the way here to Hawai'i.

"Ka manao o ke komite no kekahi mau kumu i wi ai ka apana o Lahaina."

"Thoughts of the committee about some reasons an area of Lahaina is experiencing famine."

1. O ka nui o na hale wili ko ma Hawaii nei, oia he 33, aole o lakou mahiai, aka, kuni lakou I ka ai o na aina kalo. Honokohau, Halawa, Waipio, &c.—
   Because there are many sugar mills here in Hawai'i, about 33, they are not farming, but they scorch the taro fields. Honokohau, Halawa, Waipio, &c.—

2. Ma Lahaina, nui na loi a me na kula uala I piha I ka ai mamua, a I keia wa, lilo I ke kanu ko.
   In Lahaina, there are many taro patches and potato fields that were abundant with food before, and nowadays, it turned in to planting sugar cane.

3. Nui ka wai I loaa I ka poe mahiai mamua, a I keia ed a lilo ka wai I ke ko; a he nui ka hooikaika ana a na haole kahi poe I ka mahi kalo, uala, maia, ipu &c.
   There was a lot of water supplied to the farmers before, and now, the water is supplied to the sugar cane; and foreigners made great efforts farming taro, potato, banana, gourds and such.

4. O ke kiekie loa o ke kumukuai o ke ko, kapa ai na kanaka I ka mahi kalo, uala, ipu, he poho, a makemake nui I ed ala, aole he nui o ka ai oia ka hewa.
   The price of sugar cane is so high that the people left tending to taro, potato, gourd, it wasn't worth it and the dollar was highly desired since there was very little food, that was the problem.

5. He 250 kanaka hana I na wili ko ma Lahaina, ed al loa ma keia mau hana, aole nae he mahiai, a ua pili keia olelo I na aina kanu ko o Hawaii nei a pau; me ka luhi, a me ka inea pu.

There were 250 people working the sugar mills in Lahaina, it was very dependable, not like farming, and it was known all throughout Hawai'i; it was tiring and very hard.

6. He nui ka poe opiopio ma Hawaii nei I noho palaualelo, a waiho I ka mahiai na na elemakule palupalu.

   There were numerous youth in Hawai'i who sit idle and leave the farming for the weak elders.

7. Ma Hawaii a me Maui nei, nui na kanaka ed al, lilo I ed ala e, ohi pulu, pepeiao, ia mea'ku mea'ku, loaa ed ala, aole nae ai.

   In Hawai'i and here in Maui, there are plenty of strong people, they went to other work, gathering wool and mushrooms and things like that, you earn money, not food.

8. Ua nui ka poe ai I ka ai I keia wa, e like me ka wa o Kamehameha III; aka, ua akaka ua emi ka poe nana e mahi I ua ai la.

   Lots of people eat these days just like in the times of Kamehameha III, but it's clear, there are less people farming this type of food.

9. Aole no ke Akua keia nele, aole no ka ua ole—aka, no ka noonoo ole o ke kanaka. Manao ko Lahaina I ke pai ma ka pakuai, aole nae noonoo, he nui na aina mahiko, a ia lakou na paiai. O keia ihola na kumu o ka wi ana o ka apana o Lahaina, wahi a ke komite.

   This shortcoming is not the fault of God, nor is it because of no rain, but it is because of people not thinking. Lahaina people think it's punishment, they don't realize, there is a lot of land to farm sugar cane and they still have undiluted taro. These are the reasons there is famine in the Lahaina land division, according to the committee.

Komite Rev. D. Baldwin
    M. Ihihi
    S. W. Nailiili

Committee Rev. D. Baldwin
    M. Ihihi
    S. W. Nailiili

No ka waiho pu ia ana mai o ka hoike a ke komite me kau haiolelo no na kumu o keia wi ana, a'u i hoike ae la maluna, nolaila, aole paha e hiki ia'u ke hoonahili a hooloiele i keia haiolelo ana, no ka mea, ua akaka ae la no kekahi mau kumu nui, aka, ma ko'u noonoo ana hoi, he pono no hoi ai e hoike aku, e like me ka mea hiki iaʻu.—No laila, ke waiho nei au he ninau i mua o kakou i keia la. "Heaha la na kumu i wi ai ka apana o Lahaina?" Mamuli o koʻu noonoo loihi ana, me ke akahele loa i ka haina kupono no keia ninau, e ekemu aku ana no au ano, me ka hikiwawe.

Because the committee's report was presented along with my speech detailing the reasons of the famine, what I shown just above here, that is, I can't quite mislead and take my time on this speech because the main points are clear, and my thoughts, which should be expressed with what I am capable of. Therefore, I leave a question before us today, "What are the reasons that the Lahaina division has struck famine?" Due to my long thought process while being very careful about the best conclusion for this question, I will quickly cover it now.

1. O ka hiki nui loa ana mai o na wili ko ma Hawaii nei.
   The arrival of a tremendous amount of sugar cane here in Hawaiʻi.
2. O ka lilo loa o na kanaka i ka mahi ko.
   People shifted to farming sugar cane.
3. O ka makemake nui o kanaka i ke dala loaa koke mai.
   People wanted to earn money more quickly.
4. O ka noonoo ole maoli no o kanaka i ke ano o ka noho ana.
   People completely failed to foresee this kind of lifestyle.

E lawe mua mai kakou i ke kumu mua o ka wi ana o keia apana o Lahaina nei i. "O ka hiki nui ana mai o na wili ko ma Hawaii nei." Penei paha e akakaʻi: ma ka Mokupuni o Maui nei, aole i nui na wili ko mamua aia ma Haiku, Makawao, Ulupalakua, wale no na wiliko, aole i ike ia ka wi o keia apana ia mau la, oia elima makahiki mamua, no ka mea, na na waieha e hanai i ka poe paahana oia mau wili aole i lawe ia ka ai o ko Kahakuloa, Honokohau, Ukumehame, Olowalu e hanai i ko laila poe, aka, o ka ai nae o keia mau aina, e lawe pinepine ia ana i Hilo a me Kona maluna o Kilauea. A i ke ku ana iho nei o na wili ko ma Lahaina nei, a me na waieha, ua pau pu aku nei ka ai o keia mau aina au i helu ae nei maluna, i ka malama pu i na paahana a pau o keia mau wili, a nolaila mai ka hoomaka ana o ka na pai ai e liilii loa a hiki i 7 pauna a ka 10 no ka ekolu hapawale, a he elike me ka puhene pua-ii o Molokai, nolaila, aole o kana mai o ka hahana o ka wi ma keia kulanakauhale, o ke pai ekoluhapawalu o keia wa, ua like ia me ekolu pai ke hui ia no ka hapaha ma mua.

We should bring forth the first reason of the famine of this area here in Lahaina 1. "The arrival of a tremendous amount of sugar cane here in Hawaiʻi." It's probably best clarified like this: here on the island of Maui, there wasn't a lot of sugar mills before, sugar mills were only at Haiku, Makawao, Ulupalakua, famine was not seen in this area at this time, that was five years ago because it was the four waters that fed the busy people of these mills, food from Kahakuloa, Honokohau, Ukumehame, Olowalu wasn't taken to feed the people from there, but the food of these lands, it was often taken to Hilo, Kona and up on Kilauea. When the mills stopped here in Lahaina along with the four water sources, the food of these lands I mentioned above were unproductive due to the busy nature of tending to theses mills, and therefore, it was from there that undiluted taro began to significantly decrease to seven pounds from ten pounds for ⅜, just like the tiny fish of Molokai, and so, the famine of this town is unbelievable, the ⅜ amount of this time, it's similar to three amounts when added to the ¼ before.

Eia hoi kekahi, ma mua aku nei, aole au i ike iki i ka ai o Waipio, Hawaii e lawe ia mai ana i ko Lahaina, aka, i keia wa, ke hoopiha pinepine ia mai nei ka opu o kekahi moku kona o Halawa kona inoa, e ko Waipio poe, a lawe mai i Lahaina, no ka hapalua o ke pai ai hookahi—A i keia wa, aole he lawe hou o Kilauea i na pai o Olowalu, Ukumehame, Honokohau, Kahakuloa, ua akaka lea keia, o ka wi o keia apana no ka nui o na mahi wiliko.

It also should be noted, before, I've never seen food from Waipio, Hawai'i being brought here to Lahaina at all, but nowadays, those of Halawa are being frequently fed by the people of Waipio and it is brought to Lahaina, because of the decrease of undiluted taro and nowadays, Kilauea won't take undiluted taro from Olowalu, Ukumehame, Hanokohau, Kahakuloa again, this is very clear, it's because of the famine of this area which is all because of tending to sugar cane.

2. "O ka lilo loa o na kanaka i ka mahi ko" He mea akakalea keia ma ka nana iho, no ka mea, i ka hiki io ana mai o keia mea he wili ko ma Lahaina nei, ua hoopapau loa na kanaka ma keia mea he mahi ko. No laila, haalele kekahi poe i ke kanu ana i na Kuleana aina i ke kalo, uala, maia, uhi &c—a paulele loa ka manao ma keia hana me ka manao e ola ana ka pololi ma ia mea. Eia hoi, no keia hana he mahi ko, ua lilo nui ka wai o na kahawai, a he nui na Kuleana aina kalo i ka maloo, a lilo i mea ole. I ka makahiki i pau, a me keia makahiki e naue nei, he nui ka hoopaapaa o na kanaka me na haole: o na kanaka me na kanaka, o na wahine me na kane, o na keiki me na keiki no keia mea he wai, o ke kumu o keia hoopaapaa no ka pau loa o ka wai i ke ko, a nele na aina mahi kalo. Eia hoi, no keia lilo o na kanaka i ka mahi ko, ua hana ino loa ia kekahi ai kupono e pale ai i kekahi manawa wi o keia aina, oia hoi ka ulu. O keia ai, he ai i aloha nui ia e ko Lahaina nei keiki, kau ae na maka iluna o ka ulu, a nana aku e pala mai ana ke au, a helelei mai ana, a laila, i iho ko Lahaina keiki, e ola auanei, no ka mea, ke hoi mai nei kiaiole, aka i keia mea he mahi ko, ua nui na ulu i

oki wale ia, a hoolilo ia i wahie no na wili ko, e aho no la hoi ia, hala kekahi la makaponiuniu. I kuu manao, o keia oki ana i ka ulu a o ka wa kahiko, ina paha ua pau i ke kipaku ia i ka aina, e like me Kaululaau i ke kipaku iai Lanai, no ke oki ana i ua ulu nei. A oia ka mea i oleloia e ka poe haku mele, penei.

"Halau Lahaina molale malu i ka ulu,
Malu-mai ka pea lau loha a ka makani,
I neo punohu maalo ke aka i kai,
I ke kai waiho lua a ka lai o Lele,
I unuhi a oki me he waa kialoa la,
Ka oili a ka pua i ka malie."

2. *"People shifted to farming sugar cane." This is something very clear when you look at it, because when mills arrived here in Lahaina, people were devoted to this work of farming sugar cane. Coincidentally, people abandoned planting their kuleana land with taro, potato, banana, yam and such—and they truly thought that if you continued, you would pass away because of hunger. Lo and behold, farming sugar cane, it took a lot of the fresh water, many of the taro patches on kuleana lands went dry and became nothing. Last year as well as this year, people were arguing with foreigners: all people, women, men, children because of the water, the reason being, all the water went to sugar cane and the taro patches were without water. And, since the people shifted to sugar cane, a food that would help through a time of famine in this area was destroyed, that is the breadfruit. As for this type of food, it was so favored by the children of Lahaina, they would set their eager eyes on the breadfruit and would observe it til it was ripe, it would then fall and the children knew they would be just fine, but this farming sugar cane thing, lots of breadfruit trees were chopped down and became firewood for the sugar mill. This is probably better, days of dizziness will pass. My thoughts are that cutting down the breadfruit, it is the reason the land was abandoned, like Kaululaau banished to Lanai for chopping down the breadfruit trees here. That is what said by music composers, like this:*

"Halau Lahaina molale malu i ka ulu,
Malu-mai ka pea lau loha a ka makani,
I neo punohu maalo ke aka i kai,
I ke kai waiho lua a ka lai o Lele,
I unuhi a oki me he waa kialoa la,
Ka oili a ka pua i ka malie."

3. "O ka makemake o na kanaka i ke dala loaa koke mai" He oiaio keia, no ka mea, i ka lohe ana o kanaka ua makaukau ka wili ko ma Lahaina nei, he nui ka poe i hele mai me ka manao e komo i ka hana, mai Molokai mai, Lanai a me na kuaaina mai no hoi, me ke manao nui e loaa koke mai ke dala, no ka mea, hookaa ia ana ke dala i kela pule keia pule, a pela e uku mau ia'i a pau ka uku mahina. A pela paha i hana mau ia'i ma na wahi wili ko a pau o Hawaii nei—Eia hoi kekahi mea e akaka'i o kekahi manawa ina aole e hele mai kekahi oia poe i kahi o ka Luna nona ka Wili ko, a nele ka wili i ke kanaka ole, a laila, hoolimalima keia Luna i poe nana e imi i kanaka, a laila, hele keia poe Luna e kepa kanaka me na olelo maalea, me ka ninau aku i ke kanaka. "Aole nae paha ou makemake e komo i ka hana?" Pehea ka uku? ma ka mahina paha? ma ka pule paha? wahi a ke kanaka. Ia manawa la, pane akula ka Luna, ma ka mahina no hoi ka uku, he umi dala, ke iwakalua nae dala ohi mua. Ia wa, pihoihoi no ke kanaka, me ka olioli pu o ka naau i ka loaa koke o ke dala, a o ka lilo no ia ma keia hana no keia dala hikiwawe. Eia hoi kekahi, ua hiki pinepine mai na manao i ini i waena o ke kane a me ka wahine, no kekahi mea maikai paha iloko o na hale kuai, lole pahoehoe paha, lole Silika paha, noho lio paha &c—eia nae aohe wahi e hiki wawe ai o ka loaa, o ka hele koke no ia e noi dala i ka Luna Nui o a wili ko, a komo i ka hana, a ua kapa iho kakou ia lakou, he Kumakahiki—O ke kumu ihola no ia, o ka makemake i ke dala loaa koke mai, a i ka loaa ana mai o ke dala, i hea ka ai e loaa'i. No ka makemake i keia dala loaa koke mai, haalele wale ia na kuleana kalo, aina kula mahi uala, a hoolimalima paha i ka aina me na haole.—Iloko aku nei o ka M.H. 1866, ua hoolimalima aku kekahi o na ona o kahi wili ko o Lahaina nei, no na makahiki he iwakalua, no ka makemake i ke dala loaa koke mai me ka luhi ole.

3. "People wanted to earn money quickly." This is true because when people heard the mills were ready here in Lahaina, there was a lot of people who came with the intentions of entering this field of work, from Molokai, Lanai and citizens here, they really thought money can be earned quickly because, pay was weekly and it was like that for the entire month. And it was like that at all the sugar mills throughout Hawai'i—Here's something to be clarified of a situation if people didn't show up to the boss of the sugar mill, and there weren't enough workers, the boss hired people to search for people and then these people who contract people with convincing words to one, "Don't you want to work in this field?" What is the pay like? Is it monthly? Is it weekly?" The person would inquire. It's then the boss happily responded, "It is a monthly rate of ten dollars, first pay is twenty dollars." It was then that the person became interested with great enthusiasm to earn money quickly, and they enter this field because of quick money. And so, both men and women desire something fab-

ulous in stores such as good quality clothing, silk clothing, a horse saddle. But here's the thing: there are no other places to earn money like this, so they immediately go to the main boss of the sugar mill, and start working, we call them Kumakahiki— the reason of this is they want fast money, and when they get paid, where is the food. Because of the desire for fast money, caring for taro patches and field of potatoes are just abandoned and they rent their land to foreigners. In the year 1866, some of the sugar mill owners rented land for twenty years because they wanted quick money with little work.

4. "O ka noonoo ole maoli no o kanaka i ke ano o ka noho ana." He mea maopopo no keia, no ka mea, ua lawa kupono no hoi kahi pai ekolu hapawalu i kekahi wa, no ke kane a me ka wahine, a lawa ole no hoi i kekahi manawa, aka, no ka noonoo ole maoli io no hoi kekahi. Penei paha e akaka'i, i ka wa i mahuahua ai ka ai a me ka ia, alaila, ua hoomaunauna ia no, no ka mea, ike ihola ia ua nui ka ai, o ke ai pinepine ihola ia, ekolu paha ai ana o ke ao, elua paha o ka po, a i kekahi manawa oi aku ma mua o keia mau aina, aole hoi he malama pono i na rula kupono o ka ai ana, e like me na haole, aole i loaa iki i keia ano, no ke aha, no ka noonoo kupono i na rula o ka ai ana. Eia hoi kekahi o ko kakou manao wale no i ka ai i ka poi, aole e hiki ke noonoo ka manao, a hoolilo ma kekahi ai ano e ae, e like me ka palaoa, raiki, papapa, pia, ia mea aku ia mea aku e like me na haole. Ma Lanai au i ka la 21 o Feberuari o keia maka- hiki, mamua iho oia mau la, aole o kana mai o ka wi oia mokupuni, no ka mea, he mau la ua ia, a no ia ino i loohia mai, aole e hiki i na waapa ke holo mai i pai i Lahaina nei, nolaila, hoao lakou me ka hooikaika e ai i na hua pi, ki, raiki, a i ka hoao ana, ua hala kekahi mau la oia wi me ka pololi, a owau pu kahi i komo iloko oia mau la pololi, a ua noho wale hookahi la a me ka hapa o ka la, a na ka wai o ke ki a me ka pi i hoopau i ka pilikia o na la. Ina paha kakou e manao me ka ai i kekahi mau ai e like me na haole, ina no ka hoi aole e pilikia kakou i ka wi. E nana aku i ko kakou Moi Wahine kane make Kaleleonalani ia ia i holo aku nei i na Aupuni nui o Europa, Amerika Huipuia, a ole he poi kana ai ia ia e noho ana i ko laila mau kulanakauhale. [Illegible] i hoopiha ia i ka nani a me ka hanohano, aka, o ka berena paa, palaoa, a me ia 'ku ia mea 'ku oia kana mau mea i ai no ia mau la ana i noho aku ai, ka mea hoi nona keia mau wahi lalani mele malalo nei—

4. "*People completely failed to foresee this kind of lifestyle.*" *This is known because ⅜ for undiluted taro was sufficient at one time for men and women, and then it wasn't sufficient, but also for not thinking clearly. Here is how I would clarify it, when food and fish were plentiful, and then, it was squandered because one could see that there was lots of food, there was frequent eatings, perhaps three meals during*

the day, maybe two at night and sometimes more than these meals, there wasn't a good rule of thumb in regards to consuming food, like foreigners, there wasn't such a practice, why so, because of not making a rule about eating. And here is another thought about eating poi, it was never thought to spend money on different foods like bread, rice, beans, yeast and so forth like foreigners. I was on Lanai on the 21st of February of this year, before this time, famine was unbelievably extreme on this island because it rained and due to this misfortune, boats couldn't reach Lahaina therefore they tried to be strong and eat beans, peas, tea, rice and during these attempts, days of starvation past and I too suffered in these starving days, and it was tea and beans that ended the troubles of the day. If we had thought about food the way foreigners did, if so, we would not have been suffering because of famine. Look at our deceased king Kaleleonalani, when he traveled to Europe, America, he wasn't eating poi when he was staying in those royal towns that were decorated and famous, their food and bread and flour and those types of foods, that's what he ate for all the days he stayed there, for which these lines of this mele speaks of—

"Maikai ka Wakini he nani ke nana,
Ka hemolele oia uka me ke onaona
Ua hele wale a nohopu i ka lehua makanoe
Ua ike maka iho nei i ka nani o Aipo
E li ana ka io i ke anu o Hanaiiki
I ka hana hemolele a Kukaiakamanu"
[*not translated*]

Eia hoi kekahi, ua hiki pinepine mai ka lono io kakou nei, no ka wi o ka Apana o Kona Hawaii. A he mea oiaio keia, ke huli kakou a noonoo i ka lakou hana ana i ka ai o ko lakou aina. Penei ka hana ana a kanaka oia wahi, mahiai nui lakou i ka uala a loaa na mala nui, a hiki mai i ka wa e o-o ai ka uala, a laila, he ai wale no ka hana a hiki i ka manawa e pau ai, a i ka hoomaka ana e mahi hou, ua hala ka wa pono, nolaila, ua hiki mai no ka wi. Ua akaka no ke kumu o keia wi ana, o ka noonoo ole maoli no, a hoolilo i mea hoomaunauna wale, aka, o keia olelo maluna, ua pili i ka poe i hana maoli ia mea.

Here something else, we often hear news about the famine in area of Kona, Hawai'i. And this is something seriously true when we investigate and think about them tending to food production of their land. This is the people's livelihood, they farm sweet potatoes a lot and they have huge gardens all the way up till the sweet potatoes matures, and then, all that is left to do is eat them until there are no more, and when farming happens again, the season is over, therefore, famine arrives. The

*reason for the famine is clear, it's due to poor planning and then it becomes some-
thing just wasted, but as for these words above, it was about the people who truly
do this work.*

Aka, ke noho mai nei paha kekahi poe o oukou me ka i iho iloko o kona
naau, aole he mau wili-ko ma Lanai, a me Molokai a me Honolulu, eia ua hiki
mai ka wi ma ia mau wahi. Ke pane aku nei au malaila, me ka hai aku i ke kumu
o ka wi o Lanai. Eia no ia, o ko Lanai poe, ua kau mai ke ola o ka noho ana i
Lahaina nei, no laila, ina e wi o Lahaina; o ka wi pu ia me Lanai. O Molokai
hoi, ua ano like kekahi hana a ko Molokai poe, me ko Kona Hawaii, ma ka
hoolilo ana i ka uala i mea awaawa, a o ka hope oia hana, o ka hoomaunauna
aku i na hoa e kupono ana ma ia hana hookahi, pilikia ma na aina mahi kalo
ole o Molokai. O ko Honolulu hoi, he mea maopopo keia, no ka mea, e like
me ka nui o ke kulanakauhale, pela no auanei ka nui o na kanaka, o ka nui o
na kanaka, oia ke kumu o ka wi, no ka mea, he hapa loa na aina nana e malama
ana ia kulanakauhale, o Manoa, Waikiki, Palolo, Kalihi, Kapalama, no laila,
ua ikaika ke kumukuai o ka ai, ua ike pono loa au, oiaio, ma Honolulu, elima
dala o ke kihene pai hookahi, a ewalu kekahi, a i keia mau la aku nei o ko M.
H. 1866 & 1867, ua pii ae ke pola poi hapaha, he hapalua, ua akaka no, o ka nui
o na kanaka nana e ai, a he hapa ka poe nana e mahi.——-Nolaila, ua maopopo
aela na kumu o ka wi ana o Lahaina nei, a pela no hoi paha na apana e ae o keia
mau mokupuni o Hawaii nei; a o ka mea i koe, o na kumu e pau ai keia wi ana.

*However, some of you folks are sitting about, saying inside your soul, Lanai,
Molokai and Honolulu don't have sugar mills, and yet, famine struck these areas. I'm
responding about those places, by sharing the reasons for the famine crisis in Lanai.
Here is what I think, for Lanai people, their lives are settled here in Lahaina so if
there is a famine in Lahaina, there is also famine in Lanai. As for Molokai, some
of what's going on with the people of Molokai is similar with the people of Kona,
Hawai'i, by way of turning sweet potato in to something unpleasant, what's behind
this happening is that people who are knowledgeable in this area squandered it away.
As for Honolulu, this is understood because the majority of the towns are the same
so that's what it will be like for the majority of the people there, as for the amount of
people, that is the reason for the famine because the lands that was tended to in these
towns are less than half such as Manoa, Waikiki, Palolo, Kalihi, Kapalama so the
price of food is high. I seen it with my own two eyes, I am serious, in Honolulu, it's
$5 for a bundle of food, some are $8, there are many people who need to eat and only
half actually farm. So the reasons for the famine here in Lahaina is understood, and
it's probably that way in the other areas of island here in Hawai'i. What remains to
be seen is the reasons to end this famine.*

"Pehea la e pau ai keia wi?"
"How in the heck will this famine end?"

1. E hoʻopiha pono i na Kuleana Aina i na mea ai o kela ano keia ano.
   Properly plant a variety of crops in Kuleana Lands.
2. E mahi nui ma ka ai i maa ia kakou.
   Cultivate the foods that are familiar to us.
3. E malama pono i na rula o ka ai ana.
   Take into consideration the rules of eating.
4. E hooikaika i na hana e pono ai ke kino.
   Strengthen the work that is needed for the body.

E hoomaka kakou e noonoo ma ka manao mua. 1. "E hoopiha pono i na Kuleana Aina i na mea ai o kela ano keia ano." I kuu wa 9 makahiki mai ka hanau ana mai, oia paha ka makahiki 1846; aole paha au e poina ana a me oukou a pau, i ke ano, a me ka noho ana o Lahaina ia manawa, a ma koʻu hoomanao ana ae, aole he kulanakauhale o Lahaina, he mahinaai no ka Mokupuni o Maui. No ka mea, ma kahi o ka hale e ku ana; e ulu ana na pae uala, na kalo, na maia, na pu ko, na uhi, na pu, &c. Na keia mau mea i hoopale ae i ka wi o ka aina ia wa.

Let's start to reflect on the first thought. 1. "Properly plant a variety of crops in Kuleana Lands." In my ninth year after birth, that was probably around 1846, I never forgot, just like you folks, the type of living took place here in Lahaina at that time, and if I remember correctly, Lahaina was not a town, it was farm land belonging to the island of Maui. Because, right around where the houses are now standing, sweet potato patches were growing, taro, banana, sugar cane stalks and yam. It was these things that sustained us and protected us from famine.

A ina e like hou ana o Lahaina me ia wa aʻu i hai aela ma luna, alaila, o ka pau no ia o keia wi ana. Ua ike pinepine loa au ma na Kihapai mala ai o na haole o kela ano keia ano i hiki mai i Hawaii nei, ua piha pono na kihapai i na hua o kela ano keia ano, a o ka hope kupono oia mea, i ka hoopau aku i ka wi mai ka ainaʻku. Aia ma ka Mokupuni o Lanai, e noho ana kekahi haole me kana mau keiki ekolu, iaʻu i hiki ai malaila, hookipa kela iaʻu e moe ma kona hale, mamua ae o ka paina ahiahi, lawe mua kela iaʻu e makaikai i kona mala mahiai, a i kuu ike ana ma ia mala, e ulu ana ka palaoa, ka uala kahiki, uala maoli, akaakai, &c. A iloko o keia kau wi oia Mokupuni o Lanai, ua lohe ia na leo uwe no kanaka no keia wi puni, aka, o keia haole, aole ona leo uwe no keia wi, no ka mea, ua piha pono kona mau mala ai, a pela no na haole a pau, nolaila, he akioma keia, he mea moakaka lea.

And if Lahaina was the same then, at the time when I highlighted just above, then, famine would immediately be gone. I frequently saw in gardens in small land divisions belonging to foreigners of all types that arrived here in Hawai'i, the gardens were full of the various fruits and the results of this is beneficial because it fought off famine from entering those areas. On the island of Lanai, a foreigner was dwelling there with his three children, when I arrived there, they hosted me and I slept at his house, right before dinner, he took me to sight see his gardens and what I saw when viewing these gardens, wheat, white potatoes, sweet potatoes, onions and such. Within this time of famine on the island of Lanai, crying voices were heard because of the lack of food, but, for this foreigner, he did not cry because of the famine because his gardens were full and it was that way for all the foreigners so this is a testament, it's very clear.

2. "E mahi nui ma ka ai i maa ia kakou." Mamua aku o ke ku ana o na wili ko ma Lahaina nei, ua ike ia aku na kahawai o Kaaula, Kanaha, Kahoma, ua piha pono i ke kalo, a me na mea maluna iho o na kuauna, kapiki, maia &c., ua ike ia na kanaka o Lahaina e mahi nui ana i ke kalo, nolaila, ua maopopo no, ua kaawale aku ka wi, a o ka lako o ka aina ka mea akaka.

2. *"Farm the foods that are familiar to us." Before sugar mills were situated here in Lahaina, the rivers of Kaaula, Kanaka, Kahona were seen, it was full of taro and other food on top of the banks like cabbage, bananas and such. The people of Lahaina were seen tending to the taro a lot, so it's known, there was no famine and the well fertile land was obvious.*

E nana aku i ke aupuni o Kina, Eha haneri miliona kanaka ma ia Aupuni, a ua manao wale ia, oia ka hapakolu o na kanaka o ka Honua, e ola ana lakou no ka raiki, no-laila, ua hooikaika lakou e kanu ia mea, no ka mea, ua maa lakou ma ia ai. Pela no hoi ko Helani poe, ua ola lakou no ka uala kahiki wale no, eia nae, ua mahiai nui loa lakou ma ia mea, no ka mea, ua maa lakou ma ia ai. Nolaila ua kupono i ko Lahaina e hana mau ma ka ai i maa ia lakou, a ina pela ko Hawaii nei a pau, alaila, o ka mea maopopo e pau ana keia wi. A i ka nana 'ku pela no na Aupuni Nui o ka Honua e noho nei, ua ike maopopo keia ma na hana a kanaka oia mau lahui i hiki mai i o kakou nei.

Look at the nation of China—400 million people in this nation, and it was simply thought, this is ⅓ of the people of earth, they survive on rice so they increased the planting of this food because they are familiar with this type of food. Same for Hebrew people, they survive on only white potatoes and so they farmed a lot of this kind of food because they are familiar with this type of food. Therefore, it is only appropriate for Lahaina to produce the food they are most familiar with and if all of Hawai'i was like that, then we know it will end famine. And it looks that way for the Great Nations of Earth that are living here, I truly know, by the work of the people, the nation will continue for all of us.

3. "E malama pono i na rula o ka ai ana." I ko kakou nana ana i na Haole, ua mahalo lakou i ka manawa o kela hana keia hana a pela i holo ai ka lakou mau hana a paa. A pela no hoi i malama ai lakou i ka manawa o ka ai ana—a ina pela kakou e malama pu ai i ka manawa, a laila, ua maopopo no e pau ana keia wi. Eia hoi kekahi, ua ike pinepine ia keia pilikia ma keia lahui i kekahi manawa. I na he makua me kana mau keiki, alaila, o ka hana a kekahi poe makua me na keiki, i na e hele na keiki, aole e kali na makua a ai like, a pela no hoi na keiki ina e hele na makua i kahi e aole no hoi e kali ana na keiki, a ina e malama pono ia ana ka manawa, alaila, e pau ana no ka wi, i na pela kakou e hana ai, aka, ke i mai nei paha oukou, i pono no paha ka malama ana ina rula i ko kakou lako i na wati ina aole he mau wati, "pehea la e pono ai ke malama i na rula" Ke i aku nei au ia oukou, ma ka nana aku, ua hiki no ia kakou ke malama ina rula me ka wati ole, no ka mea, o ka la e hele nei he manawa kupono loa ia, na kakou e nana, a ina paha e manao ana kakou o ka puka ana o ka la, oia ka aina kaka-hiaka, a o ke kupono ana o ka la, oia no hoi ka paina ahiahi, a ua like no keia manawa me ka wati ina he hiki ia kakou ke manao pela.

3. Take in to consideration the rules of eating. When we look at foreigners, they appreciate the time spent in all types of work and that is how they perform their work until complete. And this is how they are when eating—and if that is how we also spent our time then there would be no famine. Here's another thought, this problem is often seen in our nation at times. If there is a parent with a child, then one thing that the parent does if the child walks, the parent doesn't wait and eat the same, and it's the same way for the children, if the parents go somewhere, the children aren't going to wait and if time is well kept, then famine would not exist if we did it that way, yet you folks are probably saying, if we practice this rule with our supplies, with watches, if we don't have a watch, "how the heck do we practice this rule." I'm saying, by looking at things, we can practice this rule without a watch because when it's day time, it's a very good time for us to take notice and if we perhaps think when the sun rises, it's breakfast time, and when the sun is upright, it's dinner time so this time is similar to a watch if we can think like that.

E nana aku i na moku e holo ana i na kai lipolipo uliuli o ka moana, a hoomaka ka moku e haalele i ka aina i ku ai, a laila, o ke kapena a me na kela o ka moku, e malama ana i ka latitu a me ka lonitu, a me ke panana, a me ka hoailona makani. A me ka ohe nana la, no ka mea, me keia mau mea e kaawale ai ka pilikia mai ka moku ae, a i ole e malama ia keia mau mea, a laila, e ili mai ana na poino maluna iho oia moku, aka, no ka malama ana i na rula o ka holo moku, ua holo pono no hoi ka holo ana. Eia hoi kekahi mea a kakou e hoomanao ae ai, ma ko kakou paina ana, ua huikau na mea ekolu a ke pa hookahi, a pela no hoi i ka umeke poi, aka, ma ia ao huikau ana, ua wikiwiki kekahi me ka manao e maona e ia, a o ka mea e wikiwiki ana pela, ua lawa pono ia, a o ka poe ai me ke akahele, aole like ka lawa pono, nolaila, he pono paha ia kakou ke hoomanao ae i na haole, aia ma ko lakou papaaina, ua hookaawale ia kela mea keia mea pakahi, me kaua pa, pahi, o, a pela aku, a i ka ai ana, ua lawa like. Ma keia alanui i hahai ai ko Lahaina poe, a me na kula hanai e ae, ua lawa kupono no, no ka mea, ua malama kupono ia na rula o ka ai ana.

Look at the boats sailing towards the deep and dark area of the ocean, the boat is starting to leave land where it stood, then, the captain and the sailors of the boat, they note the latitude and the longitude with a compass and wind signs. And with binoculars because with this thing they can avoid problems coming towards the boat or keep these things or else unfortunate things may happen to the boat, but if they follow the rules of sailing, the journey safely continues. Here's something else for us to consider: when we eat, the three dishes are mixed on the one plate and it's the same for a calabash of poi, but this confusing practice, some are quick to think you'll be satiated, for those who are quick like that, they are content, for those who are careful, the fullness isn't the same so it's best we think of western ways, on their dining table, the individual dishes are separated with a plate, knife, fork and so forth and when eating, the amount is the same. It was this path that the people of Lahaina followed as well as boarding schools and it was just enough because the rules of eating were followed properly.

"E hooikaika i na hana e pono ai ke kino." O kekahi poe naauao, ua hooikaika lakou e imi i na Kanawai o ka honua, o Nutona, oia kekahi mea i hooikaika loa ma ia mea, a loaa ke kanawai o na mea haule, a ua pomaikai ke ao nei ia ia, o keia ike i loaa ia ia, o kona waiwai no ia, a me ka pono o ka noho ana. O Feranekelina kekahi i hooikaika ma ia mea, a loaa ia ia na kanawai o ka uwila. A pela no o Felavi, Melifi a me Kenita, a me Semeatona ka poe nana i ike mua i ka huli ana i ke panana, a oia no ke alakai o na moku, a mamuli o ko lakou hooikaika ana, ua loaa no ka pomaikai, a o ka waiwai i loaa mai mailoko mai o keia hana, he mea no ia e hoopau ai i ka pilikia o ka noho ana, nolaila, hooikaika kekahi poe i ka imi naauao, a hooikaika kekahi poe i ka lawaia, a i ka mahiai, a pela aku. Ua hiki no ia kakou ke ike i ke ano o ka hooikaika ana, no ka mea, o kekahi poe, ua hooikaika aku malalo o kekahi poe, a o kekahi ua hooikaika nona iho, a o ka loaa, ua loaa no i kela mea hana keia mea hana ana i hanaʻi malalo iho o ka la. O ka poe hooikaika ma ka mahiai i ka aina, e maona ana no ia, wahi a Solomona 28:19.

"Strengthen the work that benefits the body." Some wise people tried to find the Laws of the land, Newton, he was the one who worked very hard in this matter and found the law of things that have fallen and it was a blessing to teach him, as for this knowledge he gained, it became his wealth and the proper way of living. Francis was also improving in this matter and he found the laws of electricity. And it was that way for Felavi, Melifi and Kenita, along with Semeaton who first saw the use of the compass and that is life on the ships, and because of their efforts, they were successful and the wealth obtained from this work was the means to eliminate the hardship of living, therefore, some people strive to seek knowledge, while others strive to fish, farm, and things of that nature. We can also see the nature of improving, because some people studied under others, while others worked for themselves, and what was earned was earned by each person for what he performed under the sun. Those who work hard to cultivate the land will be satisfied, according to Solomon 28:19.

"O ka mea mahiai i ka aina, e maona oia i ka ai. O ka mea hoopili mea ai ma hope ua poe lapuwale, e piha oia i ka ilihune." Nolaila, ua akaka a e la na kumu o keia wi ana, a me na kumu e pau ai o keia wi, a he nui aku no paha na mea i koe ia'u, a ke nonoi aku nei au ia oukou, i na ua hemahema keia, e kala mai no, a maanei ke hooki nei au i ko'u haiolelo, me ka mahalo no.

D. KAHAULELIO

"As for the one who farms the land, he will be satisfied from its production. For the one who attaches himself behind one who is foolish, he will be destitute." Therefore, the reasons for this famine is clear and all the reasons to end this famine as well, and there are probably more things that I didn't bring forth and I'm asking you folks, if this is a bit awkward, forgive me, here is where I will end my word with great appreciation.

D. KAHAULELIO[30]

*   *   *

IV. The El Niño Southern Oscillation Climate Impacts on 19th-century Famines.

Famine is, but is not only, an anthropogenic phenomenon of unequal distribution under modern markets. The ongoing 1866 famine in Lahaina coincided with a number of El Niño events that would accelerate into the twentieth century.

Waialua, O'ahu and Ni'ihau also had a famine in 1866, suggesting larger regional climate factors in common with the famine in Lahaina:

O WAIALUA HEIHEI LIO, UA WI.—Ua hiki mai ia makou nei ka lono
no ka uwe ana o na kanaka o Waialua I ka wai. O kahi aina nui mau no ka
hoi o ka ai, eia ka! E wi ana, a ke holo aku nei na kanaka I Koolau a I Ewa,
a I Honolulu nei e imi I wahi ai. O ka hope no keia o ka heihei lio, a me
na I hana uhauha e ae I hana ia ma Waialua I ka makahiki I hala ae nei.[31]

*Waialua Horse Race, there was famine.—The news reached us concerning
the cries of the people of Waialua about the water. As for the large area of land,
lo and behold, famine is taking place and the people are relocating to Koolau
and to Ewa as well as to here in Honolulu where they search for a place. The
very last of these are the race horses and the other wasteful activities being done
in Waialua in the year that just passed.*

In his analysis of nineteenth-century famines, Mike Davis paid particular attention to the role of natural forces, particularly the El Niño Southern
Oscillation (ENSO) in synchronous drought. The massive shifts in the season
location of principal tropical weather systems and the drought they caused was
one of the great scientific questions of the nineteenth century.[32] It was not until
the late 1960s that Jacob Bjerknes, a researcher at the University of California,
Los Angeles, demonstrated the ways the equatorial Pacific Ocean was acting
as a "planetary heat engine" that coupled to trade winds and thereby impacted
non-tropical areas as well. El Niño events consisted of rapid warming of the
eastern tropical Pacific that caused drought by weakening monsoons. In 1876,
Madras, India saw only 6.3 inches of rain, whereas it had seen 27.6 inches in
other years that decade.[33]

The impact of eastern and western Pacific El Niño events on Hawai'i
remains a contested scientific question. However, it is generally agreed that
there was a significant impact. The concentration of major El Niño events
during the period leading to the 1867 Lahaina famine indicates these climate
events were a contributing factor. In 1860, S. C. Limaikaika wrote of their
travels through Maui. Limaikaika noted foreigners burning sugar in Makawao,
where all was green but the sugar crop was damaged in the dry season due to
lack of rain. "Akahi wale no pilikia ko Makawao poe no ka nele loa i ka wai
ole"—this is the first time the people of Makawao are in trouble because of
a lack of rain.[34]

Throughout this period, Kanaka Maoli communities continued to die at
alarming rates. In 1869, the Kingdom's Minister of the Interior, Rev. J. S. Green
of Makawao, Maui, noted 118 deaths in his district in six months, 116 of which
were Hawaiians. Green stated: "I need not say this is a greater percentage of

Table 6.1 Year and magnitude (0 = moderate, 1 = strong) of major El Niño events, 1800–1987

YEAR	MAGNITUDE	YEAR	MAGNITUDE	YEAR	MAGNITUDE
1803	1	1886	0	1918	0
1806	0	1887	0	1923	0
1812	0	1871	1	1925	1
1814	1	1874	0	1930	0
1817	0	1877	1	1932	1
1819	0	1880	0	1939	0
1821	0	1884	1	1940	1
1824	0	1887	0	1943	0
1828	1	1891	1	1951	0
1832	0	1896	0	1953	0
1837	0	1899	1	1957	1
1844	1	1902	0	1965	0
1850	0	1905	0	1972	1
1854	0	1907	0	1976	0
1857	0	1911	1	1982	1
1880	0	1914	0	1987	0
1884	1	1917	1		

Note: Data are from Quinn et al. © American Geophysical Union.

Source: Table 1 from Andrew R. Solow, "An Exploratory Analysis of a Record of El Niño Events, 1800–1987" 90 (429) *J. Amer. Statistical Ass'n* 72, 73 (Mar. 1995).

deaths than I have ever known since my residence on the Islands; and if other districts have sustained as large a loss, the people are fast waning."[35]

V. FAMINE WAS ONE OF MANY VECTORS OF KANAKA MAOLI MASS DEATH.

In 1786, the surgeon aboard the French ship *Boussole* assessed the abject situation of "Maui's Native population," the "greater part of" which were affected by leprosy, venereal disease, and other infectious diseases.[36] By 1800, "the majority of the people from Hawai'i to Niihau had died."[37] Hawaiian historian David Malo wrote of a devastating famine in Maui between 1806 and 1807. "No rain falls from October 1806 to April 1807. Plants, including taro—the staple food of Native Hawaiians, wither and die. Stricken imported livestock often rot where they fall because people are too weak from searching for water and food to remove them. The death toll from malnutrition and dehydration is high."[38]

In 1836, the district of Lahaina reported the population of Maui had fallen to 24,248 people. On Lāna'i, the death rate was double that of the birth rate.[39] In 1851, Reverend Dwight Baldwin—father of Pioneer Mill's Henry Baldwin— reported that in six months, there had been 132 deaths and only 24 births in the district of Lahaina.[40]

Lahaina's 1866 famine occurred after many rounds of epidemics in Hawai'i, three of which occurred only in the nineteenth century: the ma'i 'ōku'u of 1804 (likely typhoid, but some sources note dysentery and cholera), the epidemics of 1848–'49 (which included measles, whooping cough, dysentery, and influenza), and the smallpox epidemics of 1853, which lasted into January 1854.[41] In 1853, the death rate was over 105 per 1,000 persons.

By 1860, the native Hawaiian population had fallen to 66,000 persons and by 1870 would be 52,000.[42] This situation applied to Lahaina, where Reverend Baldwin reported 139 deaths and only 58 births in 1862. He reported: "One half" the people in the Lahaina district "are getting to be old men and women."[43] Historian David Stannard summarized the dire impacts of colonial disease and infertility on Hawai'i:

> By 1885 the native population of Hawai'i was down to about 44,000— compared with the 130,000 just fifty-five years earlier and probably at least 800,000 in 1778. By 1893, when American Marines and local white sugar planters topped the government, it was less than 40,000.[44]

It is in this context of nearly a century of rapid population collapse that Kahaulelio and other Hawaiian writers were rendering advice with particular emphasis on care of one's body as a means to end the famine.

During this period, there were also changes in Kingdom governance as King Kamehameha V (Lota Kapuāiwa Kalanimakua Ali'iōlani Kalanikupua-pa'ikalaninui, born on December 11, 1830, died on December 11, 1872) ascended as the the fifth monarch of the Kingdom of Hawai'i from 1863 to 1872. King Kamehameha V is credited as the first king to encourage reviving of Kanaka Maoli traditional and customary practices. He repealed laws prohibiting "kahunaism," and assembled a Hawaiian Board of Medicine that included licensed la'au lapa'au practitioners.[45] King Kamehameha V paid particular attention to Kanaka Maoli health, reportedly rejecting a 1865 bill to repeal prohibitions against the sale of liquor to Kānaka Maoli as a "death warrant of my people."

VI. Sugar Agribusiness Flourished on Government Subsidies and by Displacing "Cheap" Laborers from Their Lands.

The Hawaiian government largely supported the development of industrial plantations. With the decline of whaling and loss of most of the Kanaka Maoli population, governmental entities sought new sources of income in ventures that included an expanded sugar trade and taxes.

In 1850, the Hawaiian legislature passed the Master and Servant Act, which provided the legal framework for indenturing contract laborers from especially Asian countries. Foreign planters, newly entitled to own real property, especially sought this labor in light of the previously lukewarm receipt on their attempts to divorce Kānaka Maoli from subsistence and non-market economies.

In 1856, R. C. Wyllie, of the Royal Hawaiian Agricultural Society (RHAS), published his complaint against what he perceived as a Kanaka Maoli lack of knowledge in regard to the benefits of collaborative labor.[46] Wyllie opined, "The natives have yet to learn how much they are able to achieve by *combining their labor*" in order to construct, "local roads, grounds fenced in, water courses dug and embanked, new and roomy houses built and thatched, and even churches and school-houses erected."[47] This push for a kind of development cognizable to white settler colonists like Wyllie was further connected to a desire to enter Kānaka Maoli into a liberal capitalist economy: "the source of all wealth is labor; that without labor neither taxes, nor duties could be paid, the government would derive no revenue, and having no revenue, it could not even exist, and far less make roads, improve harbors, or undertake any other work for the good of the people."[48]

Payment of wages for Kānaka Maoli and Asian laborers on plantations in Hawai'i was reportedly less than that paid by plantations in the U.S. R. C. Wyllie wrote to RHAS:

There is reason to believe that the want of labor is less severely felt now than it was several years ago; that the wages of natives and of coolies including their food, does not exceed 33 cents per day; and that it is cheaper than slave labor in the United States, if Mr. Pease was right in stating it at the average of 37½ cents day, as he did in his essay of 1850, see page 63 of Report No. 1, volume 1. If Mr. Pease did not include, in his calculation, the interest on the value of the slave, the difference will be still greater in favor of such labor as we can procure in these islands. From all that has been said, the inference is warranted that with good and economical management the prospects of coffee planters in this Kingdom, are encouraging.[49]

The U.S. Civil War, which devastated the Louisiana sugar industry, solved many of the issues that hampered previous sugar planters in Hawai'i, including a lack of capital investment. In 1860, Hawai'i experienced a sugar "boom" initiated by the war that lasted six years.[50] This coincided with the closing of the Hawaiian mission, and the resulting need for missionaries to search out new avenues of income. Also, 1860 saw the collapse of the whaling trade, which had previously been a significant commercial activity in Lahaina.[51] These economic shifts, as well as the large-scale sale of government lands especially on Maui during the early 1860s, encouraged new plantation development by settlers with sufficient capital.[52]

Industrial plantations then emerged in Hawai'i, marked by their increased investment, organized labor recruitment and control, and production processes.[53] In 1861, the "Ahahui Hana Ko" (Sugar Makers Association) organized the "Ko Lahaina Ahahui Hana Ko" (Association of Lahaina Sugar Makers) in Lahaina, including King Kamehameha IV as one of the founders, donating $1,000 of the initial $15,000 startup funds.[54] The announcement published in *Ka Hae Hawaii,* titled "Ahahui Hana Ko," stated:

> This work will be of great benefit to the people who reside there in the shelter of the breadfruit at Lele. It is believed that there will be an income of at least $40,000 each year, divided between the sugar planters and the people who own kuleana land....[55]

Also in 1861, H. Dickenson and others founded the Lahaina Sugar Mill. On April 18, 1863, *The Polynesian* reported James Campbell and Henry Turton established the Pioneer Sugar Mill, and celebrated their efforts as "public benefactor[s]."[56] By this time, the lands from "Kaanapali to Olowalu, the low ground is one succession of cane fields." The "whole community"—"[t]he possessors of every little kuleana or patch of kula in and about Lahaina"—were enticed to "bring their cane to the mill of these 'Pioneers' to be ground and manufactured on shares, and it is an interesting and hopeful sight to observe the native owners of a cart-load of cane watching the great rollers (once made of wood, now of iron), by the aid of a team of mules, crushing the long stalks, while the rich juice runs in a continuous stream through a spout."[57] *The Polynesian's* description of an enthused community reception of Pioneer Mill departs markedly from the earlier descriptions by, for example, Royal Hawaiian Agricultural Society (RHAS) reports of "Hawaiian disinterest in plantation work" in 1850–1856.

In 1866, the Kingdom established a "Board of Immigration" to recruit laborers for these new plantations. However, at a "Planters' Meeting" in 1869, S. G. Wilder noted: "Campbell & Turton employ natives alone, but even they admit that labor is becoming scarce, while it must be remembered that they have the only mill in Lahaina, and that the natives must work with them or not at all."[58] Campbell & Turton's plantation may have been the only option for Kānaka Maoli seeking to work at this time. On the other hand, "Campbell & Turton, Lahaina, say they employ only native Hawaiians—have never had coolies, and do not want them. Consider the Hawaiians as good laborers as are needed, but acknowledges their inexperience as to coolies. They anticipate that the need for more labor will before long become pressing, and favor the introduction of natives of the Southern groups on this ocean, to supply the want. The immigration business should be kept in the hands of the Board [of Immigration], so long as they do the work properly; if no, abolish the Board."[59]

Campbell and Turton cut short their time in Lahaina. In 1870, the Campbell and Turton partnership dissolved, with the Hackfeld agency taking over. Campbell used the proceeds from the sale of his interest in Pioneer Mill to purchase two large tracts of land on Oahu, one at Honouliuli, including the lands of Ewa plantation and part of the lands at the Kahuku plantation.[60] However, during their tenure together, they fostered a relationship with Henry Perrine Baldwin, who became an infamous actor in Hawai'i's plantation oligopoly. As noted in his memoirs, Baldwin did not initially intend to work on plantations:

> In 1863, when twenty-one years old, he began to work for his brother Dwight, who was planting sugar-cane at Lahaina and selling his product to Messrs. Campbell and Turton. It was his intention to earn enough money to finance the completion of his education at Williams College, and afterwards to take a course in a medical college. This ambition was never gratified, for once started at work, he stayed at it as long as he lived.[61]

Soon after beginning to work for Campbell and Turton, Baldwin took a position under Samuel Alexander, manager of the Waihe'e plantation in the Wailuku district of Maui.[62]

Baldwin's biographers, as do others who wrote of Hawaiʻi's agribusiness oligarchs, lauded his ability to quell labor unrest and to inhabit a masculine, pioneering persona that gained respect of even the laboring classes. While working at Waiheʻe plantation:

> Mr. Baldwin alone among the lunas carried no weapons, and it was perhaps due to this fact and his ready courage and his ability to sympathize and ʻget on' with the working people, that he came through the ordeal unscathed. He did, however, carry a scar left by a stone thrown while quelling one of their riots.[63]

Baldwin's biographer credits him with making Maui's "barren and almost desert districts into a prosperous, fruitful, and well inhabited country," a claim that is wholly inconsistent with historical accounts of pre-plantation Maui.[64] His obituary in the *The Advertiser,* July 10, 1911, states, "It was a real pioneer that Mr. Baldwin became interested in the development of the sugar industry of the Islands. With an energy and optimism above praise he combated all obstacles in the way of success and set a pace in the industry which has brought unprecedented prosperity to the entire Territory."[65]

Again, this analysis of Baldwin, and the sugar industry's impacts on Hawaiʻi, is wholly contradicted by a host of historical, contemporary, and present-day accounts of the destruction caused by plantation agriculture on the physical landscape and people of Hawaiʻi. Structural means of coercing, persuading, and otherwise enticing Kānaka Maoli to leave subsistence and traditional forms of agriculture for waged work on settler-run plantations was key to the financial viability of the sugar industry in Hawaiʻi.

VII. Heaha la ia Pilikia?

While planters, government officials, and land district agents addressed a sugar plantation labor shortage by trying to drive Kānaka Maoli and foreign, especially Asian, settlers into indentured servitude, Hawaiian newspapers printed a rich discourse on Lahaina's changing rural landscape and reproductive economies.

Nineteenth-century contributors W. Sebena, D. Kahaulelio, A. L. Kamauu, J. H. Moku, Moses Palau, amongst others, documented sea changes in the society, political economy, and environmental landscape of Lahaina in granular analyses of famine in daily life. Each linked these changes to the sugar plantation's displacement of traditional agriculture, and specifically calling on Kanaka Maoli people to take roles different from those urged by government and planters.

Famine was not only a shortage of food, but a breakdown in relationships to land under their feet. Lahaina, once the "breadbasket" of Maui, began to import food. During·famine years, people were chopping down trees; "whatever grows are being cut and logs are burned to produce an income and so that one would have some pa'i 'ai from Moloka'i."[66] D. Kahaulelio commented: "I've never seen food from Waipio, Hawai'i being brought here to Lahaina, but nowadays, [the hulls of the schooner] *Halawa* are being frequently [filled with food] by the people of Waipio and it is brought to Lahaina."[67]

Lack of rain was not a common complaint in Hawaiian newspaper accounts of the Lahaina famine. "This shortcoming is not the fault of God, nor is it because of no rain, but it is because of people not thinking."[68] Instead, these authors ask, where are the people who worked the land? They register the rising price of kalo pa'i ai, that pa'i ai would have to be procured from as far away as Moloka'i, workers' dietary substitutions, and other material changes to the landscape, which had been described as a veritable garden of edible growth, most notably ulu (breadfruit) for which Lahaina was famous.

On January 19, 1860, Kaapuni wrote to call attention to the problem of vacant and uncultivated lands from Kahakuloa, Honokōhau, Kā'anapali, and Lahaina, and more specifically labor needed to work those lands. Kaapuni's writings are followed by an English translation in italics below:

Heaha la ia pilikia? wahi a ka mea ninau mai. He ninau hiki no ia e hoomohala, a wehewehe i kona ano. Oia no keia, o ka palaualelo maoli. Ua naue ae nei au e nana maka ana i na aina kahawai o ka mokupuni o Maui nei, a ua akaka lea ka pilikia no ka palaualelo.

What the heck is this problem? according to the one who asked. It's a question that can be unfolded and explained. Here it is: it's neglecting to cultivate land. I traveled about to see with my own eyes the streams of the island of Maui, and it's crystal clear that the problem is neglecting to cultivate land.

* * *

E hoomaka ana ma Honokohau, ia'u i hele aku ai mai Lahaina aku, a halawai au me kekahi mau kanaka, me na bipi maauauwa, Ninau aku la au ia laua, Heaha ko ke pai? Hai mai la laua, He ekolu hapawalu. No ke alia ka mea i hana ia ai a liilii. kaulike ole me ka makemake o ka mea kuai mai? Hai mai la laua, No ka wi. Aole anei olua e oluolu i hapaha no ke pai hookahi? I mai la laua, He ai kuai aku nei no hoi ka maua i ka mea ai, a e makemake ana hoi e hoopuka hou aku.

Starting at Honokohau, when I went there from Lahaina, I met with a few people, those who sold beef, and I asked the both of them, "How much for a heap?" They told me, "It's ⅜. It is the salt that cures it until it is preserved. Is this not fair for the one buying?" They said, "It's due to the famine." "You two kindly won't take ¼ for just one heap?" They responded, "We are selling food to buy our food, so we would like to profit."

A hiki aku la au i Honokohau, makaikai ae la au i kona loa a me kona laula, ninau aku la wau i ke kamaaina o'u e hele pu ana, Nowai kela aina i mahi ole ia. Wahi a ke kamaaina, No mea, Ninau hou aku la au, He aina kuleana anei i lima ka palapala hooko? Ae mai la ia, Ae. Pela wau i ninau pinepine ai i kuu kamaaina no na aina waiho wale, i hana ole ia iloko o na aina konohiki, a me na aina kuleana.

And when I arrived in Honokohau, I traveled about the length and the width. I questioned a local whom I was traveling with, for whom does this land that is not being cared for belong to? According to the locals, it belongs to Mea. I asked again, is this kuleana land that was rented? He said yes. That's how I asked my gracious local about these lands that were just abandoned, not cared for within the konohiki lands and the kuleana lands.

Kaupaona ae la au i ka like o na aina i mahiia, a me na aina i mahi oleia. Eia ka mea loaa, ua oi aku na eka aina i mahi ole ia mamua o na eka i mahiia. A malaila ua akaka ka leo kahea maluna, he pilikia he pilikia, no ka liilii o ke pai.

I weighed the similarities of the fruitful lands and the lands that are not cared for. Here's the conclusion: the lands not cared for were greater than the lands that were cared for. And there, the calling voice above was clear, there is a problem, there is a problem, due to very little repercussions.[69]

No ka'u olelo meia maluna, no ke kaupaona ana ika like o na eka aina i mahi ia a me na eka i mahi ole ia. Aole au i lawe i kaupaona maoli iloko o keia kaapuni ana i akaka ai ia'u ka nui o na eka i mahi ole ia, a me na eka i mahiia, eka, ma kuu mau maka no, a me na mea pili i ka noonoo, pela i akaka ai.

In regards to my conversation with him above, weighing the similarities of the acres of land that were cultivated and the acres that were not cultivated, I didn't take into consideration on this journey that he clarified with me the number of acres not cultivated and the acres cultivated, but it is with my own eyes and what I thought, that is how it was clarified.

Hiki au i Kahakuloa, i ko'u hele ana ma ke alanui, halawai au me na kanaka maauauwa me na bipi, ma Polua. Ninau aku la au ia lakou, Heaha ke kumukuai o ke pai? He hapaha no, wahi a lakou. I hou aku la au ia lakou, Ae, ua hanaia keia ai me ko kaulike i ka makemake o ka mea kuai mai, no ka mea, ua oi ae ka nui a maikai o ka ai o kela kahawai i ko Honokohau, i olelo mua ia ae nei ma keia pepa.

I arrive in Kahakuloa. When I went about the pathway, I met a peddler with meat on Tuesday. I asked them, "What is the price of a heap?" "It's ¼," they said. I asked them, "Yes, this food is prepared fairly with what shoppers desire," because the food from that river in Honokohau is much greater and better, which was previously mentioned in this paper.

Ninau hou au ia lakou, He ai anei ka oukou i kuaiia'ku me ka poe mahi ai? Wahi a lakou, Aole, na makou no ka makou ai i mahiai. I kuu nana ana i ko lakou nei mau kino, he mau kino kupono no ka lawelawe i na mea e pili ai ka lako i ke kino, a i ko lakou nei mau aahu, he mau aahu kupono ole no ka mea makemake e palaualelo. Aole pela na maauauwa o H. i olelo mua ia ae nei; o na aahu kupono no na la ano hanohano—palule papamu ulaula. Ona kino, kupono no ka lawelawe ina na hana a pau e pili ai ka lako. Aole nae pela. Noho wale no, a hele aku e kuai wale i ka hai ai, me ke kumukuai oluolu, a lilo ia ia, kuka kona naau i ka mea kaulike ole me ka pomaikai me kona mau hoa ma Lahaina paha, a ma Kaanapali hoi. Pilikia io ka! ina pela e kuka like ai na kanaka o na aina kahawai.

I ask them again: "You folks have food that is sold like the farmers?" Acccording to them, "No, the food we cultivate is for us." When I looked at their bodies, their bodies were sufficient to perform this work with supplies attached to their bodies, and their clothing, it wasn't clothing for one who does nothing. It's not that way for the peddlers of H. that was previously mentioned; as for appropriate attire for days semi-important—red checkered shirts. As for the bodies, it is good for performing all work that brings provisions. It's not like that. Do nothing and then go and buy poi at low prices, then it's spent, and then his soul debates the unfair things with blessings with his friends in perhaps Lahaina and Kaanapali. It's a real problem if that is how people of the wet lands deliberated similarly.

A hehi kuu mau kapuai i Kahakuloa, nana ae la au i kona loa a i kona laula. Ua piha ka hapa nui o ka aina i ka ai uliuli maikai, a oluolu na maka ke ike aku; lio mea maikai ka wai hooluu o ka uliuli, Uuku loa na wahi loi waiho wale a'u i ike ai, no na konohiki paha. Pela mai ke kamaaina ia'u.

My feet continue on to Kahakuloa. I look at her length and width. The bulk of land is full of good green food and it's so pleasing to the eyes; the greenish/

blueish-colored water is something good. There were very few taro patches left unkept from what I saw, perhaps belonging to the konohiki. That's what the local told me.

O ka mea akaka lea paha iloko o keia pepa hoike pilikia, ina e haalele ana na kanaka kupono i ka mahi kalo o na aina wai, pehea la e ola ai na kanaka paahana o kela ano keia ano, ko Makawao, ko Kula, Honuaula, Lahaina, Kaanapali; no ka mea, aole lakou e lawelawe mau ana ma ka oihana mahiai; he poe imi dala lakou, a o oukou ka poe mahiai. Pela e waiwai ai, wahi a ke "Kalaiaina." O ka mahele ponoia o ka hana, aole o ka hana huikau.

The thing that is very clear in this unfavorable report, if all the reliable people abandon farming taro of the wet lands, how in the world will the busy bodies of various types make it? Those of Makawao, Kula, Honuaula, Lahaina—because they are not the usual ones who do the work of farmers— they are people who look for money, and you folks are the farmers. That is how wealth is gained, according to "politics." This is the correct way of work, not a job lacking organization.

Ma na aina naauao ua mahele ponoia ka hana a kela a me keia. Ma ke kuai ana, aohe like, ma kahi kuaaina, e like me K. a me H., e hooemi i ke kumukuai, no ka mea, he hapa na kanaka; a ma L. e pii ke kuai ana, no ka mea, he nui ka poe makemake.

In enlightened lands, the various tasks are properly distributed. Through bartering, it's not the same as the areas of uninstructed people like K. and H., the price is reduced because there are fewer people and on L. there are more sales because there are many who want.

E aloha auanei me ka mahalo.

KAAPUNI.

Maui, Ianuari 19, 1860.

* * *

Kaapuni's analysis also identifies famine as a problem of unequally distributed labor, labor surplus, and specifically farmers leaving kalo lands. They found remarkable that food sellers would need to take a profit from their sale in order to buy other food (*"You two kindly won't take ¼ for just one heap?"* They responded, *"We are selling food to buy our food, so we would like to profit."*). Trading different kinds of food, particularly between mauka and makai communities, had been a common practice across the islands. Here, Kaapuni marks not just the introduction of profit as a motivation for trade, but that profit would be needed to *obtain food.*

Kaapuni's reference to the ongoing availability of work on wet kalo lands suggests plantations had not yet diverted Lahaina and Kāʻanapali streams. Later in the nineteenth century, kuleana tenants would struggle against Lahaina's largest plantation, Pioneer Mill, in *Horner v. Kumuliʻiliʻi,* 10 Haw. 174 (1895). Pioneer Mill sued sixty Kānaka Maoli who held claims to water rights in Kauaula Valley, with the lead defendant being S. Kumuliilii.[70] In their filings, Kumuliilii defendants stated: "[t]he Plantation has persecuted these Hawaiians by having them arrested and by forcibly taking their water and because one or two have been instrumental in trying to get their rights, it has determined to crush the whole settlement in the Kauaula Valley."[71] The Hawaiʻi Supreme Court's decision was remarkable. While the plantation plaintiffs sought to establish the defendants' supposed violations of an ancient system of water rights, the court ruled the plaintiffs had not respected that system. "[H]aving thus used the water upon the lands they have acquired, indiscriminately, without reference to the old right in rotation of days and nights as fixed by the ancient system, the plaintiffs claim and urge that the system must be strictly applied and enforced as to the kuleanas or kalo patches mauka."[72] The justices further found the plaintiffs sought to enforce a system that was "hardly fifty years old" and thus enumerated an eleven-day rotation system whereby all the lands could be watered. As we write today, the division of surface and ground water throughout Lahaina is newly designated as a water management area, for which the state Water Commission has particular duties to protect Kanaka Maoli traditional and customary rights.

In apparent agreement with Sebena, Kaapuni, and Kahaulelio, on September 22, 1866, the author of "Ka Malu o Lele"[73] Nupepa Kuokoa Buke 5, Helu 38 (Kepakemapa 22, 1866) described about seventy hungry Lahainaluna students and queried why this should be so where there is so much taro land and so many people who could cultivate food. The author mentions meeting with the Honorable Kahaulelio from Lahaina. Again, famine and hunger appear at the disjuncture between available land and labor that was recruited rather into sugar capital operations.

KA MALU o LELE

Iloko o kekahi o na pule i aui hope ae nei, ua holo aku au i Lahaina. Ua kuanea o Lahaina i keia wa, ua hele ia e ka wai kahe na alanui, a ua lilo i ka wai, ke i nei kekahi poe he mea mau ia i ua kulanakauhale nei. Hookahi ou po o ka noho ana ma Lahaina, loaa iho la iaʻu ke mele a kamalii, penei;

Within the past few weeks, I traveled to Lahaina. Lahaina was desolate at this time. The roads were flooded and it was taken over by water. Some were

saying that this was a common thing in the town. In one night residing there, I
received a song of a child, here it is;

> Hele au la a malihini
> Po hookahi, po pokole au maanei"
> Ua lawa no nae ka po hookahi no Lahaina.
> *One night in Lahaina was enough.*

O ke anaina kanaka nui e hoomana mau ana ma Wainee iloko o na
makahiki i hala, ua emi loa i keia wa. " Ua hele ke kahu a ke auwana nei na
hipa," wahi a kekahi ia'u. He nui na makahiki o kona hoomanawanui ana
me lakou, aka, ano elemakule, ua palupalu. Ua kahea iho nei kolaila poe
ia Rev. J. P. Green, e hoi aku a noho i kahu no lakou. Aka, aole paha oia
e ae ana no ka paa i ke kula kaikamahine ana ma Makawao. Ua nele io ia
poe i ke Kahu, he kihapai nui no hoi ia, aole loa he pono ke waiho wale ia.

As for the large audience of people who continually worshiped in Wainee
within the past few years, it has now reduced. "The pastor has left and the
sheeps are wandering," according to what someone had told to me. It has been
many years that they were patient, but, he's older now and more fragile. The
people of there called Reverend J. P. Green to return and be a priest for them.
He more than likely will not agree because of his commitment to a girls' school in
Makawao. These people were truly lacking a priest, an important parish church
and it should not be left to the side.

Ke holo nei no ke kula ma Lahainaluna, malalo o na kumu hou,
Bihopa, Kakina, a me Analu. Ma ke kanahiku ka nui o kolaila mau haumana.
O lakou no hoi kekahi i wi. No ke aha la ia, oiai he nui ka aina kalo o ia kula,
a he nui no hoi ka poe nana e mahi ka ai? Kupanaha ka wi o Lahainaluna?
Ua halawai iho nei au me ka Mea Hanohano Kahaulelio no Lahaina, i noho
iho nei iloko o ka Ahaolelo. Ua hookipa ia au iloko o kona hale. A he mina-
mina ko'u no ko'u halawai ole ana me kona hoa Hanohano H. Kahulu.
No ka pokole o kuu noho ana aohe maua i halawai. Ua halawai iho nei no
hoi au me ka Mea Hanohano J. Keohokaua, kekahi o na Lala o ka Ahaolelo no Maui Hikina nei. Ma Lahaina kahi noho mau o ka Lunakanawai
Kaapuni o keia mau mokupuni ekolu. Eia nae ka Lunakanawai ma Maui
Hikina i keia mau la kahi i hele ai mamuli o kana oihana. Malaila kahi a ke
Alii Kiaaina i noho ai.

The school in Lahaina is functioning under new teachers, Bihopa, Kakina
and Analu. Seventy is the number of students there. They too are in a time of

famine. What would be the reason for this since there are many taro patches at this school and there are countless people who can farm taro? Isn't the famine of Lahainaluna extraordinary? I recently met the honorable Kahaulelio from Lahaina who also was a part of the legislature. I was hosted at his house. I regret that I failed to meet with his friend, the honorable H. Kahulu. Because my stay was so short, we did not meet. I also met with the honorable J. Keo-hokaua, a member of the legislature of east Maui. It is in Lahaina were the honorable Kaapuni of these three islands resided. Here as well was the judge of east Maui these days who came because of his job. It was here as well where the governor resided.

On July 5, 1867, J. H. Moku, Lahaina, Iulai 5, 1867, wrote another article titled: "No ka Wi" under the section "No ka malu ulu o Lele" for *Ka Nupepa Kuokoa*.[74]

Ua pale hoi ka wela a me ka hahana loa o ka wi ma o makou nei I keia mau la. A no ka mea hoi I kekahi wa o ea ne ulu nei, ua loaa kahi pai I ka hapaha, a I ka nui loa ana mai o na pai ua hoemiia I ka hapawalu. Ina la mamua aku nei, ekoluhapawalu a hiki I ka ekoluhapaha ke kumu kuai o ke pai ea ne. A no ia mea, ua imi a ua noonoo keia kulanakauhale no na kumu I wi ai, a me na mea e pau ai ka wi ana mamua aku nei. A me he mea la, mahope iho o ka pau ana o na halawai kuka no ia mea, ua paipai ea ne ia kela a me keia mea ma ke kanu ana I ke pu, uala, kalo, ia mea ku ia mea ku, a I ka manao o ka mea e kau nei I keia, e pau ana paha ea ne pilikia o keia kulanakauhale no ka wi, I na mahina hope loa o keia makahiki.

The heat and warmth of the famine was protected by us these days. And that is because one time in this tea leaf groove, there was a heap for ¼ and when the heaps increased, it was reduced to ⅛. In prior days, this town searched and thought about the reasons for searching for food and things to end the famine before. It's as if, right after the discussion meetings about this, it was strongly encouraged to plant sweet potatoes, taro and other things like this, and in the thoughts of the one who brought this up, the famine of this town will end by the last months of this year.

Hawaiian newspaper accounts of the Lahaina famine were prescient; perceptive and formative of a desire that change, adaptation, and work may marshal collective agency to turn back systems alienating people into disre-paired waged systems and destroying cultivated landscapes. That so much of the contemporary analysis of the 1867 famine is presented as advice, prescription, and exhortation evidences an optimism, or a thought—that a people who had arrived in the present could turn back tides of capitalist modernity that were undoing traditional lifeways of especially makaʻāinana by reaching for what had worked before. Planting "sweet potato, taro, and other things like this" was not bad advice against sugar plantation incursions.

In the 1860s, the sugar plantation had not been long in Lahaina and its ascendancy could not have seemed inevitable. Nor was the future of the sugar plantation as an institutional structure for large scale Native dispossession necessarily visible. "[W]hat we commonly call 'structure' is not what we usually presume—an intractable principle of continuity across time and space—but is really a convergence of force and value in patterns of movement seen as solid from a distance."[75] From the distance of centuries, the plantation and its supporting political, physical, and market infrastructures appear to steadily engulf Lahaina, until their conglomerates turned landholdings into resort and real estate. This was not always what they looked like.

VIII. Early Incursions of Commercial Sugar Did Not Look Wholly Like Colonial Dispossession at First, and Rather More Often Appeared as Failure.

At the beginning, the sea change from traditional to increasingly industrial agriculture looked orderly and productive to some. In 1865, the following appeared in *Nupepa Kuokoa:*

> No Lahaina. Ina e nana ia mai o Lahaina mai ke kai mai, he ulu laau nui uliuli, I hui ia mai ka niu, ke kou, a me ka maia, aka he mau kiekiena palahalaha aku kahi ma ke kua aku, e ohu ae ana me he mauna la. Ke nana ia mai, mai Lahainaluna, elua mile ke kaawale aku o ia wahi ma ke kua aku, me he meaʻla he mahinaai I aila maikai ia I ka wai, a e hoholo ana mai o a o o ke kapa kai ekolu mile ka loa. He ololi na alanui, a o ke kulanakauhale, ua oi aku nae ka maikai ia wa; na helehelena o ka naauao aole I like aku me Honolulu. Ka ko aila kanaka mea e hilinai nui nei I keia wa o ke kanu ko, I kanu nui ia iloko o ko aila a e momona.
>
> *About Lahaina. If one looks at Lahaina from the sea, it appears as a great green forest grove, mixed with coconut trees, kou, and bananas. But there are also open heights and expanses of the ridges, and the mountains are adorned. To look at it from Lahainaluna, there are about two miles that separate that place from the mountains, and it is like a garden through which the water flows*

well. It is about three miles long, from one boundary to the other. The roads are
narrow, and the goodness of the town exceeds any other at this time. There is
an appearance of intelligent thought, unlike Honolulu. The people here at this
time endeavor in the planting of sugar cane. It is being extensively planted, and
there is the wealth.[76]

This picture of industry resonates with Kaapuni and Kahaulelio's invocation towards making the land more productive. Yet, though the land was being extensively planted and bringing wealth, the wealth was increasingly concentrated in the hands of a foreign sugar planter class.

By 1866, Maui hosted twelve plantations that produced 7,750 tons, more than half of all of the sugar produced on all islands at the time.[77] While the earlier sugar mills of the 1850s relied on existing communities of Hawaiian workers, by the 1880s, the larger industrial plantations were worked by especially Asian migrant labor. It was in this context that D. Kahaulelio stated to the Hawaiian legislature in 1870: "It would be better for the people in general if they would remain at home and cultivate their own lands, instead of contracting for a term of months or years to work for a foreigner."[78]

Sugar was not an indominable modernizing force at its onset. Hawaiians grew sugar and ran small sugar mills in Lahaina as early as 1837.[79] In the early 1840s, the Hawaiian government promoted development of commercial agriculture.[80] Historian Carol Maclennan describes the officials' rhetoric from this period as harkening towards a vison of a commercial society. In his May 1, 1847 speech to the legislature, King Kamehameha Ill stated:

I recommend to your most serious consideration, to devise means to promote the agriculture of the islands, and profitable industry. [. . .] What my native subjects are greatly in want of, to become farmers, is capital, with which to buy cattle, fence in the land and cultivate it properly.[81]

Despite the government's enthusiasm, commercial agriculture remained a relatively limited part of Hawai'i's economy in the 1840s and 1850s, as most of the people in Hawai'i operated within a subsistence economy, planting kalo and other native crops for use and not export.[82]

In 1849, "Parson's old mill at Lahaina" was considered typical.[83] It consisted of a battery of wooden rollers, perhaps 18 inches in diameter and two feet long, mounted vertically and driven by animal power. The profits from the sale of the thick syrup produced mainly proceeded from whalers who presumably used it for making rum. The cane trash needed to be supplemented with indigo in order to boil down the cane juice. "The area cleared was subsequently used for the first planting of seed cane brought by Captain Edwards, of the whaleship *George Washington*. This cane was subsequently called 'Lahaina.' "[84] No great amount of investment was needed for these "screeching nuisances" and the mills seem to have been portable and changed hands frequently.[85] The native wild cane milled at Lahaina was only incidentally watered, grown on the banks of taro patches.[86] Parson's mill moved to Makawao in about 1850 and sugar milling was discontinued at Lahaina at that time.[87] By 1857, the only Maui sugar plantations were Brewer Plantation and East Maui Plantation—both at Makawao.[88]

With the passage of the Māhele law of 1850, the Hawai'i lands could be sold to foreigners, including those who sought to construct sugar mills. King Kamehameha III appointed land agents to broker land sales. John T. Gower, an American sugar planter and store owner in Makawao, served as a land agent on Maui.[89] According to Interior Department records, however, John Gower pocketed the income from land sales he arranged. Although the government discovered his practice and sought repayment from him for the funds he took, Gower remained in the position of land agent.[90]

Post-Māhele, rural Hawai'i changed as many Hawaiians turned away from subsistence agriculture and towards day work on nearby plantations, or even distant ones.[91]

In the 1850s and through the 1860s, Kanaka Maoli workers at commercial mills were often day laborers. They preferred to work under teams, hiring themselves, and sometimes their oxen, out for a day or week at the time. This was one means by which these workers resisted the harsh authoritarian plantation system.[92] Though Chinese workers arrived in 1852, Hawaiians—both women and men—formed the majority of the plantation workforce through the 1870s.[93] By the 1860s, Hawaiians were also signing lengthier, one-year contracts. Laborers in other sectors were also struggling against consolidating settler capital and concomitant industrial relations. In May 1867, the Honolulu Longshoremen went on strike to raise their wages from $1 to $1.50 a day and were replaced by scabs.

Though Kahaulelio and his co-committee writers appear to fault the desire of people for "fast money"[94] or to earn it quickly, there is little discussion of the then-recent government requirements for cash payments. New government laws regulating property and taxes that required cash were perhaps more of a push for Kanaka Maoli subsistence labor to transition to commercial plantation waged work.[95] "By 1860, cash became a requirement for all but road taxes, which were still paid in labor on the local roads."[96] Also, by this time, many were prevented from access to forests, pasture, and coastal areas by the division of lands into private parcels, thereby also prevented from subsistence economies and forced into plantation labor.[97] During the 1860s, Hawaiian adults were required to pay $5 per year for various taxes—poll, school, road, dog, horse, cart, property, and other taxes.[98] These taxes were specifically designed to force Hawaiians into a cash economy and to meet the demands of planters who required increasing amounts of labor.

Another challenge to traditional farming operations was industrial plantations' monopolization of water sources. The period between 1856 and 1878, particularly at Lahaina, saw "considerable activity both in the organization of new plantations and in the development of irrigation resources by those which already were in operation."[99] By the time the historic *Horner v. Kumuliilii*, 10 Haw. 174 (1895) was decided, Pioneer Mill had adversely used Kauaula stream water against kuleana tenants, including "D. Kahaulelio," for at least 20 years.

This period also falls between the cessation of English-language publications of the *Transactions of the Royal Hawaiian Agricultural Society* in 1856 and the 1875 publication of *Thrum's Annual.* Maclennan attributes the tendency of accounts of Hawai'i sugar industrial development to skip this early period to, amongst other things, this paucity of documentation, as well as the relatively high failure rate of these early sugar mills.[100] Yet, many of the foundational changes in law, technology, and economic systems occurred during this time.

IX. 1877 LAHAINA FAMINE

On July 12, 1877, Moses Palau wrote "Na Anoai o ka Malu Ulu o Lele" from Lahaina Prison.[101]

> "No ka wi.—Nui loa ka wi ma keia mau la, oiai mawaena o kekahi poe, he neo ma ka waihona, ua hoolilo lakou i ka ehako i ola, a i hala hoi kekahi wa pilikia, oiai, ua pii hoi ke kumukuai o ke pai ai i kekahi wa 75 keneta a $1.25."
>
> *"Concerning famine.—There is a lot of famine these days, meanwhile for some people on average, there is nothing in the cabinet, they turned "suffering" into their daily lives, and suffered a time of trouble, while the price of undiluted taro went up 75 cents to $1.25."*

Though some believed the famine would end in 1867, famine in Lahaina was again noteworthy in 1876–1877. "Na Nu Hou Kuloko" *Nupepa Kuokoa* Buke

15, Helu 46 (Nowemapa 11, 1876) included the following advisory, warning that the people should plant taro in order to prevent famine:

KE HOPOHOPO nei makou i keia manawa malia e hiki mai ana he wa no kakou e wi ai. Aole no paha e liuliu ana a hiki io mai. Aole makou ma ka ano kaula keia wanana e ana i o la honua, aka ma ka ike iho, ke miki mai nei na pake i na aina mahi kalo e lilo ia lakou ma ka hoolimalima, a e hoopiha i ke kanu ana i ka laiki. Ina ua punihei aku nei oukou, e hiki io mai no ka hopena o ka wi.

He mea no hoi kekahi i maa ia makou, ina e puka ana ka ai i kekahi mau makahiki a ina hookahi makahiki e haule ai, o ka palaleha mai la no ia o na kanaka i ke kanu ana. Molowa iho la a manaka i ke kanu hou aku. No keia mea makou e paipai pinepine nei i keia mau malama elua, e kanu i ke kalo o wi auanei kakou. Ke hoolohe mai nei paha oukou, aole paha. Aka "he kuli ka make a he lohe ke ola."

We are now concerned that maybe a time of famine will fall on us. And in no time, it will surely arrive. We are not prophets who predict what will happen here on earth, but we see that the Chinese [persons] are eager for taro patches and they rent these lands and then they fill them by planting rice. If you folks are gullible, the outcome of a famine will surely be here.

This is also something familiar to us, if we grow food some years and then one year there is none, it's because people neglected planting. Continuously planting is lazy and boring. It is for this reason we frequently encourage these two months, plant taro or a famine will eventually happen. Perhaps you folks are listening, perhaps not. But, "Ignoring is a death sentence; listening ensures life."

On May 21, 1877,[102] A. L. Kamauu, of Hulikanahele, Lahaina wrote of the continuing famine:

"Ka wi. Ke holapu hopo ole mai nei ka wi ia Lahaina nei, ke pinana loa aku nei na wahi pai ai liilii o Kauwe mai, I ke ¾ a I ookah dala.

Hele I ka pule. I ka manuwa Fantome I hiki mai ai, ua hoopae ia mai kekahi mau koa I ka pule Bihopa a me Katorika, malalo o ka malama ana a kekahi o ko lakou mau alii.

Lokahi ka manao. Lahui like ia ka Lunakanawai Hoomalu o Lahaina me ke Lii Kiaaina, e hui pu ma ka hooikaika I ka pono o ka Haku, ke uleu nei, lana ka manao.

Ke hooki nei au maanei me ka adieu I na hoa hanohano o ka Papa Pai."

"Famine. Famine is spreading here to Lahaina without a doubt, tiny food bundles from Kauwe are very much so increasing from ¾ to $1.00.

Go pray. In the time when Fantome arrived, some warriors landed in the prayer of the Bishop and Catholics, under the care and guidance of some of their chiefs.

Thoughts were united. A unified nation, the presiding judge and the governor will convince for the purpose of strengthening the expectations of the Lord, it's moving quick, hopefully.

I will end things here with a farewell bid to the famous friends of Papa Pai."

The recurrent famine condition is unsurprising. Few traditional farmers were able to retain title to their kuleana parcels, and even those that had done so were at risk of losing them to encroaching industrial plantations or being cut off from customary water sources. These authors alternate their focus on broad concepts—nation, market, God, and daily lives—yet consistently measure famine in the cost of kalo and the absence of cultivated loʻi kalo. Though people ate other famine foods, like banana shoots, use of paʻi ai as a metric for famine shortages remained at least through the 1870s.

In her book about how change happens, Lauren Berlant observes: "When things stop converging in reliable patterns of social and material reproduction, they also threaten the conditions and the sense of belonging, but more than that, of assembling."[103] As above-noted, Kahaulelio earlier observed: "Here is another thought about eating poi, it was never thought to spend money on different foods like bread, rice, beans, yeast and so forth like foreigners." Kahaulelio's advice was practical to the extent that food is a commodity and a tool for survival. Beans, wheat flour, and rice have cultural and ecological relationships foreign to traditional Lahaina. And they have very different historical-ontological relationships as compared to kalo and Hāloa. Reticence to incorporate imported haole foods into daily lives may have signaled something like resistance to giving up a vital tool of assembling the very lifeways that settler colonial agriculture threatened.

X. CODA

Who talked about famine in Lahaina matters because it seems only Kānaka Maoli did so. And when they talked about famine, they talked about new arrangements of life, land, and desire—for "fast money" for "something fabulous in stores such as good quality clothing, silk clothing, a horse saddle." Newspaper authors talked about how people could mobilize as a people and in making individual decisions about how to live. That it worked through a form of call and no-response is inbuilt to the newspaper format. But this does not mean the limits of the genre defined the authors' sense that their world could be otherwise and better, if only people would do otherwise and do better.

At base was an optimism for the possibilities of learning from the past (about how to survive famine) and for arresting what was new and perilous (about abandoning the land for waged work). The authors located in their audience a kind of person who would be a "potential conversion space for not reproducing capitalist, imperialist, racist, and patriarchal lines of descent."[104] Though cabined into plantation work by converging climate phenomena, global markets, and missionaries turning to capitalism, the people of Lahaina were still seen—at least by these authors—to have the ability to maintain identity, dignity, and land. "Perhaps you folks are listening, perhaps not. But, 'Ignoring is a death sentence; listening ensures life.' "[105]

NOTES

1.   A transcription of W. Sebena, N., "No Ka Wi o Lahaina Nei," Ke Au Okoa, aoao 2 (June 4, 1866). The original author's name is difficult to discern fully. A contemporaneous author writing out of Puehuehu, Lahaina is named "Sebena W. Nailiili" and may be the same person.

2.   Kahealani Lono produced all translations in this text unless otherwise noted.

3.   "Lele" is another name for Lahaina, often associated with the phrase: "Ka Malu Ulu o Lele" or the breadfruit shade of Lele (Lahaina).

4.   Translator's note: "hoʻō" can mean food provisions for a journey, or to provide the same. The author and their friends may be scavenging and trying to be resourceful with food production by producing as much as possible and then sharing it out even though it is not the favored food.

5.   Robert Schmitt, *Historical Statistics of Hawaii* (Honolulu: University of Hawaiʻi Press, 1977), p. 114.

6.   "European Summary," *The Pacific Commercial Advertiser*, p. 3 (May 30, 1868).

7.   "The Famine in India," *The Pacific Commercial Advertiser*, p. 3 (November 10, 1866).

8.   "Terrible Famine and Distress in Mantchuria," *The Pacific Commercial Advertiser*, p. 3 (December 3, 1870).

9.   "Famine," *The Pacific Commercial Advertiser*, p. 3 (April 4, 1868).

10. *The Pacific Commercial Advertiser*, p. 3 (June 27, 1868).

11. *The Pacific Commercial Advertiser*, p. 1 (November 14, 1868).

12. *The Pacific Commercial Advertiser*, p. 3 (June 30, 1866).

13. *The Pacific Commercial Advertiser*, p. 1 (March 23, 1867).

14. *The Pacific Commercial Advertiser*, p. 2 (Jan. 19, 1867).

15. *The Pacific Commercial Advertiser*, p. 4 (August 10, 1867).

16. *The Pacific Commercial Advertiser*, p. 3 (February 2, 1867).

17. *The Pacific Commercial Advertiser*, p. 3 (February 15, 1868).

18. F.A. Schaefer, Consul, Prussian Consulate, "Notice," *The Hawaiian Gazette*, p. 3 (Apr. 22, 1868).

19. *The Hawaiian Gazette*, p. 1 (Oct. 6, 1869).

20. Mike Davis, *Late Victorian Holocausts* (London & New York: Verso, 2001), p 9.

21. Karl Polanyi, *The Great Transformation*, rev. ed. (Boston: Beacon Press, 2001), p. 167.

22. Ibid., p. 168.

23. Ibid.

24. Davis, *Late Victorian*, p. 21.

25. Ibid.

26. Ibid., p. 29.

27. D. Kahaulelio et al., "No ka Wi," *Nupepa Kuokoa*, aoao 4 (Apelila 12, 1867) (trans. K. Lono).

28. "No Lahaina Mai," *Au Okoa*, at 2 (May 30, 1867) *available at*: nupepa-hawaii.com/2017/05/29/news-out-of-lahaina-1867/

29. Maly's translation is contained in D. Kahaulelio et al., "No ka Wi" (About the Famine) *Nupepa Kuokoa*, aoao 4 (Apelila 12, 1867), by Kepā Maly, *He Wahi Moʻolelo no Kauaʻula a me Lahaina i Maui* Vol. 2 (May 25, 2007) (Maly Lahaina V.2).

30. Judge Daniel Kahaulelio wrote of his life in Lahaina in "Ka Moolelo o ke Kaulanakauhale o Lahaina," a five-part series published in *Ka Lei Rose o Hawaii* (1898), translated in this volume. Judge Kahaulelio had sons, including David Kahaulelio, who also graduated from Lahainaluna, in 1886, and Job Frank Kahulelio. "Lahaina Letter," *Pacific Commercial Advertiser*, at 5 (September 6, 1887); *Hawaiian Gazette* at 9 (November 18, 1890). Judge Kahaulelio also participated in the legislature. In 1870, he objected to a law concerning reasons for divorce because "the law would be too hard on the people." Mr. Kalakaua also opposed the bill "as he thought its working would be hard and severe on the lower classes." *Pacific Commercial Advertiser*, p. 3 (July 2, 1870).

31. *Nupepa Kuokoa*, Buke 5, Helu 9 (Malaki 3, 1866).

32. Davis, *Late Victorian*, p. 13.

33. Ibid., p. 25.

34. S.C. Limaikaika, "Holo I Maui," *Ka Hae Hawaii*, Poakolu, helu 2 (Augate 15, 1860).

35. "Excessive mortality," *The Pacific Commercial Advertiser*, p. 3 (Aug. 21, 1869).

36. David Stannard, "Disease and Infertility," *J. American Studies* 24, no. 3 (Dec. 1990): 325, 330 quoting M. Rollin, M.D., "Dissertation on the Inhabitants of Easter Island and the Island of Mowee," in J. F. G. de la Perouse, *A Voyage Round the*

World Performed in the Years 1785, 1786, 1787, and 1788, Vol. II (London: A. Hamilton, 1799), p. 337

37. Stannard, "Disease and Infertility," p. 330 quoting David Malo, "On the Decrease of Population in the Hawaiian Islands," *Hawaiian Spectator*, p. 125 (April 1839).

38. David Malo, *Hawaiian Antiquities*, 2nd ed. (Honolulu, 1951), p. 22, 43. In 1977, a settler historian noted the "most mysterious and least known of historic Hawaiian famines reportedly took place on Maui in 1806 and 1807." Robert Schmitt, *Historical Statistics*, p. 111.

39. Stannard, "Disease and Infertility," p. 332.

40. Ibid., p. 335, citing Dwight Baldwin, Lahaina, Maui, Mission Station Report (HMSC, 1851).

41. Kerri A. Inglis, "Kōkua, Mana, and Mālama ʻĀina," *Hūlili: Multidisciplinary Research on Hawaiian Well-Being* 2, no. 1 (2005): 216, 218 citing R. C. Schmitt, "The Okuu—Hawaii's greatest epidemic," *Hawaii Medical Journal* 29 (1970): 363.

42. Stannard, "Disease and Infertility," p. 335.

43. Ibid.

44. Ibid., p. 337.

45. Malcolm Nāea Chun, *Must We Wait in Despair? The 1867 Report of the ʻAhahui Lāʻau Lapaʻau of Wailuku, Maui on Native Hawaiian Health* (First Peoples Productions, 1994).

46. "Discourse on Roads," read to the R.H. Agricultural Society, July 31, by R.C. Wyllie, *RHAS* 2, no. 3 (1856): 75.

47. Ibid.

48. Ibid.

49. "Discourse on Coffee," R.C. Wyllie, Foreign Office, July 22d, 1856 *RHAS* 2, no. 3 (1856): 64.

50. Carol A. MacLennan, "Foundations of Sugar's Power: Early Maui Plantations, 1840–1860," *The Hawaiian Journal of History* 29 (1995): 53.

51. *But see* Sydney Iaukea, "Re-storing Lahaina," in *Tourism Impacts West Maui*, ed. Lance D. Collins and Bianca Isaki (Lahaina: North Beach-West Maui Benefit Fund, 2016), noting Lahaina was only a whaling town between 1842 and 1860.

52. Carol A. MacLennan, "Hawaiʻi Turns to Sugar: The Rise of Plantation Centers, 1860–1880," *The Hawaiian Journal of History* 31 (1997): 117.

53. MacLennan, "Foundations of Sugar's Power," p. 54.

54. Maly V.2 at 6 translation of "Holo ka Hana!" (Work Progresses!) *Ka Hae Hawaii*, p. 34 (May 29, 1861)

55. Ibid.

56. Maly V.2 at 928 citing *the Polynesian* (April 18, 1863).

57. Ibid.

58. "Planters' Meeting," *The Pacific Commercial Advertiser*, p. 1 (October 16, 1869).

59. Ibid.

60. H.A. Wadsworth, University of Hawaiʻi Associate Professor of Irrigation Practice and an Irrigation Specialist with the Hawaiʻi Sugar Planters' Association Experiment Station, "A Historical Summary of Irrigation in Hawaiʻi," p. 143 (University of Hawaiʻi Press, Dec. 1933) reprint of the *Hawaiian Planters' Record* XXXVII, no. 3 (Oct. 1933): 145.

61. Arthur Douglas Baldwin, *A Memoir of Henry Perrine Baldwin, 1842 to 1911* (U. Michigan Press, 1915), p. 27.

62. Ibid.

63. Ibid., pp. 27–28.

64. Ibid., p. 28.

65. Ibid., pp. 99–100.

66. W. Sebena, N., "No Ka Wi o Lahaina Nei."

67. Translation of Kahaulelio et al., "No ka Wi." "No Lahaina Mai," *Au Okoa*, p. 2 (May 30, 1867) *available at*: nupepa-hawaii.com/2017/05/29/news-out-of-lahaina-1867/

68. Ibid.

69. Translators' note: The author's tone is chiding, saying the people were lazy, uninterested, and lacked forward thinking. The "kahea maluna" is like a heavenly calling from God, which told him there is a problem.

70. The individuals sued were named as follows; K indicates Kane (male) and W, Wahine (female): Kumuliilii (K), Kalua Kanawaliwali (K), Kukue (K), Kukaia (K), Ilaika (W), Kauahikaua (K), Wahinepio (W), Kahai (K), Kalua (K), Charles Liilh (K), Henry Hairama (K), U. Kahaulelio (K), Noa Kahaulelio (K), Keao (K), Kawahamana (W), Kaaeae (K), Kapili (K), Kahooneeaina (W), Piimoku (W), Kealo (K), Maikeike Ihihi (K), Kaleihoomio (K), Kahulikaa (K), Elia (K), Kulu (K), Kukue (K), Punihele (K), Kaminamina (W), A. Pali (K), Wili Aholo (Boy), Mrs. Iiattie Ayers (W), Wm. White (K), Henry Smith (K), Kualau (W), Waihoioahu (K), Kanelawahine (K), Liliuokalani (W), Likua (K), Opunui (K), Palakiko (K), D. Kahaulelio (K), Kahoino (W), Hoohilahila (W), Joe Paniole (K), Rev. J. Waiamau (K), Uilama Hinau (K), Kahalepuna (W), Moku (K), Mrs. Sylva, Mrs. Espinda, J. Espinda (K), Mrs. Pratt of Honolulu, Kaloiele (K), Mrs. J. F. Brown of Honolulu, G. K. Halemano (K), S. Koko (K), J. F. Brown, M. Makalua, Kanekoa (K), and C. Aiiwai.

71. J. A. Magoon, Defendants' Brief, *Pioneer Mill vs. Kumuliilii et al.*, First Circuit Court (1895).

72. *Horner v. Kumulii*, 10 Haw. 174, 179 (1895).

73. "Malu o Lele," *Nupepa Kuokoa* Buke 5, Helu 38 (Kepakemapa 22, 1866).

74. J. H. Moku, Lahaina, Iulai 5, 1567, "No ka malu ulu o Lele," *Ka Nupepa Kuokoa*, Volume VI, Number 28, p. 4 (13 July 1867).

75. Lauren Berlant, *On the Inconvenience of Other People* (Durham: Duke University Press, 2022), p. 25.

76. *Nupepa Kuokoa*, Apelila 6, 1865 (aoao 1), translated by Kepā Maly (Maly V.2 at 9).

77. MacLennan, "Hawaiʻi Turns to Sugar," pp. 97–98.

78. "Legislative Proceedings, Monday May 23, 1870," *The Hawaiian Gazette*, p. 1 (June 1, 1870), referring to a An Act to repeal Sections 1417 to 1425 inclusive, regarding the Master and Servant Law upon its 2nd reading. Here, Kahaulelio was speaking in support of a proposal to repeal parts of the Master and Servant Act of 1850. The Master and Servant Act would later be abolished under the Republic of Hawai'i under a new law enacted in February 1895.

79. MacLennan, "Foundations of Sugar's Power," p. 41.

80. Ibid., p. 34.

81. Ibid.

82. Ibid., pp. 35–36.

83. Wadsworth, "A Historical Summary."

84. Ibid., p. 138.

85. Ibid.

86. Ibid., p. 139.

87. Ibid., p. 143. S.C. Limaikaika wrote of their travels through Maui, noting foreigners burning sugar in Makawao, where all was green but the sugar crop was damaged in the dry season due to lack of rain, writing: "akahi wale no pilikia ko Makawao poe no ka nele loa i ka wai ole"—"this is the first time the people of Makawao are in trouble because of a lack of rain." S.C. Limaikaika "Holo I Maui," *Ka Hae Hawaii*, Poakolu, helu 2 (Augate 15, 1860) *accessed via* nupepa.org

88. MacLennan, "Foundations of Sugar's Power," p. 47.

89. Ibid., p. 43. Gower succeeded John Richardson, a part-Hawaiian Wailuku taro farmer and Maui circuit judge.

90. Ibid., p. 44.

91. Ibid.

92. MacLennan, "Hawai'i Turns to Sugar," pp. 97, 110.

93. Ibid., p. 109.

94. *See also* translation of Kahaulelio et al., "No ka Wi."

95. MacLennan, "Foundations of Sugar's Power," p. 44.

96. Ibid.

97. Ibid.

98. MacLennan, "Hawai'i Turns to Sugar," p. 111.

99. Wadsworth, "A Historical Summary," p. 143.

100. MacLennan, "Foundations of Sugar's Power," p. 33.

101. Moses Palau, Lahaina Prison, July 12, 1877, "Na Anoai o ka Malu Ulu o Lele," *Ka Lāhui Hawai'i*, Buke 3, Helu 29 (Iulai 19, 1877).

102. A.L. Kamauu, Hulikanahele, Lahaina (Mei 21, 1877) *Ka Lāhui Hawai'i* Buke 3, Hule 23 (Iune 7, 1877).

103. Berlant, *Inconvenience*, p. 95 (footnote omitted).

104. Ibid., p. 77.

105. "Na Nu Hou Kuloko," *Nupepa Kuokoa* Buke 15, Helu 46 (Nowemapa 11, 1876).

CHAPTER 7

SARAH KALE KANĪ'AULONO DAVIS
A Transitional Life in West Maui

'Umi Perkins

Lu'ulu'u 'Eke i ka 'eleua
Ke ka'awili nei i ke one o Honokahua
Lawakua ka 'ahu'ula kūlōlio 'o Pi'ilani
Pihana papau i nā lani mai nā kupuna mai.
Aia he anoano i ka hi'i kapu,
Ho'opālama ke kia'i i konapiliahi o Keauhou

'Eke is overladen with heavy rains
Kneading the sands of Honokahua,
Pi'ilani's feather cloak tightly plaited
Closely gathering our sacred ancestors
Reverently bearing the kapu—
The watchful, powerful guardians of Keauhou[1]
—Kapulani Landgraf, "Honokahua"

'ŌLELO MUA

When I was a boarder at Lahainaluna, and in subsequent years throughout the 1990s, I used to go fishing with my former track coach, lifelong Nāpili resident Dennis Nakamura. One area we often visited was a bluff of short cliffs, and it was here, perhaps, that I felt most connected throughout my entire life. I later discovered that this bluff was the edge of the ahupua'a of Honokahua, given, indirectly, by Kamehameha I to the subject of my study: Kale Davis.

Much is known about the advisors to Kamehameha I, John Young and Isaac Davis. Their exploits at the battle of Kepaniwai in ʻIao Valley, Maui, where the waters of ʻIao Stream were dammed by the bodies of the dead, are part of Hawaiian historical lore. Even John Young's descendants are known because their line led to Queen Emma, who was the daughter of Young's daughter Fanny Kekelaokalani. Far less is known of the descendants of Isaac Davis. This chapter tracks the life of Davis's daughter, called by Hawaiians "Kale." But because Kale lived so early in the historical period—to illustrate, I was not able to find birth or marriage records for her in the Hawaiʻi Archives—I lay out the shape, or silhouette, of her life based on those who surrounded, and in most cases loved, her. From a Hawaiian perspective this is appropriate in that individuals are situated within a social context—a web of relations. I also use the place over which she exercised kuleana as a proxy for her character: Honokahua.

Sarah Kale Kaniʻaulono Davis was born in 1797 and lived until 1867, when she passed away at about age 70. One genealogical source cites Waimea, Kauaʻi as her birthplace.[2] A mele written about Davis associates her with Hilo. Other genealogical sources claim that she was named Sarah after her father Isaac Davis's sister in Wales. As Wanda Adams noted in the *Honolulu Advertiser*, Kale Davis was "the last chiefess of Honokahua Valley, the portion of land known today as Kapalua."[3] The noted Hawaiian history expert Clarice Taylor wrote in her *Honolulu Star-Bulletin* column that "Kale was not the Hawaiianized form of Sara. [. . .] It was short for Kalekoolani."[4]

Moʻokūʻauhau—Genealogy

Sarah Kaniʻaulono Davis, often called "Kale Davis," was the daughter of Isaac Davis and the "Big Island chiefess" Nakai-a-Kalimaʻaluʻalu.[5] According to modern genealogical sources, her mother was born in 1778 (the year of Cook's arrival) and died of the maʻi ʻōkuʻu in 1803. Maʻi ʻōkuʻu has not been pinpointed but is thought to have been cholera or perhaps the bubonic plague. David Malo claims that half of the Hawaiian population died in 1804 of the disease. Nakai was probably 19 years old when she gave birth to Kale. Her name followed the traditional chiefly practice of marking the father's name: Nakai of Kalimaʻaluʻalu. Nakai's parents were Kuwaluluka and Uwaikikilani, both born around 1714, according to the Len Kong Farm genealogy.[6] An article in the *Honolulu Star-Advertiser* reviewing a historical novel about Kale Kaniʻaulono Davis's life describes her mother as "a Big Island chiefess." Maʻi ʻōkuʻu, which killed her mother and a large portion of the Hawaiian population, was most likely cholera. Called "the squatting disease," it was an extreme form of diarrhea that could eventually cause organ failure. A *Maui News* article notes that her mother was "a descendant of Kihapiʻilani, who built the Alaloa road around Maui, also known as the King's Trail."[7]

Kale's siblings included Betty Davis, who married Humehume, the son of Kauaʻi King Kaumualiʻi, and George Huʻeu Davis.

In 1861, six years before her death, *Nupepa Kuokoa* printed a mele for Kale, entitled "He Mele no Sale Kaniaulono":

> O Kale wahine i ka ua kanilehua,
> Ua kanilehua o Hilo i ka nahele,
> Ke hoomu la i ka liko o ka lehua,
> Ka'o ka pua hala ka-a-o i ka ua,
> Ka puneki oho kalole o ke ki,
> I lalena i ka ua ia e ka ua,
> I nahea kou hiki ana mai,
> Inehinei no—e.
> Inehinei ka la o ka makemake.
> Hiki lailai i o'u nei ke aloha,
> Me kuu ipo pua kaunoa i ke kula,
> Ina la i ke kula i ke kaha o Kanehili,
> Me kuu kane hauwai opu o Kalena,
> Kau ke ano ihi ka nahele o Malama,
> I ka mapumapu aala o ke kupukupu,
> Aala ka uka o Maunauna,
> Mai mauna ia e oe ka hoa i loaa.
> O luhi oe auanei i ka imi.
> He hana inea—a—e,

> NA I. A. KAHANUI.

Below is a direct translation (without any kaona, or hidden meanings) by Pili Keala-Quinabo:

> *Kale, woman of the Kanilehua rain*[8]
> *Kanilehua rain of Hilo in the forest,*
> *That silences the bud (child or descendant) of the lehua*
> *Bare is the overripened hala flower in the rain*
> *The straight cluster of ti leaves*

A day tinted yellow by the rain of the rain.[9]
When will you arrive
Yesterday indeed
Yesterday was the day of desire
Love arrived to me in serenity
With my love kauna'oa flower in the plains
If in the plains, in the place of Kanehili
With my man diving in the cool waters of Kalena
Settled in the slight reverence of Malama
Wafting in the rising scent of the kupukupu ferns
The uplands of Maunauna are fragrant
Don't you waste the friendship had
You are tired of searching
A task that brings suffering

By I. A. Kahanui

Isaac Davis

Sarah "Kale" Kanī'aulono Davis's father, Isaac Davis, was a crew member of the sloop *Fair American,* whose crew were all killed in a revenge attack (for humiliating one of the Hawai'i chiefs)—all except Davis, that is, who was spared because he fought bravely. Davis was brought before Kamehameha, where he saw John Young, and the two were made an offer they couldn't refuse: either be killed or become assistants to Kamehameha. Their choice became a history-changing one.

Isaac Davis was born in Milford Haven, Pembrokeshire, Wales in 1758—he was likely the same age as Kamehameha. He joined the crew of *Fair American* under Captain Simon Metcalfe, who was involved in the Olowalu Massacre, outside Lahaina, which left fifty Hawaiians dead and was called Kalolopahu (the spilled brains).[10] Davis assisted John Young with the cannon Lopaka at Kepaniwai, the Battle of the Dammed Waters at 'Iao Valley. This battle was the site at which Kamehameha made his famous speech:

Imua e nā pōki'i, e inu i ka wai 'awa'awa, 'a'ole hope e ho'i mai ai
   Go forward my dear younger brothers, drink of the bitter waters, there is no turning back

According to the National Park Service:

It is clear that Isaac Davis and Kamehameha became close friends. Ebenezer Townsend of the *Neptune* noted in 1798 that:

> On leaving Davis the king embraced him and cried like a child. Davis said he always did when he left him, for he was always apprehensive that he might leave him, although he had promised him he would never do it without giving him previous notice.

> In 1810 he negotiated terms of peace for Kamehameha with Ka'umu'a-li'i [*sic*], the king of Kaua'i. When Ka'umu'ali'i journeyed to Honolulu on board a foreign vessel to see Kamehameha, some lower chiefs conspired to kill him and proposed to Kamehameha that a sorcerer perform this deed. The king refused and even had the sorcerer slain. The chiefs then hatched a plot to kill Ka'umu'ali'i secretly as he journeyed into the interior. Learning of these plans, Davis warned Ka'umu'ali'i to return on board ship. Shortly thereafter, Davis died by poisoning, possibly in retaliation for this act of loyalty to Ka'umu'ali'i.[11]

Isaac Davis died in 1810, the same year Kamehameha conquered the islands, and at a time when Kale would have been about 13 years old. Some sources say the poison he ingested was intended for King Kaumuali'i of Kaua'i. John Young adopted Davis's orphaned children. Davis had married into Kaua'i ali'i, and still has descendants today. Many of these descendants stem from the lines of Kale Kanī'aulono Davis, who married her stepbrother James Young Kanehoa (the son of John Young), Captain Alexander Adams and three Hawaiian men, including Kanekuapu'u and Kaholokahiki. But descendants appear to descend from Adams and Kanekuapu'u, either mainly or exclusively.

Pō'aiapili—Historical Context

The Hawaiian Kingdom in the years 1797 to 1867 saw massive shifts politically and socially. After the aforementioned ma'i 'ōku'u, Kamehameha conquered the archipelago in 1810, when Davis was 13, conquering and thereby uniting Ko Hawai'i Pae 'Āina—Hawai'i's Islands. The 'aikapu—the separate-eating institution that ordered Hawaiian society by gender—was abolished in 1819 when Kale was about 22 years of age. In Lahaina, she would have seen Kamehameha's second son, Kauikeaouli (King Kamehameha III), transform the kingdom into a constitutional monarchy in 1840. By the time of Kale's death, Kamehameha V would be on the throne, having promulgated a third Constitution in 1864. Kale would have known of the missionary work throughout the islands. She would have definitely been familiar with the missionaries William Richards and Dwight Baldwin, and the latter's residence on Front Street in Lahaina. She may have even known my great-great-grandfather Keli'imakekauonu'uanu, who assisted Baldwin, was said to be Baldwin's "Right hand man" and whose brother's name was very like her mother's: Nakaielua. Because she lived in the Lahaina moku (district), Davis would have had a front-row seat to these, at times, traumatic changes, centered as they would have been at Moku'ula, the capital and royal residence of Kamehameha II and III.

Kale Kanī'aulono Davis was the ali'i of the Honokahua area of North Lahaina moku (district, although Māhele records list the district as Kā'anapali)—the place where the first burials were discovered desecrated by the Ritz Carlton hotel in the mid-1980s, sparking a movement to deal with Hawaiian burials in a manner that is pono (righteous). This troubling historical coincidence suggests that some of her relatives may have been disinterred in this disrespectful and desecrating manner. Kale Kanī'aulono Davis's own grave is believed to be intact.

Kale Davis was given the ahupua'a of Honokahua, North of Lahaina, by inheritance from her father.[12] She sailed there from Honolulu after a bad divorce from John Kanehoa Young (who had discovered the destructive allure of alcohol in Honolulu), and on the voyage met her future husband, Captain Adam Alexander.

HONOKAHUA

Smith notes that there are two spellings of the 'āina over which Davis was kono-hiki: Honokohua and Honokahua.[13] The name Honokahua can be broken into the words *Hono,* meaning bay, and kahua: foundation, but the term can also mean a declaration of principles. This is apropos in that it came to stand for the principles guiding the proper treatment of 'iwi kūpuna beginning in the mid- to late-1980s.

According to Hawaiian history blogger and former director of DLNR, Peter Young, "Honokahua Valley has been described as having lo'i lands. Sweet potatoes were reportedly grown between the Honokōhau and Kahaku-loa Ahupua'a."[14]

The "Alphabetical Index of Awards by Awardee" for the Māhele lists, in the district of Kā'anapali, Honokahua, consisting of 2650 acres, granted to "Davis, Kale." The land consists of two Land Commission Awards (LCAs), 8522-B and 6146-B, granted under Royal Patent 2236. It is by far the largest land grant in Kā'anapali.[15]

The King's Mahele lists Davis's lands under "Kale" as a surname. The book lists "lands [. . .] claimed for Kale" among those that were "for the apportionment of Isaac Davis' lands among his three children, George Hueu Davis, Kale (Sarah Davis) and Peke (Betty Davis)":

LCA 8522-B
RP [Royal Patent] 2236 Honokahua ahupuaa, Kaanapali, Maui 2,650 ac
RP 2236 Kapaa, ahupuaa, [N.] Kohala, Hawaii, by name only . . .
RP 2236 Wakahekahe, ahupuaa, Puna, Hawaii by name only[16]

Honokahua was much later the site of a struggle between Hawaiian activists and the Ritz-Carlton developers over 'iwi (burial remains), and to many became synonymous with the burial movement that emerged from the site. The Maui activist and poet Dana Naone Hall of the Hui Alanui o Mākena noted that while the site was not the first of such desecrations,

> this was the first time anybody latched on to what was happening [. . .] and slowed the process down enough so that we could really see and understand what was going on and [. . .] the uproar could occur. Honokahua allowed for the final necessary element to be put in place, which is that the people whose culture it is were able to begin to make the decisions about what happened to these important sacred places.[17]

The 'āina with which Kale Davis was entrusted later became a symbol of the beginning of Hawaiian control of sacred space within the islands. A leader in the movement for the pono treatment of 'iwi, Edward Halealoha Ayau, reflected back on the significance of Honokahua, noting, "The events at Honokahua revealed that a significant kuleana was missing from the Hawaiian conscience: how to culturally care for 'iwi kūpuna and moepū that had become exposed and how to healthily process the resulting kaumaha (physical, emotional and spiritual trauma)."[18]

Nae'ole similarly summarized the significance of Honokahua in the struggle to treat burials in a pono manner:

> Honokahua changed the history of Hawai'i. They have set precedent that we will never ever go back to this complacency and complete disregard for the iwi of our kupuna. Honokahua has created the laws, Honokahua is the law, this stands as the kāhili [feather standard, a sign of royalty] for all burial

sites from here on to perpetuity. This is the battleground, this is the piko [navel, umbilical cord] of these new laws.[19]

OTHER LANDS

Another estate in which Davis had an interest was that of John Young. It states in *The King's Mahele: The Awardees and their Lands:*

> Persons interested will of John Young, Sr': John Young [Keoni ana], Jas. [Kanehoa] Young, Fanny [Kelelaokalani] Naea, Grace [Kamaikui] Rooke, Jane [Gini Lahilahi] Kaeo, Geo. [Hueu] Davis, Sarah [Kale] Davis, Betty [Peke Davis] Silva and Mary Kuamoo [Kaoanaeha].[20]

This estate would have certainly included Young's compound at Kawaihae, near the Kona-Kohala district border, upon which an archaeological survey was done. This survey strongly suggests by the foreign and native implements present that Young would have been considered a wealthy man. This is also the likely site of Kale Davis's upbringing in the aftermath of her father's death.

KONOHIKI

What does it mean to be a konohiki? In the Māhele, ali'i received lands in their capacity as Konohiki—because of their kuleana of managing lands, not merely because of rank. As Honokahua was sold in 1894 intact (except for the very small parcel containing Davis's grave), it begs the question: Why did Honokahua remain intact? In other words, why didn't the maka'āinana living under Kale Davis's leadership divide out their interests and claim small kuleana parcels from her 2,650-acre holding? In some cases, it is said that konohiki persuaded maka'āinana to continue to live in the old way—this could have been particularly effective if a konohiki was trusted or beloved. It is possible that this was the case with Kale Davis, resulting in no kuleana parcels being "cut out" of her extensive holding, as was normally done. It is also possible that kuleana were claimed from her lands, but that those kuleana were reabsorbed into the larger parcel before or after its 1894 sale.

MARRIAGES

The *Lahaina News* lists Davis's five husbands: "She married James Kanehoa Young, Captain Alexander Adams, Pahaaikaua, Kanekuapu'u, and Kaholokahiki," and her six children: "Isaac Adams of Niu, 'Uwaikikilani Halstead of Maui, Amelia Nakai Davis of Waikoloa, Mele Kuamoʻo of Lahaina, [and] Fanny and James Kanehoa Young Davis of Honokahua."[21]

James Young Kanehoa

James Young Kanehoa was a member of the House of Nobles, the Land Commission, and the Privy Council, and served as governor of Maui, Molokai and Lānaʻi.[22] He lived from 1797 to 1851. In *The King's Mahele:* "James Kanehoa Young, born ca. 1798, was the son of John Olohana Young by his first wife, Namokuelua, who died in 1804." It also states: "KANEHOA Sarah Davis no issue." The couple had no children but adopted a child of James's sister Jane Lahilahi. The child was named Keliʻimaikaʻi Kaeo as he was the son of Peter Kaeo, who attended the Chiefs' Children's School (Royal School). *The King's Mahele* notes the testimony of Dr. T. C. B. Rooke, who claimed under oath that James Young Kanehoa "had an adopted child named Keliimaikai 'but not formally adopted before a judge by agreement in writing' he [Alebada Keliimaikai] died on the 13th of October last [1850]." Katherine Smith's novel alludes to the gradual dissolution of this marriage due to James's discovery of alcohol/rum. He accompanied Liholiho (Kamehameha II) on his trip to England in 1824–1825.[23]

Alexander Adams

Like her father, Isaac, Kale's second husband was a close confidante of Kamehameha. Alexander Adams was born about 1780 in Arbroth, Forfarshire, Scotland. According to the Kekoʻolani genealogy, Adams was:

> born on 27 Dec 1780 in Abroath, Angus, Scotland. He died on 27 Oct 1871 in Niu Hawaii. He was buried in Nuuanu Cemetary, Oahu, Hi. He married[3] Sarah Kaniaulono Davis (Sally, Kale) about 1816 in Niu Hawaii. Alexander was employed as Brig Pilot for the Kaahumanu, formerly the Forrester, purchased by King Kamehameha in 04–16–1816. He was baptized on 30 Aug 1784 in St. Vigeans, Angus, Scotland.[24]

His father was John Alexander, the Earl of Fyfe. This is a high rank in the British peerage system, below only duke. However, some sources claim that there was a dispute over the earldom between the Adams and the Duff lines over Fyfe. It is possible that this led Alexander to seek his fortune elsewhere. Arriving in Hawaiʻi in 1811, immediately after unification, he became brigadier of *Kaʻahumanu* for Kamehameha I. Some credit Adams with designing the Hawaiian flag. A *Honolulu Star Bulletin* article from 1925 tells of one of his contributions to the Kingdom—the Hawaiian national ensign. Debate continues today over this flag, and it remains contested whether Adams designed it, or merely had a part in doing so:

> Captain Adams is said to have inspired the designing of the Hawaiian flag, when he refused to fly the British colors at the masthead of the "Kaahumanu," and suggested to Kamehameha that the kingdom should have its own individual ensign. Although claims have been put forth by others as to the designing of the flag, and historians have differed on the relative merits of such claims, descendants of Captain Adams are confident that he did actually place the British Union Jack in the upper left-hand corner of the Hawaiian flag.
>
> The story goes that Kamehameha I laid out the field of the flag with its eight stripes, representing the eight inhabited islands of Hawaii. "Now, what shall I use for a head?" he is supposed to have asked his followers. Various suggestions were made, including that the royal insignia or the crown be used. None met with the monarch's approval, and he declared that he would wait for the return of "my Haole" (Captain Adams) from a sea trip before hoisting the new flag of the country. Upon Captain Adams' return, it is asserted, he took the eight stripes and laid thereon the Union Jack as a head for the Hawaiian flag, and the national emblem was completed.[25]

Adams was married three times in total, and had fifteen children. His two other wives were the Harbottle sisters, and eight of his children were from the younger Harbottle sister. In his blog, "Images of Old Hawai'i," Peter Young notes that:

> Adams died October 17, 1871. He is buried next to his friend and fellow Scotsman Andrew Auld in the O'ahu Cemetery. Their common tombstone contains the following inscription in the Scots dialect: 'Twa croanies frae the land of heather; Are sleepin' here in death th'gether.'[26]

Kanekuapu'u

According to a genealogy on the website Family Search, Kale Davis had four children by Kanekuapu'u (one apparently named for her former husband, and one for her stepsister): John Kanehoa Kanekuapu'u, Amelia Nakai Kanekuapu'u, Kuamo'o Kanekuapu'u, and Fanny Kanekuapu'u.[27]

Nā Keiki—Children

Isaac Young Adams

Because his father, Alexander, was granted land at Niu in Southeast O'ahu (now called Niu Valley), Isaac Adams maintained his residence there. Isaac Adams was the second husband of Princess Ruth Ke'elikōlani, but they later divorced. An 1863 article reported sightings on Adams's property of "the wild man of Niu," who had "lived in a wild state for 18 years."[28] This is the property on which Hawaiian wayfinder Nainoa Thompson lives, as he is a descendant of the Harbottle family (Alexander Adams's wife).

Amelia Nakai Kanekaupu'u

Amelia Nakai Kanekaupu'u was born in 1827 and died in 1895 at age 68.[29] It seems that she married her first cousin George Hu'eu Davis, Jr., the son of Kale Davis's brother, and they had one child who survived, William Kahiukahi, and three who did not.

Ua Hala

Death of Kale Kanī'aulono Davis
According to a *Maui News* article:

> For 150 years, the Davis family grave was preserved by Maui Land & Pineapple Co., set off in a pineapple field by a white rail fence and marked with one papaya tree. The grave itself was reserved from sale by the family in 1894 and remains the property of Davis family descendants.
>
> Clifford Nae'ole, cultural director at The Ritz-Carlton, Kapalua, said Sunday that Kaniaulono is buried at the site above Kapalua, but there may be others there. There is a burial mound, but another flat area nearby could be another burial area, though there is no record of others being laid to rest there, he said.[30]

Mo'opuna—Descendants

A *Maui News* article lists the families who descend from Kale Davis:

> On Maui, descendants include the Mahoe family of Lahaina, Kaeo and Davis families of Moloka'i, and the Wilcox family of Waihe'e. The Adams

family of O'ahu descends from Kale, as does the Davis family of West
Hawai'i.[31]

'ŌLELO HOPE

I have attempted here to trace the life of a historical figure of the second tier—
that is, she lived her life in the shadow of more famous people, such as her father,
Isaac Davis. Kale Davis represents a transitional figure, coping with the changes
that modernity and the encroachment of Euroamerican "civilization" wrought
on Hawaiian society. She is also the product of these forces, but attempted to
dispense her kuleana in a traditional way—if she had not, she may have been
better known to history. That Honokahua became a symbol of Hawaiian resistance to an over-development that literally trod on native remains—perhaps
symbolic of the way she lived her life.

NOTES

1. "Honokahua," Nā Wahi Kapu o Maui, Kapulani Landgraf, 2003.
2. familysearch.org.
3. Wanda Adams, *Honolulu Advertiser,* 18 Jun 2006, p. 60.
4. Clarise Taylor, "The Isaac Davis Family," *Honolulu Star-Bulletin,* April 7, 1960.
   Taylor's column was called "Tales about Hawaii" and ran for many decades. The
   name is reminiscent of the Keko'olani 'ohana of Hawai'i Island. Other sources
   claim that "Kale" was a transliteration of "Sally."
5. Adams, 2006, 60.
6. Len Kong Farm genealogy (website).
7. "Grave site opportunity brings woman's descendants together," *The Maui News,*
   Mar. 18, 2013.
8. Kani-lehua, name of a mistlike rain famous at Hilo. *Lit.,* [rain that] lehua flowers
   drink. An alternate interpretation is "rain that makes lehua flowers rustle"
   (Keala-Quinabo).
9. lena-6. *(Cap.) n.,* Name of a yellow-tinted rain famous at Hanalei, Kaua'i, and
   on Maui.
10. Kamakau, 1992.
11. nps.gov site for Pu'ukoholā Heiau.
12. Puhipau and Lander, Who will Save the Bones? *Nā Maka o ka* Āina (film), 1986.
13. Katherine Smith, *The Love Remains,* 2006.
14. Peter Young, "Honokahua," Images of Hawaiian History (weblog).

15. Land Commission Awards, Alphabetical Index, Pae ʻĀina Productions.

16. *The King's Mahele: the Awardees and their Lands,* Dorothy Barrere (comp.), 1994.

17. Salnoiraghi, "Honokahua." *Manoa,* vol. 19, no. 2, 2007, pp. 24–35. *JSTOR,* http://www.jstor.org/stable/25474966. Accessed 1 May 2023.

18. Ayau, *Ka Wai Ola,* Jan. 30, 2020.

19. Naeʻole, DLNR.

20. *The King's Mahele: The Awardees and their Lands,* Dorothy Barrere (comp.), 1994.

21. "Descendants to beautify Kale Kaniaulono Davis' grave site," *Lahaina News,* Mar 21, 2013.

22. *The King's Mahele: The Awardees and their Lands,* Dorothy Barrere (comp.), 1994.

23. Kuykendall, 1947, 280.

24. kekoʻolani.org.

25. "The Story of Hawaii and Its Builders," *Honolulu Star-Bulletin,* 1925. Edited by George F. Nellist.

26. http://imagesofoldhawaii.com/captain-alexander-adams/.

27. familysearch.org.

28. *Pacific Commercial Advertiser,* Feb. 12, 1863

29. Len Kong Farm Genealogy.

30. "Grave site opportunity brings woman's descendants together," *Maui News,* Mar. 18, 2013.

31. Wendy Osher, "Descendants to Gather at Kupuna Gravesite in Kapalua," *Maui News,* Mar. 18, 2013.

CHAPTER 8

THE TORRENS SYSTEM OF LAND TITLE REGISTRATION, AS ESTABLISHED IN 1903 IN HAWAI'I AND THE PHILIPPINES

Lance D. Collins

This chapter provides a broad understanding of how the Torrens system of land title registration—that is, the system that determines who owns what pieces of land and what ownership itself means—came to be established in Hawai'i and the Philippines in 1903.[1] In some countries, systems of land title develop over time, such as with the development of English, and then American, land tenure systems. The chapter will present the historical progression of how land was understood and controlled—towards a simplification of land ownership resulting in full rights of alienation. The American system of recording deeds, which entailed a government register of title transfers, was an early solution to the problems settler colonial societies encountered with the private system of land transfers within the English system. The Torrens system of land registration, first proposed in the mid-1850s by Sir Robert Richard Torrens in South Australia, was a later solution to the problems a settler colonial society encountered with the common-law English system of proving landownership. The problem, in brief, was how to recode the control of indigenous or communal land through state-centered forms of private property recognition.

In the then-newly occupied countries of the Philippines and Hawai'i, American colonial officials sought to experiment with this new method of controlling land. The application was not without problems. In the Philippines, even while mandated to be the only method of transferring land title, the Torrens system was a failure—in terms of land formally registered—until the early 21st century, when grants from the European Union funded the surveying necessary to allow widespread acceptance and use of the system. In Hawai'i, the Torrens system has been extensively deployed, even though it is voluntary. In part, the problems and the value of the Torrens system arise from the way that it clarifies land ownership by creating a clear registration system for land ownership and transfer. All ambiguities in ownership are terminated. The system is not simply a bureaucratic procedure; it is also a key political strategy for securing ownership of land, often to the detriment of indigenous peoples.

Both the Philippines and Hawai'i offer examples of how the Torrens system arose in colonial contexts. This chapter will briefly look at one semi-urbanized barangay[2] in a rural province in the Philippines where the Torrens system has legally been present for over a century, but where the cadastral surveys had not been completed, to get an understanding of what kind of land would be registered. The chapter will then turn to examining the first and last of the 16 land court applications filed for West Maui lands to secure ownership through the Torrens system. The chapter will thus seek to identify a unifying logic for both cases to register land in Hawai'i based on the needs of the Territory of Hawai'i in 1911 and Pioneer Mill in 1957.

ENGLISH AND AMERICAN LAND TENURE

Anglo-Saxon land tenure in England was an amalgamation of land control practices shaped by Celtic, Roman and other European tribal experiences. Land ownership was typically tied to long-standing verbal agreements between lord and serf. However, the somewhat stable and relatively comparable practices that developed in England suddenly shifted following the Norman Conquest, which necessitated a way to maintain domination of the lands conquered. The Normans divided the country into lands tied to the military, to agriculture, to the church, and to the court lands. William I of England created four types of land tenure that correspond to those four: military tenure, socage tenure, frankalmoign tenure, and serjeanty tenure. Modern American land tenure primarily derives from socage tenure, which is thus tied to an agricultural image of land control.

William I distributed land first acquired by forfeiture and commendation as spoils to reward his followers and allies, and then to so-called "tenants in capite." These individuals with large tracts of land would distribute control over portions of these lands to their own followers, who were described as "mesne" tenants "seised in service." Later, control over the smallest portions of land were given to the actual users of the land, who were described as "seised in demesne." Each grant created a relationship wherein the lord protected the tenant and safeguarded his landholding in exchange for service and products rendered to the lord by the tenant. The lord received primarily economic, and sometimes military, returns from this relationship.

Military tenure was a life grant from a lord to his loyal warriors. When the warrior died, the grant could go to a "regrant on death," or it would escheat to the lord. As the immediacy of the Norman Conquest faded, the regrant on death could substitute a payment of relief for a showing of usefulness to the lord in order to keep the grant. Similarly, the requirement of providing service for the lord under military tenure was replaced by a cash payment, called "scuage," in lieu of military service. This evolved into the paying of "aids." The Magna Carta further limited aid to three situations: the ransoming of the lord's body, the knighting of the lord's eldest son, and the first marrying of the lord's eldest daughter. This was further developed by statute.

The regrant on death eventually evolved into the right of inheritance. Problems arose, however, when the tenant died with only infant children. The lord would take wardship of the infant and could again directly control his land. To prevent his land from going to strangers, the law came to recognize a power in the lord to decide whom his former tenants' children could marry.

Wardship and marriage were widely abused in military tenure. Wardship, marriage and escheat persisted through centuries. However, given the lack of a need for local armies to protect local feudal lords, military tenure would eventually disappear.

Socage tenure was a relationship between lord and tenant based upon service other than military service—which meant agricultural service or money payment. It could be expressed either in a definite amount of work, or defined by a quantity of some product of the land or a cash payment. The obligations attached to the relationship of land tenure were thus similar to military tenure. The tenant owed his lord aid.

On death of the tenant, the lord had the right to escheat or to grant relief. The forms of wardship and controlling the marriage of tenants was absent from this form of tenure. If a socage tenant died with infant heirs, those relatives disqualified from inheriting (the widow, for example) would become the guardian of the lands until adulthood of the infant. Modern guardianship law is based upon the customs developed by socage tenants.

Land grants to the Church were called frankalmoign tenure. In the Middle Ages, the Church argued that God was a conveyee of the land, and therefore ecclesiastical courts were the proper forum for disputes regarding lands under frankalmoign tenure. The king agreed only if a jury were summoned and determined first that God had a sufficient interest in the dispute for the ecclesiastical courts to preside. New grants of land to the Church without royal assent ended after 1290.

Finally, servants in the household of the lord were given serjeanty tenure, meaning that they obtained the use of lands in exchange for their ongoing services to the lord's household. However, this form of tenure was soon integrated into military and socage tenure as money payment (i.e., rents), and was substituted for the specific services required of a tenant.

Real property law in England developed in response to problems regarding alienation of land. Tenants could alienate their land subject to the higher lord's power of veto—which eventually turned into a "fine on alienation." If the tenant made the money payment, he could convey his interest by "substitution" or by "subinfeudation." Substitution was the process whereby the conveyee took the place of the conveyor. Subinfeudation was the process by which a tenant became a lord over the person to whom he conveyed his interest. Lords disliked subinfeudation, and along with grants to the Church, the process was stopped in 1290 upon adoption of the Statute of Quia Emptores. The fine on alienation was likewise abolished on all tenants other than the tenant in capite. The simpler system worked until the seventeenth century, when the number of tenants in capite became significantly greater, and the burdens imposed by the king on them increased—the "incidents" of these land tenures were historical and byzantine, and many times only corresponded to the call of custom as opposed to need.

In 1660, Charles II agreed to convert all military tenure and socage tenure in capite into common socage tenure. All future land grants would only occur in socage tenure. Wardship and marriage rights attached to land disappeared, fines on alienation by large landowners also disappeared, and the "aid payments" on all types of land disappeared. What survived was the concept of escheat, relief as a form of inheritance tax, and the concept that land is "held" and not "owned." In exchange, Charles II obtained a royal revenue.

The Statute of Quia Emptores and the Act of 1660 had the ultimate effects of generalizing all alienable land into one type, and of minimizing and eliminating temporally bound relationships and "incidents" connected to land. English feudal life, which was characterized primarily by subsistence, was in the process of transforming to market-based agriculture, and the legal system for the control of land followed a similar process. Land not subject to specific subinfeuded tenure included common lands for the use of all. However, the enclosure movement also occurred during the transition from feudal to market life. In short, land had become free from complex social, legal, and political structures that limited its ability to be alienated and acquired like a commodity.

The colonization of the American continent was an expression of this move from feudal economics to market economics, and thus an expression of the property system on which the new market economies relied. As settler colonial governments relied less upon indigenous communities, there was a decrease or ending of recognition of the power or authority of indigenous communities over their lands. Settler colonial governments decoded native land of native control and recoded the land through English forms. Ownership was not simply transferred, or taken; the idea of ownership was imposed. In legal terms, control of land developed from English common-law principles.

Applying American Land Tenure in Hawai'i

During the 19th century in Hawai'i, the native land tenure was replaced with a system devised primarily by American advisers to the king. The emerging system was modeled, in certain important ways, after Anglo-American land history—the starting point of "privatizing land" was to make the king—in this case Kamehameha—the feudal suzerain (overlord) and the chiefs his feudatories. The king's lands were divided into three parts: the king's lands, the government's lands, and the private lands held by the chiefs. A land commission was appointed to quiet land titles. After the initial division of lands, native tenants filed claims that were then adjudicated by the land commission, and awards were issued. The commission did not grant patents for land; it only ascertained the nature and extent of each claimant's rights in land and then issued awards constituting good evidence of title. Upon payment of the commutation tax, if any, the claimant obtained a royal patent, extinguishing any residual interest of the king.

The process of making the control of Hawaiian land operate under the system of rules of nineteenth-century American common-law principles was part of a process by which Hawaiian land was increasingly taken out of Hawaiian hands. The king and the chiefs often resisted this process in many ways, and derivative claims continue to persist today. However, in large part, the mechanisms by which these forms of resistance were maintained was through the political process, which, after the overthrow, was dominated by the non-Native economic elite. The nature of land tenure and how the land was transferred was thus intertwined.

Transferring Land

In English common law, ownership of land was transferred with a written deed. A deed was a special agreement entered into between the grantor and grantee. In the case of a land sale, this was a contract between seller and buyer. A deed was not valid unless the grantor had the power to transfer the land—and the grantor only had this power if the person who transferred the land to him had the right to transfer it. This backward investigation would continue until one came upon the first transfer of land by the Crown to its first owner, or until the longest statute of limitations had lapsed for any undiscovered claims. This process was known as proving a chain of title. Unfortunately for the efficient working of the system, the majority of historic deeds were held in private hands, which required both the grantee and grantor to employ attorneys to examine all of the deeds to ensure the grantor had good title to transfer.

One problem with this system, however, is that flaws in earlier titles would be passed down to the present holder even if nobody knew of that flaw. Deeds held in private hands were also susceptible to fraud and forgery.

Until 1535, the transfer of title required the "feoffment by livery in seisin," meaning there had to be a ceremonial delivering of possession to the transferee. The purpose of feoffment by livery in seisin would be attacked by someone claiming to hold adverse possession. After 1535, the conveyance of the deed— that is, the execution of the deed and the deed's delivery—was sufficient. Physical delivery of possession was no longer necessary. However, the change to paper transfers of title in 1535 did not stop people from claiming to hold adverse possession. The entire system was thus based on the interaction of varied, problematic, and dispersed documents. As has been said, "On the one hand, no matter how good a title is, there may in theory always be a better. On the other hand, no matter how bad a title is—how short the period of possession—the possessor has a title good against all but better claimants, which he can convey or devise by will" (Brookfield).

The American experience differed from the English experience due to the confiscation of lands from American Indian tribes, which meant that the amount of land available to be bought and sold was far greater and ever-expanding: the title did not have to be traced back to distant generations, and the amount of land changing hands was much greater. From these differences, American jurisdictions adopted public recording systems for titles so that ownership of land was a public fact. Instead of deeds being held privately by the owner of the land, a copy of the deed was recorded in a public register so that ownership of a parcel could be determined without needing to obtain the private holdings of deeds. Under English common law, when a person had properly conveyed his interest in property to another, there was no circumstance in which he could then purport to convey that interest to yet another. In other words, if a landowner sold his property to Person A on Monday and then attempted to sell that property again to Person B on Tuesday, Person B obtained nothing from the seller. The possibility of fraud in this way was far less likely in the English system than the American system.

Because of the possibility of fraudulently twice selling one's land in the American system, two types of recording statutes in the United States were devised to set the significance of recording a deed. When a deed is recorded, that recorded deed is evidence of title. In older "race" statutes, the first deed to be recorded signifies that the grantee of the first recorded deed is the owner even if the first recorded deed was executed—that is, when all of the formalities of completing the deed were completed—after the second recorded deed and the person who recorded their deed first knew about the other deed. Under former so-called "notice" statutes, a person without notice of a previous deed at the time he obtained his deed, notice actual or constructive, is the owner of a parcel regardless of subsequent events. Half of U.S. states follow the "notice" regime and half follow the "race-notice" regime. The "race-notice" regime adds an additional step to the second grantee: he has to record before the first grantee in order for his deed to have the effect of transferring title.

The Hawaiian Kingdom, under the advice of American advisers, quickly adopted a system of recordation after the Westernization of land tenure had occurred. The Bureau of Conveyances, created in 1859, records the instruments of conveyance and provides evidence of title or ownership in the new buyer. Under this system, a purchaser of land must examine the chain of title that has been recorded at the Bureau.

SPANISH LAND TENURE AND THE PHILIPPINES

Before turning to the specific example of the Philippines, it is necessary to first consider the land tenure system in Spain, which was to dominate the formal legal processes in the Philippines for centuries before the American conquest in the late 19th century.

Rather than a Norman invasion leading to a central figure seeking to ensure the longevity and legitimacy of his sole rule over the English, Spain was created from the struggle of certain Christian elites against the Muslim rulers of the Iberian Peninsula over a long period of time. Land use in early medieval Spain for both Christian and Muslim peoples was characterized by agriculture, and the Christian princes helped to expand agricultural settlements in the West. Rather than one conquering king, there were several already-established kingdoms.

By the twelfth century, great estates became more numerous and were controlled primarily by Church entities and, to a lesser extent, by military orders referred to as *latifundios*. Control of land was allowed by purchase, exchange, marriage, donation, inheritance, or usurpation. The manorial system of England did not develop in Spain. Rather, most great estates had a central portion of land, as well as the various buildings, that was the landlord's "reserve," whether the landlord was a secular lord or religious or military entity. Serfs or day laborers worked the reserve, as did tenants with obligations for service to the landlord. The bulk of an estate was composed of the lands of the tenants, common pasturage lands and forest. Depending on the topography, type of agriculture, and surrounding areas, tenants could be grouped together or scattered throughout the land. Land ownership was generally not distributed.

In the transition to a Christian Spain, tenants held land through grants of an indefinite term in exchange for rent. These types of grants became lifetime tenancies and then became inheritable. Sometimes, a tenancy required the tenant to do some service for a period of years, allowing that tenant to eventually become the owner of some portion of the land granted. Sharecropping was the most common status in areas with large Muslim populations. In Muslim sharecropping, the landlord provided the land, tools, animals, and a portion of seed, and in exchange received between one-sixth to one-half of the produce. In Christian sharecropping, the sharecropper owed the landlord rent in the form of produce. Tenants were subject to obligations to the landlord in addition to rent, and landlords in some cases claimed the power to kill their tenants.

The Christianization of Spain corresponded with the establishing of colonies in the Americas. Similar to the English in North America, there was no recognition of indigenous peoples' claims in the New World. Landownership in Spanish America was founded by a series of edicts by the Roman Catholic pope recognizing Spanish and Portuguese sovereignty over lands in the Americas and Africa on the basis that non-Christian peoples could not own land. Mass exterminations and re-concentrations of native peoples off their lands created newly available land to be then granted to military officials and the Church. These grants of land supported Spanish colonial purposes and developed along the lines of the *latifundios* as *encomiendas* and *haciendas*. In other words, rather than an increasing individualized private ownership system as was common to England, the Spanish system in the Americas reinforced social hierarchies through land ownership. Whatever land was not held privately was deemed to be owned by the Spanish king.

The Spanish followed this same process in their colonization of the Philippines. *Encomiendas* were issued to religious orders and the military officials who then were allowed to extract tribute from the people who lived within their unclear boundaries. Unlike Spanish America, where Spanish settled and extensively both exterminated certain native peoples and intermarried with other native peoples, the Spanish did not widely settle or intermarry with Filipinos. As military officials passed away, their lands were more frequently donated to the religious orders or, after defaulting on mortgages to religious orders, were foreclosed upon. In the late eighteenth century, a native and Chinese mestizo elite began to follow Spanish practices and individually secured colonial government-recognized ownership to certain lands, although native or mestizo landlords of large private estates did not become significant until the mid-nineteenth century.

Land that was held in private hands was not subject to a uniform practice or set of laws, and land tenure laws comprised "numberless single decrees forming a casuistical, disconnected, complicated and confused mass." In 1893, the *Ley Hipotecaria* (translated as the Spanish Mortgage Law) established a title registration process that was mostly unworkable and therefore ignored. The confusion was compounded at the very end of Spanish rule by a fire in Manila that destroyed the repository of documents relating to recognized property rights in land. While changes to land laws for upper classes that increased regularized procedures for formally acquiring title came during the nineteenth century, it was "commonly recognized as a fact that comparatively few holders of real estate in the Philippines can trace their titles to their origin in the Spanish Government, and this remarkable fact exists in the face of the evident and persistent effort made by that Government to induce landholders to avail themselves of the opportunities afforded by law for converting their mere rights of possession into legal titles" (Report of the Philippine Commission 2:320).

When the Treaty of Paris ceded the Philippines to the United States in 1898, the document indicated that all property owned by the Crown as well as royal public works were ceded to the United States, but that the peaceful possession of property by private individuals, local governments, and religious entities would not be disturbed. The United States thus acquired a largely medieval Spanish system of land ownership, and a considerable amount of land, where the recorded title system at the core of American land ownership was impossible to implement. As with the situation in Hawai'i, a theoretical solution would be found in settler colonial Australia.

TORRENS LAND REGISTRATION

In nineteenth-century Australia, colonial settlers to South Australia found the English system of landholding and conveyancing to be rife with fraud and injustice as persons would purchase land, make improvements, use the land, and then discover later that some flaw or fraud dispossessed them of ownership. South Australia was Australia's only non-convict colony. As a settler colonial society, all settlers but the very poor could become landowners—that was one of the main draws for voluntary British settlers to move to Australia. Land title reform was therefore a popular and pressing issue in South Australia for settlers.

The registration of deeds, as practiced in the United States and elsewhere, was a reform of conveyancing—taking the private holding of the papers constituting a chain of title and making them public and more secure. But deed registration is not directly a reform of the land titles, only of how those titles are available to research. Deeds must still be examined and a chain of title established and verified.

Robert Richard Torrens, an Irish-born settler to South Australia, was a politician who advocated for land titling reform in the 1850s. He had advocated for a system in which a registered title to land would be as valid as the original patent granted by the Crown. The so-called Real Property Act of 1858 was given royal assent, although the support for it was not unanimous. Challenges in the courts and other problems required amending, and the final act was embodied in the Real Property Act of 1861. When the law passed, Torrens resigned from his seat in the South Australia Parliament and became its first registrar. The South Australian Company, the major landowner in early South Australia, planned and then brought vast tracts of land into the Torrens title system, making its holdings more easily marketable. Reducing potential legal challenges went hand in hand with denying property rights to aboriginal peoples, which was core to the overall system.

This system proved to be popular with colonial officials in reducing problems with land conveyancing and ownership and was adopted throughout Australia and New Zealand. It was eventually also adopted throughout the areas of the British Empire that followed the common law, such as Canada, Malaya, freehold lands in Fiji, British Honduras, Jamaica, British Papua, Trinidad and Tobago, Palestine, Ireland, Sri Lanka, Gambia and the Leeward Islands. Beginning in the late nineteenth century, U.S. states began adopting versions of the Torrens system of registering title. As discussed below, however, in most instances the system was subsequently repealed or terminated.

The Torrens system of land title registration was considered to be "progressive" and "efficient" compared to private conveyance systems and even deed registration systems. The Torrens system works on four basic concepts. First, the land title register reflects completely the facts of title to a particular parcel. Second, the certificate of title contains all legally recognized information regarding ownership. Third, the state guarantees the validity of title to land and will indemnify for any errors caused by fraud or by errors of the registrar. Finally, title was indefeasible, meaning that it was no longer subject to attack. The result was a land-titling system that removed ambiguity and freed the current owner of the title from many potential challenges to ownership.

ADOPTING TORRENS LAND REGISTRATION IN THE PHILIPPINES AND HAWAI'I

The economic elite who dominated Hawai'i's political and legal system since the overthrow considered themselves to be progressive and economic liberals in line with their racist beliefs about the nature of civilization and the position of white Europeans in relation to non-white Pacific Islanders. The colonial officials who went to the Philippines after the Spanish-American War also considered themselves to be progressive and economic liberals. And in many instances, these groups were classmates at the same Ivy League schools on the East Coast of the U.S. Both groups of ruling elites also faced similar issues connected to establishing control over the land. It is thus no surprise that the Torrens land title registration system would be quickly adopted by both governments, although in practical terms, vast portions of Philippine lands remained unregistered for over a century.

In the Philippines during the American occupation, the law was that unless a person had obtained title to their lands, all lands within the Philippines were owned by the state. The only exception to this was recognized by the U.S. Supreme Court in *Carino v. Insular Government,* wherein ancestral communal ownership of land by indigenous tribes in specially governed non-Christian areas was recognized absent titling. The Torrens land system was adopted as the only lawful land titling system. But because title registration was generally expensive due to the need to survey, land title registration occurred mostly in urban areas and as part of large-scale land development projects. Land grants issued from the public domain were also registered.

However, for practical purposes, land transfers of unregistered lands outside of the Torrens system continued under claims of ownership through the Spanish Mortgage Law or earlier questionable Spanish grants, and land-ownership that was unregistered would be recognized administratively—but it only had a legal effect on the parties to a particular transaction. During Martial Law, Ferdinand Marcos sought to abolish this shadow land title system existing under the veneer of the Spanish Mortgage Law, and gave those holding title through the Spanish Mortgage Law six months to seek registration of their title through the Torrens system or find their documents forever barred as evidence of ownership.

Nevertheless, Marcos also continued the administrative procedure of allowing the recording of conveyance documents for lands that were unregistered. "Ownership" of unregistered lands involved a process of changing the name of the person listed as the owner on the tax declaration. However, if the owner were to register his unregistered land, he would legally be obtaining a patent of public land—regardless of whether he might have been able to establish a century-long chain of ownership through the unregistered administrative process.

The Torrens system was also supported by certificates of title issued through the cadastral process. Within ten years of civilian colonial government in the Philippines, a Cadastral Act was adopted to survey and map the entire archipelago. One of the provisions allowed under the act was for the government to survey a tract of land and then have certificates of title issued to all those who owned land within the tract. Once issued, the lands were considered registered under the Torrens system, and all transfers thereafter followed the Torrens process. The process would have provided a clear foundation for the Torrens system. However, it is worth considering that the cadastral surveys of the archipelago were finally completed only in 2015—more than one hundred years after the passage of the Cadastral Act.

The limitations of the Torrens system in practice can be illustrated by looking at one semi-urbanized barangay within a generally rural municipality in a rural province, where we discover very few lands that had their titles registered in 2012. All parcels had an "owner" as reflected administratively in the tax records, but almost none had registered title. Most of the record owners of the titled land were dead, and the common feature of those who did register the title to their land was that they had worked in Hawai'i—away from the land itself. A few parcels with registered title have owners who were alive yet who did not live in the municipality, but rather in Manila or elsewhere. In other words, the title registrations occurred as a way to protect one's purchase of land from being "stolen"—through fraudulent sales or simple squatting—in the absence of the owner's full-time presence on or near the land in question.

With the completion of the cadastral surveys, however, registering land titles no longer required the expensive hiring of a surveyor and similarly costly procedures that limited who could register title. Rather, the process has brought much of the land in the Philippines under the Torrens system. It is unclear whether the completion of the cadastral surveys and the broadening of access to the registration of titles will have any significant impact on the continuation of the administrative process of recording informal conveyance documents. The structure and mechanisms are established, however, for the Torrens system to incorporate and supersede the various land title systems that had previously operated in the Philippines.

In Hawaiʻi, the Torrens land system was established as a voluntary system supported by the government. The deed registration system that had been adopted by 1859, known as the regular system, continued to operate, while the Torrens system became known as the Land Court system and could be utilized to move a parcel of land's title into the Torrens system. Most registrations of land into the Torrens system involved some aspect of quieting title and required a formal adjudication of title; therefore, it came to be known as Land Court. In other words, unlike the Philippine experience wherein the initial registration of title was similar to Australia, where no previous private ownership existed, most privately held land in Hawaiʻi had been set into private hands more than fifty years before the establishment of the Torrens system. So, the court process of determining title was incorporated into the Hawaiʻi Torrens system.

The biggest benefit for land developers and financial institutions in the Torrens system is that title is indefeasible, which, from the opposite perspective, means that people who might have claims to the land have their status erased permanently. The emphasis in practice was to establish the land title to the point that it could be registered. In Hawaiʻi, the Torrens system of land titling has generally been used for property destined for land development, whether for agriculture, tourism, or housing.

Whereas many Big Five companies and their subsidiary plantations and ranches utilized extremely liberal adverse possession laws to dispossess Hawaiians of their ancestral lands, Torrens' indefeasibility principles meant that registered land could not itself be subject to adverse possession or subsequent counterclaims by Hawaiians. As a result, we find condominium and hotel resort projects have had the land on which they are built registered through Land Court—the entirety of AmFac's Kāʻanapali Resort land and most of the Mākena Resort lands, for example. Almost the entire Island of Lānaʻi was likewise the subject of one consolidated Land Court application, and half of Molokaʻi is subject to Land Court registration. On the other hand, very small portions of Maui, Kauaʻi and Hawaiʻi Island are registered. Half of Oʻahu is registered, primarily in connection with resort and condominium construction.

With the advent of modern title insurance, the decrease in the amount of lands with unclear title, and staffing limitations at the Land Court in processing applications and transfers, the Torrens system has fallen out of favor, even with developers and lending institutions. The bureaucratic overhead that once provided reliable documentation has become burdensome. Most land speculation companies in Hawaiʻi typically find a successful quiet title action to be sufficient to eventually market and sell their land claims. Legislation has even been passed that allows time-share interests in condominium projects as well as other registered properties to deregister from Land Court (Act 120 of 2009).

WEST MAUI LANDS REGISTERED

Within the context of the Hawaiian land title systems, the first application submitted to the Land Court regarding West Maui land concerned the title over Pā Pelekane, referred to as Land Court Application No. 109.

In 1802, Kamehameha I built a red brick palace in the style of British brick houses at Keawaiki Point in Lahaina. The area came to be known as Pā Pelekane. Kaʻahumanu set up a traditional thatched house next to the brick palace where she resided, preferring traditional architecture to the foreign version. After Kamehameha's defeat while attempting to invade Kauaʻi, though, he moved to Honolulu. The building was used for government purposes until 1845. In 1848, the ahupuaʻa of Paunau was assigned to Victoria Kamāmalu during the Māhele.

In 1850, three petitions were raised to the Privy Council regarding Pā Pelekane.

On March 5, 1850, H. S. Swinton applied to purchase the land. The Privy Council opposed the sale, "as it is a place to which many historical associations are attached, and which has already been set apart as a place not to be sold." In May of 1850, Swinton applied to lease the land. The Privy Council disapproved, saying that "the government may require it for public buildings."

In August of 1850, the Privy Council issued another resolution regarding a claim filed by Kekūanāoʻa on behalf of Princess Victoria Kamāmalu that "the premises known as Beretania, in Lahaina, Maui, be and is hereby confirmed as government property and that Governor Kekūanāoʻaʻs claim therefore is hereby negatived." Kekūanāoʻa had attended the Privy Council on behalf of Princess Victoria Kamāmalu, claiming Pā Pelekane and the adjoining wharf lot as land belonging to Kaʻahumanu, and Kamāmalu being the heir to Kaʻahumanu.

In July 1852, the legislature authorized the minister of the interior to establish a battery and mount guns at Pā Pelekane, which did not impact the formal ownership of the land.

Finally, in 1854, the Land Commission awarded Paunau to Victoria Kamāmalu (LCA 7713: Apana 26) and patented the award in 1861 (RP 4775). The award and patent conveyed the ahupuaʻa without a survey or a description other than the name Paunau. In 1855, land adjoining Pā Pelekane was awarded to Kanaina (LCA 8559), and the land of Pā Pelekane was referred to as government land. In 1859, Governor Kekūanāoʻa petitioned the Privy Council to "restore" Pā Pelekane to Princess Kamāmalu.

From the late 1860s through 1883, the lands of Victoria Kamāmalu descended to Bernice Pauahi Bishop. In 1885, the lands of Bernice Pauahi Bishop descended to her estate. In addition, between 1879 and 1882, the Kingdom's Ministry of the Interior held receipts of rents to portions of Pā Pelekane that it rented to commercial outfits. Up until the overthrow of the Hawaiian monarchy, therefore, ownership of the area by a series of Hawaiian aliʻi and the government was contested and ambiguous.

In 1910, the Territory of Hawaiʻi sought to register the land. At that time, the Pioneer Mill Co. (a subsidiary of H. Hackfeld & Co.), through its hotel company, ran a hotel built in that location, and H. Hackfeld & Co. (later renamed American Factors) directly ran a lumber yard. Both of these operations occurred under leases from the Bishop Estate. In addition, a Chan Wa and a Shimamura ran a retail store, and Messrs. Sato, Komaia, Kimura, Okomoto and S. Yagi conducted fish markets, all under leases from the Estate of Elizabeth Nahaolelua. Mr. Sing Kee ran a coffee shop under a lease from an F. C. Ah Chong. The Territory maintained the streets, a park, and the wharf. The U.S. government operated a lighthouse. The Territory and U.S. government asserted ownership over the area as successors to the Kingdom of Hawaiʻi.

The Territory's application went to trial, as the various persons and entities denied the Territory's claim of ownership. The case was tried before the Land Court in Honolulu, and at the close of the Territory's case the other claimants moved that the case be dismissed. They argued that the Territory had failed to meet the burden of proof regarding ownership, based largely on the disparate written documents connected to the land. The Land Court agreed and dismissed the case. The Territory appealed.

The Supreme Court sustained the Territory's appeal, vacated the Land Court's decision, and remanded the case for a new trial.

No new trial was ever held, however. After some negotiating, the parties agreed that the street and esplanade lot, the lot that presently contains the makai portion of Lahaina Library and a small strip fronting Main/Front Street, would be registered, and the remaining "lots" of Pā Pelekane would not be registered. The specific lots would thus remain government property and be included in the Torrens system, while the unregistered lots would remain under the regular system claims of the various purported owners.

The last application submitted to the Land Court concerning West Maui occurred in 1955, 40 years after the first one. The case, Land Court Application No. 1744, involved 306 acres of West Maui lands then claimed to be owned by Pioneer Mill that made up the area now occupied by Kā'anapali Resort and the resorts of the North Beach subdivision. The area to be registered included two significant areas of land: Apana 2 to William Shaw, and Part 1 of Apana 3 to Lot Kamehameha. It also included:

- (LCA 3925-C) Apana 1 to Kahope
- (LCA 3925-C) Apana 1 to Olamana
- (RP 3023) Apana 3 to Holona
- (RP 4603) to Amai
- (RP 3336) Apana 3 to Makuahine
- (RP 6169) Apana 4 to Hanuna
- (RP 3559) Apanas 1 and 4 to Kahanaumaikai
- (RP 4173) Apana 1 to Pa
- (RP 3939) Apana 1 to Mai
- (RP 2567)

as well as several land grants by the Territory of Hawai'i.

By examining deeds recorded at the Bureau as well as court judgments regarding land and estates, the examiner of title determined that Pioneer Mill did not have good title to some or all of the lands awarded to William Shaw, Kahope, Makuahine and Pa. He also noted problems with the claims to other lands within the application. The details of the transfers or lack thereof help illustrate the complex legal situations that can arise.

William Shaw's lands had descended to three of his children: Patrick Shaw, Phoebe Shaw Dawson, and Mary Shaw Gohier. Patrick Shaw deeded his shares to Henry Turton, Isenberg and Horner (Turton's business successors in West Maui Sugar), and Lahaina Agricultural Co. However, the court-appointed examiner noted that if Patrick were married, his wife had not released her dowry. Similarly, Mary Shaw Gohier conveyed her shares to Patrick, although no consent of her husband was evident. Patrick claimed to have canceled the deed, and his wife did not express consent to that either.

Phoebe Shaw Dawson conveyed her interest to George Shaw. When he died, his wife, Maunahina, obtained half of his interest, while his four brothers and sister, along with Becky Shaw Cockett, Patrick, Phoebe, and Mary, obtained the other half. Maunahina conveyed half of her interest to George Shaw, Jr., who conveyed to Turton. The other half was conveyed to Joseph and Charles Cockett, who both conveyed to Turton.

Becky Cockett conveyed to George Cockett, who conveyed to Isenberg and Horner.

Phoebe Shaw Dawson did not again convey in her life, and her heirs were never determined. A Sarah Dawson Fisher conveyed her interest to Joseph Cockett. Joseph Cockett, Sr. died, and he had four children: Lizzie, William, Sarah, and John. John's mother, Mahiki, conveyed his interest to Isenberg and Horner, and that conveyance had been later confirmed by the circuit court.

Mary Shaw Gohier died intestate, meaning that there was no will, but the probate court appointed her husband, Charles, as the guardian of a minor son, Charles Gohier. Charles Gohier in turn conveyed his inheritance to William N. Shaw, Jr., who conveyed his interest to Isenberg without his wife's release. An Adrian Charles Gohier conveyed his interest to Campbell and Isenberg.

Kahope died in 1860. Apana 1 was awarded to his widow, Akahi. Other of his lands were awarded to his son Kekawewe. Edwin Jones recorded a deed purporting to transfer Kahope's lands to L. M. Baldwin.

Makuahine never recorded any deeds transferring his property. However, Wahineaea, Kamoku and Hana Maria each deeded portions of Makuahine's lands, claiming their interest in the land from grants by heirs of the estate of Kukahaoa.

Pa perfected his Land Commission Award by patent in 1858. Someone named Pa also occurs in a lease as lessor in 1896, and then gives a deed in 1909. But, as the examiner noted, "It is highly improbable that this could have been the same person who went before the Land Commission in 1851 to secure his/ her award."

The examiner also noted a host of other issues regarding wives or husbands not giving the necessary consent to the transfer of title.

Without further investigation, the solution to the failure to include these unknown persons as parties was to publish a legal notice called a "citation" in the newspaper, indicating that the lands at issue were subject to the court proceeding and that interested persons needed to appear and defend their claims.

At the return hearing on the citation, the Territory of Hawai'i, the County of Maui, William Cockett, James Cockett, James Gohier, Adolph Gohier, Eleanor Gohier, and Robert Gohier appeared. All other parties were defaulted. The Cocketts then failed to file an answer required by the process and were defaulted. The Gohiers promptly deeded their interest to Pioneer Mill for a cash payment. Pioneer Mill then asserted that no natives were exercising any native rights, and the Court registered title, including title free of any reservation of native rights as to Part 1 of Apana 3 of LCA 7713.

These two cases of the Territory's application for Pā Pelekane and Pioneer Mill's application for what is now Kā'anapali Resort offered different situations and raised different legal issues. In both cases, however, legal and political issues connected with the earlier land title system as well as the Torrens system (Land Court) can be seen.

In Application No. 109, the Hawai'i Supreme Court viewed the threshold question as whether the land had ever been alienated from the Crown in the first instance. Implied by the Territory having standing to pose that question was its status as successor to the Crown and government lands of the Kingdom of Hawai'i. Presumed but not mentioned were the Newlands Resolution and the Organic Act, which asserted cession of lands from the Republic of Hawai'i and control over those lands not set aside by the U.S. president to the Territory. Therefore, the framing of the threshold question itself obscures how land ownership was tied to the shift from Hawaiian sovereignty to the Territory as the successor to the Kingdom. The Territory attempted to assert settler sovereignty over historic land uses of the area. In the end, however, it settled with Pioneer Mill and the Bishop Estate trustees so that it registered the roadways, park, and esplanade, and did not further pursue the claim to the rest of the lands. In other words, its power to assert the claims of the Kingdom of Hawai'i were invoked, but without monopolizing control over all entitled lands, and at the same time yielding to the power of the sugar plantation interests. The political struggles of the time thus limited the ability of the state to fully utilize the Torrens land registration system to perfect its claims.

In Application No. 1744, Pioneer Mill was unable to demonstrate perfect title for nearly any of the parcels it included in the application. There were nearly insurmountable defects with four parcels, including the large Shaw parcel. Unlike today, when a substantial showing of diligent inquiry must be shown before resorting to publishing legal notices in the newspaper, in 1955, it was permissible to publish official notice in the newspaper with no showing of any diligence. Several of Shaw's descendants and heirs' assigns appeared and eventually settled with Pioneer Mill. But other than those six individuals, nobody else appeared, and Pioneer Mill was deemed owner by default. The process, cloaked in the authority of law, was used to erase all of the myriad ownership claims and insert in its place a clear and simple title wherein Pioneer Mill owned all of the land.

If Pioneer Mill had adjudicated the case as a regular adverse possession claim in the Maui courts, there would remain the possibility that someone with an interest might set aside the judgment for being void as to their ownership interest, or for some other reason, at a later time. It would also be possible, in theory, for someone to subsequently claim adverse possession of some part of the land after ten years (until 1973, and after twenty years thereafter). However, in the Torrens land registration system, the title being held by the owner becomes indefeasible one year after the judgment is entered and the title registered. In other words, after a year, even if title is found to be based upon an erroneous or void judgment, the registration cannot be undone. Instead, the government is only liable to pay damages to one wrongfully ousted of his title.

CONCLUSION

The Torrens land registration system thus removes the early modern Anglo-American system of land tenure, which itself had torn asunder the motley feudal ties that bound a person to his "natural superiors," leaving in its place naked self-interest and a money-based transactional system. The Torrens system replaced a varied and chaotic paper trail establishing ownership to a single system supported by government money and institutions. The Torrens system of land titling focuses on the ownership of a thing, leaving the history of the land, its present uses, and its relationship to people of generally no consequence. In Hawai'i, where the Torrens system has always been a voluntary system, it has been used to establish perfect title for resort and condominium development primarily for the benefit of absent owners and the banking institutions that finance them. In the Philippines, where the Torrens system is the only legal system of conveyance and land ownership, we find that it was also used primarily by absent owners in rural settings and more broadly adopted in urban settings. But with the completion of the nationwide cadastral survey, it is increasingly used by a broader group of people to secure their rights of ownership—where informal negotiations of control of land have become replaced by formal, legal processes backed by the power of the State. Over the last two centuries, land has increasingly moved from being a factor of production to a commodity itself. However, as the main uncertainties and risks of the regular recording system recede into the non-electronic past, and with the ubiquitous availability of title insurance policies in Hawai'i, we see that the function the Torrens system served may no longer be necessary. In the Philippines, where all land has come under a cadastral survey and there is no separate system for titling or registration, there has been a significant increase in registrations, as securing title has become affordable for a much larger part of the population.

NOTES

1. An earlier version of this paper was presented at the 2017 West Maui Conference on Pacific Peoples and their Environments at Mokuhinia, Lahaina.
2. The smallest geopolitical unit of political administration in the Philippines, it was previously termed *barrio*.

SOURCES

Bello, Walden. *The Anti-Development State: The Political Economy of Permanent Crisis in the Philippines.* Quezon City: University of the Philippines Press, 2004.

Chinen, Jon. *Original Land Titles in Hawai'i.* Honolulu: Jon Chinen, 1961.

Hinde, George W. *The New Zealand Torrens System Centennial Essays.* Wellington: Butterworths, 1971.

Hogg, James. *Registration of Title to Land Throughout the Empire.* London: Sweet & Maxwell, 1920.

Kame'eleihiwa, Lilikalā. *Native Land and Foreign Desires: Pehea Lā E Pono Ai?* Honolulu: Bishop Museum Press, 1992.

Kusaka, Wataru. *Moral Politics in the Philippines: Inequality, Democracy and the Urban Poor.* Quezon City: Ateneo University Press, 2017.

McBride, George. *The Land Systems of Mexico.* New York: American Geographical Society, 1923.

McKenna, Rebecca. *American Imperial Pastoral: The Architecture of US Colonialism in the Philippines.* Manila: Ateneo University Press, 2017.

Ortega, Arnisson. *Neoliberalizing Spaces in the Philippines.* Manila: Ateneo University Press, 2018.

Patton, Rufford G. and Carroll G. Patton. *Patton on Land Titles.* St. Paul, MN: West Publishing, 1957.

Perez, Padmapani. *Green Entanglements: Nature Conservation and Indigenous Peoples' Rights in Indonesia and the Philippines.* Quezon City: University of the Philippines Press, 2018.

Philippine Commission. *Report of the Philippine Commission to the President.* Washington D.C.: Government Printing Office, 1901.

Powell, Richard R. and Patrick J. Rohan. *Powell on Real Property.* New York: Matthew Bender, 1949 (1995).

Thompson, David. *Thompson on Real Property.* New Jersey: Matthew Bender/Lexis, 1998 (2009).

Van Dyke, Jon. *Who Owns the Crown Lands of Hawai'i?* Honolulu: University of Hawai'i Press, 2007.

Vassberg, David. *Land and Society in Golden Age Castile.* Cambridge: Cambridge University Press, 1984.

ABOUT THE CONTRIBUTORS

LANCE D. COLLINS is an attorney in private practice on the island of Maui. He holds a PhD in Political Science from the University of Hawai'i at Mānoa. He was the compiler and indexer of the seventeen-volume *Proceedings of the Charter Commissions of the County of Maui* (1966–2012) and served as its Chair in 2021. He co-edited *Tourism Impacts West Maui* (2016), *Social Change in West Maui* (2019), and *Civil Society in West Maui* (2021). His research interests focus on the Philippines, Hawai'i, American colonialism in the Pacific, and legal and political history.

FRANK EZRA KA'IUOKALANI DAMAS was born and raised in Wai'anae, O'ahu. He is an Assistant Professor at Ka Haka 'Ula o Ke'elikōlani at the University of Hawai'i at Hilo. After completing his BA and MA in Hawaiian language at Hilo, he is now doing his doctoral work on nineteenth-century spoken Hawaiian language in the Hawaiian and Indigenous Language and Culture Revitalization program at the same school. He and his wahine, Kau'ilani, are raising their two daughters in Waiākea Uka, Hilo, Hawai'i, with Hawaiian as the household language. Ka'iuokalani hopes to normalize the use of Hawaiian language through his family and his work.

SYDNEY LEHUA IAUKEA is a Native Hawaiian educator who holds a PhD in Political Science. Sydney has taught over 80 college courses, and she was also the Hawaiian Studies program manager for the Department of Education. She currently works at Kamehameha Schools Hawai'i as a senior design specialist. Sydney is the author of two books, *The Queen and I: A Story of Dispossessions and Reconnections in Hawai'i* (University of California Press, 2011), which received a Ka Palapala Po'okela Excellence in Publishing award, and *Keka'a: The Making and Saving of North Beach West Maui* (North Beach-West Maui Benefit Fund, 2014). Sydney is also the author of two TED-Ed animations entitled "The Dark History of the Overthrow of Hawai'i" and "The Epic Tale of the Wind Goddess's Gift."

BIANCA K. ISAKI is a writer, solo legal practitioner, community activist, and a director of the North Beach-West Maui Benefit Fund. She received her doctorate from the University of Hawai'i at Mānoa Department of Political Science for research on Asian settler colonialism and plantation labor organizing, completed a postdoctoral fellowship at the University of Illinois at Urbana-Champaign, returned to Hawai'i to teach Women's Studies, and then graduated *summa cum laude* from the William S. Richardson School of Law. She has contributed to other West Maui book projects including *Tourism Impacts West Maui* (2016), *Social Change in West Maui* (2019), *Civil Society in West Maui* (2021), and *Water and Power in West Maui* (2021).

KAHEALANI LONO is a Hawaiian language instructor at Kawaihuelani Center for Hawaiian Language for more than fifteen years where she teaches introductory and intermediate Hawaiian language courses. She was raised in Kāne'ohe, Ko'olaupoko, O'ahu, home to the makani known as Ulumano, and she continues to learn the teachings of our 'āina.

ADAM KEAWE MANALO-CAMP is a writer, cultural practitioner, and ethnohistorian. His academic interest and background is in the anthropology of indigenuity. Adam is of Native Hawaiian and Filipino ancestry and grew up at Papakōlea Hawaiian Homestead, O'ahu.

SHILPI SUNEJA is the author of the novel *House of Caravans* (2023). Her work has been nominated for a Pushcart Prize and published in *Guernica, McSweeney's, Cognoscenti, Teachers & Writers Magazine,* and *Michigan Quarterly Review,* among other places. Her writing has been supported by a National Endowment for the Arts literature fellowship and a Massachusetts Cultural Council fellowship. She holds an MA in English from New York University and an MFA in Creative Writing from Boston University, where she was awarded the Saul Bellow Prize. She is currently pursuing a PhD in English at the University of Hawai'i at Mānoa.

RONALD WILLIAMS JR. holds a PhD in History with a specialization in Hawai'i and Native-language resources. He is a former faculty member within the Hawai'inuiākea School of Hawaiian Knowledge at the University of Hawai'i at Mānoa and was the founding Director of the Lāhui Hawai'i Researcher Center. He served as past president of the 132-year-old Hawaiian Historical Society and currently works as an archivist at the Hawai'i State Archives. He has published in a wide variety of academic and public history venues including *The Oxford Encyclopedia of Religion in America,* the *Hawaiian Journal of History,* and *Hana Hou! Magazine.*

INDEX